The Curse of Queen Kelly

The Curse of Queen Kelly

Pamela Hutchinson

Sticking Place Books
New York

ISBN 979-8-89976-056-3

For Mum and Dad

Contents

"A naughty little number"   ix

1. The Debutantes   1
2. The Business   7
3. The Legend   13
4. The Star   21
5. The Producers   31
6. The Genius   49
7. The White Knight   59
8. The Swamp   67
9. The Queen   83
10. The Palace   93
11. The Whip   101
12. The Manure Pile   119
13. The Misfit   131
14. The Yank   141
15. The Outsider   151
16. The Axe   155
17. The Scapegoat   163
18. The Hit   169
19. The Remake   179
20. The Hard Sell   187
21. The Lost   193
22. The Memoir   197
23. The Revival   203
24. The Curse   211

Acknowledgments   219
Index   221

"A naughty little number"

This is a story of how not to make a film. A story about three people who should have known better—people we could dismiss as a spendthrift, a swindler and a sadist, but who are far more interesting than that. They almost made a movie, but succeeded in creating a legend. This is the story of how a 1920s movie star, a businessman, and an artist set out to make an impossible film, the infamous *Queen Kelly*, of how they hit breaking point and threw it all away. It is also the tale of how that star spent the rest of her life trying to save the trio's beleaguered infant.

"We hear a lot lately about underground films—you know, naughty films you make with your own money—you'd think they were just invented."[1]

The date is 8 May 1967, and Hollywood star Gloria Swanson is on stage at one of the largest, most lavishly decorated cinemas in New York, teasing her audience with the prospect of something outrageous, even indecent—a relic of cinema's risqué youth. "Well, tonight I want to welcome you to the showing of a naughty little number I made in 1927 with my own money—$800,000 of it—and this film has been underground for forty years." The auditorium of the Beacon Theater, on Manhattan's Upper West Side, is full of expectant faces. She is introducing is *Queen Kelly* which, because it was never completed, was never theatrically released in the US. Had it ever been finished, it might have been pronounced a masterpiece or denounced as a scandal. Probably both.

Gloria is famously petite, just shy of five feet tall, but has more than enough charisma to hold the stage of a 3,000-seat auditorium, which is nearly at capacity, and she has a captivating story to tell. The event started late. After ten minutes of waiting for the star, the crowd started clapping "with enough intensity to shame the fans at Shea Stadium".[2] A few of those present are old enough to remember Gloria's first films, released half a century earlier. Others can recall her years of top-flight stardom in the 1920s. Many more know her from her career-reviving performance in Billy Wilder's 1950 classic *Sunset Boulevard*, her famous face now an icon of Hollywood's hidden history—the forgotten eccentricities and wild excesses of silent cinema's glory days.

Time is a slippery concept tonight. Gloria is 68 but looks much younger—graceful and gorgeous, dripping in diamonds and wearing a flowing, floor-length gown made of diaphanous chiffon, dyed a rainbow of pastel shades. In her right hand she carries one red, one white carnation. When she smooths down her dress it is apparent that her figure is just as trim as it was in her 1920s heyday. Her healthy complexion is an excellent advertisement for her famously austere diet of brown rice and vegetables, while her poise and perfect makeup evoke a lost era of Hollywood glamour. "I am older than I look, and younger than you think," quips Gloria, in case anyone in the audience is confused.

Gloria is a living piece of film history. Cinema history, too. The Beacon was opened in 1929, originally intended as a sister venue to the gigantic Roxy, opened two years earlier and named after developer Samuel "Roxy" Rothafel. The Roxy was then the largest cinema in the world—a movie palace seating nearly 6,000 patrons. The film chosen for its opening night was Gloria's first foray into producing her own films, *The Love of Sunya* (Albert Parker, 1927). That evening, the sell-out crowd gave her a standing ovation. The Roxy, far too big to survive as a

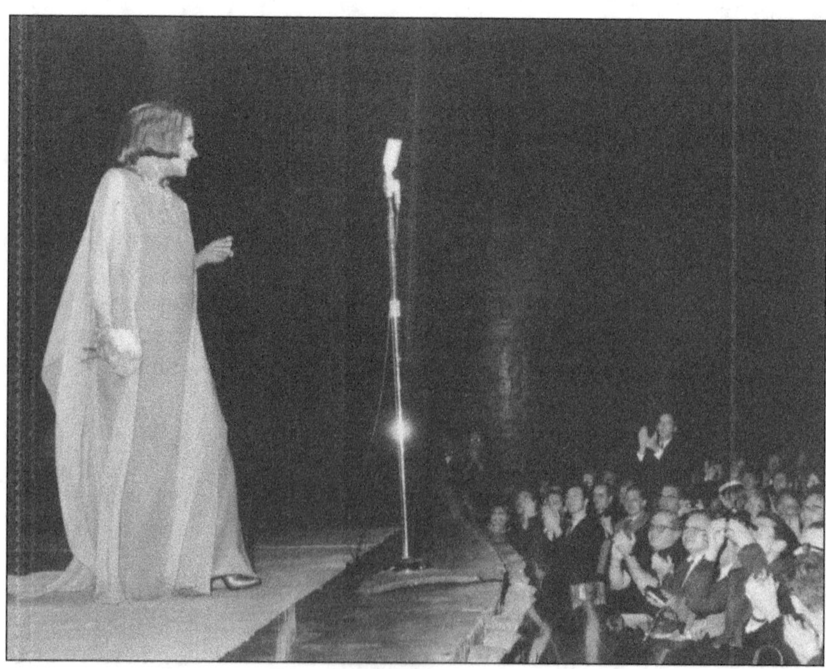

Gloria Swanson introduces *Queen Kelly* and *The Trespasser* at the Beacon in New York in 1967. UPI Photo/Author's collection.

cinema alone, was eventually demolished in 1960. To mark the occasion, Gloria posed for press photographers in the ruins of the "Cathedral of the Motion Picture", dressed in a strapless black evening gown and a scarlet feather boa.

Forty years later, Gloria is at the Beacon with a little forbidden fruit from the good old days. "I have made more than sixty pictures in more than fifty years," she tells the crowd. "I started with Chaplin in Chicago, then Hollywood, then New York, then France, England and Italy… Good ones, bad ones, indifferent ones. I've made all kinds. Probably my most famous picture is one that was never finished. And the most famous parts of it are the parts that have never been seen anywhere." This is the film she is introducing tonight. "Some people call it the first underground film made in Hollywood, directed by the daddy of them all, Erich von Stroheim." When Gloria talks about underground cinema, she means films that are made independently of the Hollywood studios, without traditional financing, outside established genres. Gloria feels a kinship with this DIY, avant-garde scene and seems to relish the connotation of pornography. In the following decade, Gloria will get to know the fringes of the underground circuit, working with Curtis Harrington as well as befriending Andy Warhol and his coterie, even attending the funeral of Candy Darling. She refuses Warhol's request to appear in one of his Factory films. But she does tell him that she would love to direct one. Underground cinema is art cinema and rebel cinema—hence its appeal to Gloria.

Gloria's "underground" film will screen tonight with a new score played on the Beacon's magnificent Wurlitzer as part of an event called From Silents to Sound, in a double-bill with Gloria's first talkie, *The Trespasser* (Edmund Goulding, 1930). The cover of the programme features a bronze sculpture of Gloria's head, crafted by… Gloria herself, who is impressively multitalented. Most exciting of all, tonight she will show that "famous" unseen footage from *Queen Kelly* and for the first time reveal the film's original, outlandish ending, taken from what she claims is the real screenplay, not the scenario that was approved by censors at the Hays Office.

Queen Kelly was Gloria's final silent movie and the most controversial chapter in her career. The cameras began turning in late 1928 and stopped in January 1929, when Gloria suddenly called a halt to the whole production. They tried again and again but the film was never finished, for reasons that have never been made entirely clear. Tonight, Gloria seems keen to stir up a little of the old controversy, hinting at a dispute behind the scenes. "Probably the most important character in the film is someone you never see. Mr Will Hays, the Hollywood czar of movie morals. With von Stroheim on one side, Will Hays on the other, and then there were the bankers loaning me the money—that's quite a triangle," she says. "And I was in the middle." Hays died in 1954, Stroheim in 1957. Gloria doesn't name the other party in question, banker-turned-film-producer-turned-diplomat Joseph P. Kennedy, patriarch of the Kennedy clan and her married lover back in the late 1920s, without whom *Queen Kelly* would never have been begun. There is a reason for delicacy. Joe is a sick man, paralysed on one side after suffering a stroke and under constant medical care.

In a theatrical and entirely fictional flourish, Gloria, who lives in an apartment at 920 Fifth Avenue, tells the audience that she has recently discovered, in her basement, a copy of Stroheim's "private script" for *Queen Kelly*. "A script I never read until yesterday. Will Hays never read this one at all." After the screening of the film and the recovered, unreleased footage, she will relate this eyebrow-raising scenario, which takes *Queen Kelly*'s story, a period romance between a prince and a convent girl in pre-World War I Europe, into shockingly seedy territory—a booze-sodden brothel in Tanzania, and a chase through a deadly swamp choked with crocodiles—before contriving a happy ending, with a wedding and a joke. A "naughty little number", indeed. Gloria is now the sole representative of the trio who made this film, and the story is hers to tell. As she informs the papers, "I own the picture—who the hell else paid for it?"[3]

A year earlier, in a much more decorous introduction on public television,[4] Gloria struck a less salacious tone, explaining that she became horrified by how Stroheim was deviating from the screenplay and creating a scurrilous film that would never be passed by the censors—so she reluctantly pulled the plug. It isn't that this story was entirely false, but like *Queen Kelly* itself it was incomplete. Perched on a divan, next to a vase of gladioli, Gloria sighed fatalistically, "This *Queen Kelly* gal was a child that somehow didn't want to be born." That broadcast, of the incomplete cut of the film, was a hit. "So many people talked about it," Gloria wrote excitedly to her *Queen Kelly* co-star Walter Byron a few days after the segment aired. "I am trying very hard to get it syndicated around the country."[5] It was not her most notable TV appearance of the year, however. That would be an episode of *The Beverly Hillbillies*, "The Gloria Swanson Story", in which she camps it up as a diva star of the silents, making a mute melodrama with Jed Clampett.

For the most part, Gloria promoted *Queen Kelly* the hard way, wearing out her own shoe leather. The Beacon double-bill is the biggest date on Gloria's own ad hoc *Queen Kelly* tour of film societies and university campuses, bringing an unreleased film to her public one screening at a time. Previewing the event, the short-lived paper *World Journal Tribune* reprinted the Roxy photograph from 1960 in what would be its last edition. It's a miracle that Gloria, who tended to the superstitious, didn't take that as a bad omen. Instead, she wrote cheerily to the paper's newly unemployed film critic William Peper to thank him for the story. "How little we knew—at least I—that in what was to be the final edition of your paper, there would be Swanson in the ruins, with newspapers going the way of theatre organs!"[6]

The Beacon show is a triumph. Letters pour in from her fans, some of them far too young to have seen her in the silent era, calling it "a thrilling experience" and taking Gloria up on her promise of an autograph to everyone who writes in. Gloria, whose next job is a run in the play *Reprise* in Chicago, continues the conversation on talk shows that summer—Johnny Carson, Merv Griffin—where she has yet more chances to reminisce about *Queen Kelly*. She will remain a popular guest on the talk show circuit throughout the 1970s, regularly answering questions about her most notorious film. It is worth losing yourself in a YouTube rabbit hole just to see her go toe-to-toe with rock star Janis Joplin on *The Dick Cavett Show* in 1970. The infamy of *Queen Kelly* keeps pace, step for step, with the unstoppable fame of Gloria Swanson. Everybody wants to know more about the film they cannot see.

Queen Kelly's incompleteness is what makes it so tricky to talk about, so controversial but also so fascinating. Film history is littered with lost and incomplete films—especially silent film history. The majority of silents, an estimated 70–95 percent, are presumed to be permanently lost, mostly now-obscure titles, but also works by directors such as F. W. Murnau or Alfred Hitchcock. Lost because their negatives were destroyed in studio fires, misplaced, worn out or decomposed; they existed in an era before film archives, when popular films were shipped around the world and screened until they gave out, and the negatives of less popular films were melted down for the value of their celluloid and silver. Of those prints that survive, many only exist with great patches of damage, missing reels or lost frames, sometimes edited in bizarre ways to appease the censors or to appeal to export audiences. Some feature films only reached posterity via a cut-down, small-gauge home cinema release. Exquisitely hand-painted versions of early films or early two-strip Technicolor sequences from feature-length movies have gone astray, or been worn down to nothing, leaving us only black-and-white echoes of what contemporary audiences enjoyed. In the late 1930s, all prints of *Queen Kelly* were officially destroyed.

Some films are incomplete in another, devastating fashion. These are the films that were released in a studio-mandated form that differs vastly from the makers' vision. In this way, *Queen Kelly* director Erich von Stroheim was the auteur of more incomplete films than most. He was kicked off films he was directing on more than one occasion and famously ejected from the editing process for *Greed* (1924) by MGM as the studio attempted to wrestle it down from a rumoured 42 reels to only ten. The *Greed* that was released was never Stroheim's *Greed*, and because much of his original footage is missing, the film he intended to make is now also lost. Orson Welles, Sergio Leone, John Huston, David Lynch and many more all fought and lost similar battles with studios. We might call these projects, including Welles's *The Magnificent Ambersons* (1942) or Huston's *The Red Badge of Courage* (1951), incomplete or unfinished films. The film that could have been, the film we are looking for, may never be found. The complete *Queen Kelly* can never be recovered.

There are other ways for a film to be lost, figuratively, though not literally, and *Queen Kelly* also joins the ranks of those films abandoned in the midst of production, such as Alfred Hitchcock's *Number 13* (1922), or Josef von Sternberg's *I, Claudius* (1937). It is one of those films whose productions were so notoriously troubled that their making-of histories became industry horror stories. *Queen Kelly* is up there with *Cleopatra* (Joseph L. Mankiewicz, 1963) and *Heaven's Gate* (Michael Cimino, 1980)—films that make studio executives' blood run cold. It may be the most terrifying of them all. As you will see, it has more than a little in common with those films that, even if more or less completed, were never released. That might be for financial or artistic considerations, as with Sternberg's *A Woman of the Sea* (1926), or, decades later, Jerry Lewis's Holocaust comedy *The Day the Clown Cried* (1972)—deemed to be in such bad taste it could never be shown to an audience.

There's a French term, *film maudit*, reserved specifically for films released to almost universal critical opprobrium, but whose true value became clear over time: Michael Powell's Soho serial-killer thriller *Peeping Tom* (1960) or Jean Vigo's satirical boarding-school saturnalia *Zéro de Conduite* (1933). A *film maudit* defies the odds, and its age, to become acclaimed as a masterpiece. As critic J. Hoberman wrote, "A true *film maudit* has a heroic saga."[7] *Queen Kelly* has that heroic saga indeed. It may not be a true *film maudit*, but anyone superstitious will see that it was, as the French term implies, a cursed film, and one with a long tale worth telling. Gloria certainly thought so.

As we picture Gloria telling that tale to the Beacon, or the TV camera, we must also place her, like Stroheim, as a *cinéaste maudit*. It took guts, luck and a lot of financial security to make it in the 1920s and 1930s as a female filmmaker, whether as a director such as Dorothy Arzner, an executive such as June Mathis, a screenwriter such as Frances Marion, even a star-producer such as Gloria. The odds were stacked against her. *Queen Kelly,* and its failure, represents the work of a Hollywood rebel, a woman better placed than most to express herself in the film industry, who still hit insurmountable obstacles. The lessons of *Queen Kelly* may resonate with later generations of filmmaking women. We have more recent examples of directors Sandi Tan and Zia Anger, who like Gloria took ownership of their own lost films and refashioned them into something else. For Tan it was the documentary *Shirkers* (2018), which tells the story of how her mentor stole the footage for her debut feature, also called *Shirkers* (1992). Anger presented the story of her own abandoned feature film *Always All Ways,* which was shot between 2010 and 2012, in the desktop performance *My First Film,* which she then adapted into a docudrama of the same name in 2024.

In a recent book advocating for the study of unfinished films, Alix Beeston and Stefan Solomon invite us to turn "away from the melancholy associations of the missing or the lost, accounting for—and stimulating—the agency and activity of those whom film industries marginalize".[8] By looking closely at *Queen Kelly,* and celebrating what has been saved, we turn away from regret at its loss and also look beyond the studio system, to admire the trailblazing spirit of a truly disruptive figure: Gloria Swanson. *Queen Kelly* can only be understood as an underground film because of the form in which it has survived. Gloria reclaimed it from the industry, from Hollywood, and championed it as something much more personal, and precarious, than any of her other films she is known for.

"Unfinished or not," Gloria told the Beacon audience, "*Kelly* has had a life of her own." This book—more elaborate than the stories Gloria told—relates how a magnificent film star, frustrated by her career options, and running out of cash, fell into an affair with one of silent Hollywood's most ruthless businessmen, Joseph P. Kennedy, whose notoriety and influence extended far beyond the movie business. Together they teamed up with Erich von Stroheim, a drastically extravagant talent, a cinematic genius, to make a masterpiece: a bizarre, beautiful, and truncated film about an illicit, strangely innocent romance in a sordid world. In the process, they created one of the film industry's most blood-curdling cautionary tales.

Joe, Gloria and Von (as he was so often known), who were fond of spending other people's money, sleeping with other people's spouses, and who could be very cruel at times, sound a little like F. Scott Fitzgerald's "careless people", his exemplars of Roaring Twenties egoism in *The Great Gatsby.*[9] But that comparison is not entirely fair to our trio. Working out what our trio really cared about helps us to understand *Queen Kelly.* Joe and Gloria cared for each other, it's true. Joe's chief concern was to leave a legacy for his nine children, to raise his family out of financial struggles and beyond criticism of their Irish-immigrant heritage. Gloria likewise was a tireless worker, who staged her own crusade against Hollywood's sexual double standards. She became the guardian and champion of their shared romantic folly, *Queen Kelly*, as she fought to preserve the memory of the silent era and all its lost films. Von cared deeply, passionately about cinema, and was uncompromising in the pursuit of his own creative truth. No one in silent Hollywood was as exacting an artist. All three might identify with the *Gatsby*'s narrator, Nick, gazing at the beautiful people across the bay: Joe, the barkeeper's son snubbed by Boston Brahmins and Harvard protestants, Gloria, mistreated by her husbands, her reputation besmirched, betrayed by her friends in the industry, and Von, living a double-life, scapegoated by Hollywood. All three wanted to make something that would live longer, mean more than they did.

That is why the history of *Queen Kelly* is so much more than just a horror story. It is also why we must finally lift what Gloria memorably termed "the curse of *Queen Kelly*".

1. All quotations from this introduction taken from Swanson's notes for the event, Gloria Swanson Archive (GSA).
2. Lee Beaupre, "Nostalgia Eve: Gloria Swanson & Organ Music", *Variety*, 10 May 1967.
3. Syndicated interview with Philip K. Scheuer, "The indestructible Gloria Swanson", *The Morning Call*, 30 September 1967, 42.
4. *A Million and One Nights*, Channel 13, TX 28 March 1966.
5. Letter from Gloria Swanson to Walter Byron, 31 March 1996, GSA.
6. Letter from GS to William Peper, 11 May 1967, GSA.
7. J. Hoberman, "No success like failure: A natural history of the film maudit", *Sight and Sound*, April 2021, 43.
8. Alix Beeston and Stefan Solomon, *Incomplete: The Feminist Possibilities of the Unfinished Film* (University of California Press, 2023), 7.
9. F. Scott Fitzgerald, *The Great Gatsby* (Charles Scribner's Sons, 1925), 216.

1
The Debutantes

The tale of *Queen Kelly* begins in 1914, when a starstruck young American woman and a mysterious Austrian man with a dubious history step into a film studio for the first time—while Boston's most promising young man of finance walks down the aisle.

Gloria Swanson, started making pictures as a teenager. She was playing lead roles by the time she was 17 and getting top billing at 19. By then she was already caught in Hollywood's teeth. Gloria Mae Josephine Swanson was born in Chicago on 27 March 1899 and raised there, with a couple of stints in Key West and Puerto Rico, where the family temporarily transferred because of her father's army career. She had a mixed European heritage; her father came from a family of puritanical Swedish Lutherans, named Svensson, her mother's family, a couple of generations back, was from Alsace—her great-grandfather had come to Chicago in 1852. Her maternal grandfather was a Polish Jew named Klanowski. She was a spoiled, beloved only child with an upturned nose, large teeth and oversized ears that her mother attempted to hide with hair ribbons. As a little girl she loved unusual clothes, playing mother to her dolls and singing. And she loved to get her own way. Although mostly raised Lutheran, she was briefly enrolled in a convent school in Florida but she protested so much that her parents agreed to have her educated at home by a tutor instead. She dreamed of becoming an opera singer and she said a prayer every night for an exciting life.

It was when Gloria was 13 or 14 that she first began to notice boys, and they noticed her too. Her father cautioned her to wait; there was plenty of time for boyfriends later. Film stars provided a safe outlet for teenage lust, though. She didn't much like the Swedish and Danish films that she had seen when she was living in Puerto Rico ("You could see people moving around waving their arms, and then some words printed in Swedish, and then more people making faces. In ten minutes it was all over."[1]) but she had a crush on an American movie star, Francis X. Bushman, a matinee idol with a muscular physique who was making films at Chicago's Essanay studios. This infatuation should have been inconsequential, but it may have changed her life because Gloria always believed in taking matters into her own hands.

One day towards the end of 1914, when the Swansons were back in Chicago, 15-year-old Gloria made her way to the Essanay studios to take a private tour with her aunt Inga. She remembered exactly what she was wearing: a large black-and-white checked skirt with a slit in the middle and a black cutaway jacket made from an Irene Castle pattern, paired with a green waistcoat and topped by a felt Knox hat. According to Gloria, she took the tour on a whim, at her aunt's invitation, and once she arrived she was horrified by the sight of comedians performing violent, messy slapstick routines, including a mêlée of roller-skaters who fell over and ended up in a heap: "I thought it was vulgar, disgusting and stupid."[2] But then she was taken to a different studio, where Canadian actor Richard Travers and Danish actress Gerda Holmes were filming a wedding scene. This was far more appealing to Gloria and it was there that a casting director, Mr Babile, spotted the diminutive visitor in the eye-catching ensemble and asked for her name and telephone number. He wasn't Francis X. Bushman, but Gloria handed over her details anyway.

Babile called Gloria the next day, asking her to come to the studio to work as an extra and to be sure to wear the same outfit. After seeking reassurance that she wouldn't be asked to roller skate in her best clothes, Gloria agreed and made her movie debut handing a bouquet to Holmes, who was dressed in a bridal gown. She received $3.25 for her day's work and treated herself to a dill pickle. The film has never been conclusively identified but may well be the lost *The Ambition of the Baron*, released in early 1915. Gloria was called back to the studio for two more days' work, each time dressing with care, as instructed. She avoided smiling to hide her teeth, learned a little something about makeup and clothes for movies, a little more about the temperament of directors, and counted herself lucky to have made $9.75, toasting her success with another pickle. She went to visit her father in New York where her mother forwarded her a letter offering her a steady job as an extra at between $13.25 and nearly $20 a week, depending on how many days she worked. Gloria said yes.

There are other versions of this story. Some friends were convinced that Gloria went to the studio that day deliberately to catch someone's eye. Bushman himself ungallantly claimed he had repeatedly seen Gloria hanging around the studio gates and had to shoo her away. It may not be Gloria's version of events but there is something appealing in the idea that whether determined to be a star, or to date her dream guy, this teenager dressed up and turned up day after day until the studio took notice. By accident or design, Gloria realised her dream of an exciting life. She left school and started work at Essanay right away, sharing a dressing cubicle with a girl called Virginia Bowker. On their first day they pencilled in their eyebrows and donned swanky outfits to appear in one of the Sweedie comedies directed by Lightning Hopper and starring Wallace Beery—the beefy star whom she would marry less than eighteen months later, on her 17th birthday.

o o o

Also in 1914, two thousand miles away in Hollywood, California, Erich von Stroheim made his debut on a much more famous film, D. W. Griffith's *The Birth of a Nation*. Five years previously, a 24-year-old Viennese man called Erich Oswald Stroheim had boarded the steamer Prinz Friedrich Wilhelm bound for New York. He had been born to Jewish parents, milliner and shopkeeper Benno Stroheim and his Czech wife Johanna Bondy, on 22 September 1885, and his CV included a brief stint in the military that ended in desertion. On arrival at Ellis Island this same man identified himself as Erich Oswald Hans Carl Maria von Stroheim—the crucial "von" designating his assumed aristocratic status. He was to refine and elaborate his legend over the following years, but his new backstory was also to comprise elite education, decorated service in conflicts of global significance (including the Bosnia-Herzegovina annexation of December 1908), and always noble birth. He would never again represent himself as a Jew.

That Von's first film engagement was the most famous, and infamous, of all silent Hollywood's output, *The Birth of a Nation*, immediately has the ring of a tall tale. But as scholar Richard Koszarski concluded after following all the evidence, this one may well be true. Various members of the cast and crew recall Von on set, not always fondly. Having worked as a salesman and completed another couple of months in the military, this time in the New York National Guard, Von travelled west to California. He took a job as a factotum at a West Point County inn where he began writing fiction and met his first wife, Margaret. Between their financial struggles and Von's drunken temper, the marriage soon hit the rocks. In summer 1914, he left the marital home to work a couple of temporary jobs, first rowing tourists across Lake Tahoe then working at a riding academy in Pasadena. This is when the call would have gone out from Griffith's team in Hollywood for extras and horses to swell the crowd scenes in *The Birth of a Nation*. Von claimed that he served as an assistant and as a stuntman, falling from a rooftop. Further, he "impersonated seven negroes"[3] in blackface.

Accounts of Von's involvements from other members of cast and crew differ. What Von mostly did was keep his eyes peeled, observing the mechanics of a movie set and a director at work. But not just any director and not just any movie. Von's first taste of filmmaking was a prophetic one, in terms of scale. Griffith was spending wildly and shooting ten or twelve times the footage he needed, a pattern that Von was to follow in his own directorial career, in which he was known for busting budgets, courting controversy, going to extreme lengths to control every detail of production, and turning in overlong cuts of his films. In the summer of 1914, Von took lessons from Griffith in the more-is-more school of film-making.

When the shoot was over, Von began working as a movie extra, just like Gloria. But unlike Gloria, he had no studio contract and for him the $3 a day was more than just pocket money—he had to live on it. Von had to hustle. When one day he got talking to actor John Emerson on the Griffith lot, he presented himself as an expert on European military uniforms and critiqued the latter's costume. A short while later, Emerson, now directing, planned to adapt *Old Heidelberg*, the play by Wilhelm Mayer-Förster, with Wallace Reid and Dorothy Gish starring. He asked Von if he had ever been to Heidelberg. Von had not, but according to screenwriter Anita Loos, Emerson's wife, he responded: "I am a graduate of the university, sir." Von claims he merely stated that Austria too had a student corps. Whether he fibbed or not, his answer convinced Emerson he had the necessary expertise, and he was hired as a technical advisor on $15 a week, which soon became an assistant director role. He also played a named part in the film and makes a considerable impression as Lutz, the young prince's tutor, a strict guardian wearing a monocle and breeches, a getup that was to become his trademark. Von was making his way up the Hollywood hierarchy thanks to his boundless chutzpah, dubious credentials, and glowering screen presence.

o o o

Joseph P. Kennedy made no claims to aristocratic birth, but he was without doubt Boston royalty. In October 1914, aged 26, Joe married 24-year-old Rose Fitzgerald, eldest daughter of Boston mayor John Francis "Honey Fitz" Fitzgerald. Joe was already well connected, the son of a powerful local mover and shaker, Patrick Joseph "P. J." Kennedy, an entrepreneurial second-generation Irish immigrant who built up his fortune and influence through running city bars, catering to Boston's Irish contingent. He expanded his empire to include several local businesses and investments, and collaborated with a few like-minded peers to found Columbia Trust, a bank—a credit union, really—for Boston's Irish community. Mostly, he was a sharp and tireless, if reserved, political operator, the highly respected boss of East Boston's ward two. Joseph, his eldest son, was born on 6 September 1888 with ambition to spare and a knack for making money. He inherited his father's charm and ruthless streak. Joe was born to as much privilege as East Boston could afford, attending the elite school Boston Latin, although he was more athletic than academic.

At Harvard, reality hit. Having been held back a year to study for his entrance exams, Joe was 20, older than his peers, and low down the pecking order, one of a small minority of Catholics and Democrats, and from a new-money family. Refused entry to the Hasty Pudding Club, he developed a sense of himself as an outsider for life. But he refused to make his home on the bottom rung and worked hard, or at least smart, to make money and improve his extra-curricular record. Scurrilous stories abound in relation to Joe's Harvard years, from blackmailing his way on to the Varsity baseball team to demanding a permit from the Mayor for an unlicensed tourist bus service to getting paid as a reporter for *The Boston Globe*, although it was a classmate who wrote the articles, unpaid. These tales can't all be true, but a peer recalled, "If he wanted something bad enough, [he] would get it and he didn't much care how he got it. He'd run right over anybody."[4]

After graduating with mixed grades, Joe found that in Boston, just as at Harvard, he had to fight against his marginalisation as an Irish Catholic. Although the Irish were in the majority, the city's best jobs in finance, the ones Joe wanted, went to the Protestant sons of Boston Brahmins. "You can go to Harvard and it doesn't mean a damn thing," Joe told a colleague years later. "The only thing these people understand is money."[5] On graduating, Joe worked as a bank examiner and invested in a local real-estate company, becoming its treasurer. He learned the ABCs of finance, discovering, as he put it: "We make a mistake when we call money hard cash. It's lively and fluid—the blood of business."[6] It could be manipulated to his own ends. In 1913, as he proudly boasted to the press, he became America's youngest bank president—or, at least, he took over the running of Columbia Trust, which was nearly the same thing.

His wedding to Rose Fitzgerald was to be another step towards self-aggrandisement, uniting two of Boston's most prominent Irish families. But the feeling wasn't mutual. Honey Fitz had long been cool on the Kennedys—P.J. had backed his electoral opponents. He had attempted to keep Joe and Rose apart but they had become college sweethearts regardless; at parties Joe filled in Rose's dance card with aliases to cover the fact that she spent the evening dancing with just one boy. Honey lost his moral authority over Rose when he resigned from his re-election campaign early in 1914. He pleaded poor health, but the truth was that his opponent was threatening to expose his adultery with a cigarette girl named Elizabeth "Toodles" Ryan, who was the same age as his daughter. Rose defied her father and accepted Joe's proposal of marriage.

Joe was a handsome groom in a top hat—six-foot tall and stocky with brown-auburn hair and blue eyes. Rose, sweetly pretty with dark curls and a sparkling smile, was resplendent in a white satin dress with a long train and a veil, plus a lavish bouquet of white orchids and lilies of the valley. Still, the wedding Honey Fitz laid on for his eldest daughter was pointedly modest; the couple were married quietly in the private chapel of Cardinal O'Connell, at nine in the morning. Nicknamed Number One because he was Boston's first archbishop to become a cardinal and because of his mighty influence in Massachusetts, O'Connell was a powerful, hardline and later controversial figure who took a lasting interest in the Kennedy-Fitzgerald marriage. Some say Joe and Honey Fitz quarrelled as soon as the wedding reception in the Fitzgerald house, but the newlyweds travelled to New York that afternoon to begin an epic honeymoon. They attended the Liberty Theatre that night to see *He Comes Up Smiling*, featuring Douglas Fairbanks in a farce about a clerk who becomes a hobo but corners the cotton market.

After three weeks, taking in Philadelphia, White Sulphur Springs and Atlantic City, the couple moved to what Rose later called a "rather a common looking little house in Brookline"[7], a largely Protestant area, and started their marriage on an uncertain footing, steeped in Joe's debts, and sexually far from compatible. The situation was not helped by the fact that Rose fell pregnant almost immediately and gave birth to their first child, Joseph Patrick Kennedy Jr, in July 1915. Eight more children would follow. Perhaps only a man as determined as Joe could foresee that this union would produce America's most famous political dynasty, even a president of the United States. No one present, one hopes, could have imagined the terrible Kennedy curse, the hard-to-shake superstition that however high the Kennedy children flew, they would be shadowed by death and disaster, a far-fetched theory nevertheless supported by a series of early deaths, terrible accidents and assassinations. Just six years after his marriage, Joe would have a premature confrontation with his own mortality when he was caught up in what was the deadliest terrorist attack yet on American soil.

1.   Gloria Swanson, *Swanson on Swanson* (*SoS*; Random House, 1980), 25.
2.   *SoS*, 26.
3.   Quoted, Richard Koszarski, *Von: The Life and Films of Erich von Stroheim* (Limelight Editions, 2001), 16.
4.   Quoted, Richard J. Whalen, *The Founding Father* (American Library, 1964), 27.
5.   Quoted, Cari Beauchamp, *Joseph P. Kennedy Presents: His Hollywood Years* (Alfred A. Knopf, 2009), 8.
6.   Quoted, Beauchamp, 12.
7.   Amanda Smith (ed), *Hostage to Fortune: The Letters of Joseph P. Kennedy* (Viking, 2001), 14.

2
The Business

The saga of *Queen Kelly* really begins in the Roaring Twenties, the years of America's booming economy and Hollywood's great rise, which offered the rich and powerful a decade of barely contained excess. It was the carnival before the fast caused by the Wall Street Crash and the coming of sound. *Queen Kelly*, in all its pomp, represents one of the last flourishes of the 1920s' optimistic hedonism—reason enough to jump to the opening of that ferocious decade. Joe is making money and his name on the east coast while Von is making movies and his name on the west coast, fighting with his studio bosses. Gloria is a Hollywood star, also about to go to war with the front office.

Let's begin where we left off, with Joe—and the blast. At one minute past noon on 16 September 1920, a bomb exploded in a horse-drawn wagon parked opposite the J.P. Morgan & Co. premises at 23 Wall Street. The bomb consisted of 230kg (500lbs) of cast-iron window sash weights strapped to 45kg (100lbs) of dynamite and a timer. Thirty-eight people plus the horse died. Hundreds more were injured and the interior of the Morgan building was torn apart, the marble walls of the facade gashed by shrapnel, the windows shattered, glass hurled across the street. The driver of the wagon was seen escaping down a side street. Although the culprits were never formally identified, blame fell on an anarchist collective called the Galleanists, who had set off similar bombs in 1919. The prestigious banking house was clearly the target but the bomb's location meant that most of those injured or killed were younger people, junior bank employees, not the partners, whose offices faced Broad Street, away from the blast. Jack Morgan himself was at a shooting lodge in Scotland.

Joe was emerging from the subway when he felt "a concussion" and was thrown to the ground by the force of the explosion. He told *The Boston Daily Globe* that he witnessed "clouds of glass flying and men and women with their heads split and blood streaming down their faces. Numbers were crying in agony and fear." Not for the last time, Joe emerged from a disaster unscathed but with a good story to tell. For generations, bankers asked each other, "Where were you when the blast occurred?" Anarchists had already become stock villains or figures of ridicule in silent films. In early 1922, Buster Keaton replayed the Wall Street attack for laughs in his two-reel comedy *Cops*, with the hero catching the anarchists' bomb and throwing it into the path of a police parade.

How did Joe make his way to Wall Street in the first place? He had been busy, very visibly so, at the Columbia Trust, running the business while managing his personal investments and trusteeships via a desk phone fitted with a muffler to protect his precious conversations from eavesdroppers. Throughout his career he did most of his business on the phone, leaving as little documentary evidence as possible. His stated aim was to become a millionaire by the time he was 35; he would amass a family fortune so vast that his children need not worry about money, and

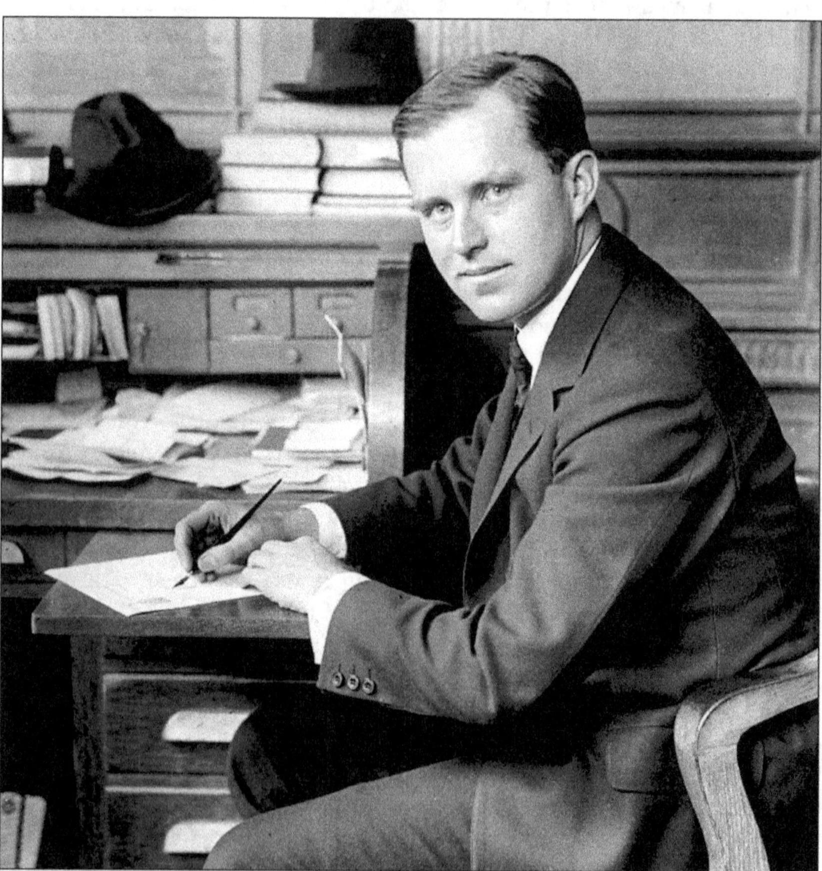

Joseph P. Kennedy, a promising young businessman.

could devote their lives to public service. Then World War I intervened, with the US entering the conflict in 1917. Joe had been entirely opposed to American involvement and more particularly the idea of facing combat himself, and tried (and failed) to claim exemption from conscription on the grounds of being a father and running a bank. His way of joining the war effort was to quit Columbia Trust to become assistant general manager of Bethlehem's Fore River Ship Building Corporation in Quincy, Massachusetts at $4,000 a year (at least $100,000 today) plus bonus. He did this with the encouragement of his new mentor, lawyer and lobbyist Guy Currier, and thanks to his father-in-law calling in a favour. He was still considered 1-A fit but the company president had sway in Washington; Joe was never officially deferred but nor was he drafted. As a middle manager at Fore River, Joe ran himself ragged putting in 60-hour weeks. When the influenza epidemic swept Boston in the autumn of 1918, the Kennedys survived but Joe was at a low ebb. By the time the war ended, he had developed his first ulcer and was sent to a health farm to recuperate. Today we would call it a classic case of burnout.

After the war, in July 1919, Joe joined the Boston offices of the Hayden, Stone brokerage and shuttled back and forth between Boston and New York. At home in Boston he played the bountiful breadwinner; each time Rose had a baby, he opened an account for the child at Columbia Trust and presented his wife with an expensive piece of jewellery. In Manhattan he did business on Wall Street and partied with chorus girls after hours—often in the company of Currier, who was discreetly but serially unfaithful to his wife, Shakespearean actress Marie Burroughs. In early 1920, Rose was very far gone with their fourth child when she learned that Joe had been dating the movie actress Betty Compson in New York. Compson ended the relationship because of Joe's promiscuity, which was far more widely known than Currier's. Rose briefly moved back in with her parents but they encouraged her to try and make the marriage work. A further crisis arrived when their second child, John Fitzgerald, caught scarlet fever and came close to death. When the boy recovered, Joe promised to be a better father, wrote a cheque to charity, and bought Rose a bigger house, also in Brookline. He also moved up to a $10,000-a-year job managing Hayden, Stone's stock exchange department.

Joe began to work towards that goal of becoming a millionaire at Hayden, Stone, where he was able to top up his salary by making his own investments. His methods were legal. Joe's boss, Galen Stone, was adept at what we would now call insider trading. Joe stumbled when he first started playing the market this way but soon came into his own. He favoured a game called stock pools, whereby a pool of brokers would appoint a manager to inflate the price of a stock, then sell it when it was high. The pool made a tidy packet, whereas all the smaller investors who fell for the rising stock would be left with losses. He also invested in companies and especially in real estate with his best friend Eddie Moore, a likeable, gentle man with a dry sense of humour, formerly in Honey Fitz's employ but soon to become Joe's most trusted adviser. Joe chased every lead to make a deal. His signature move was chatting up secretaries, sending flowers and love notes to ensure they booked him in for a meeting with their boss.

In January 1920, the Volstead Act and the advent of Prohibition presented another business opportunity. For years, stories have swirled — always denied by the Kennedy family — that teetotal Joe and his publican father ran a sideline delivering booze for clients including the media mogul William Randolph Hearst and his mistress Marion Davies. Joe was no gangster. The most likely story is that he and his father, like many others, simply squirreled away as much liquor as possible. Thanks to P.J.'s business they had a bigger cellar than most to start with. During the Prohibition years they could use this stash to entertain guests, donate generously to the occasional private function, and make a few discreet illegal sales. They were able to start selling the strong stuff again the minute that the law changed in 1933. For his own part, Joe never touched alcohol, nor did he smoke. He didn't even drink coffee.

The investment that really appealed to Joe — the fledgling movie business — carried a different kind of risk. He loved the theatre but quickly understood that a performer captured on celluloid, playing in a hundred cinemas at once, could make more money than a turn on the stage, entertaining one hall at a time. What attracted Joe to the film business was the sight of the queues outside the cinemas. He was agog when he saw how much money his friend Bill Gray was making from his chain of cinemas in New Hampshire and began to read the film trade papers, studying what he saw as a sector with potential. "Look at that bunch of pants pressers in Hollywood making themselves millionaires," he notoriously told a colleague, throwing in a casual slur against the Jewish immigrants excelling in the film industry. "I could take the whole business away from them."[1]

So now Joe was divided between three worlds: Boston, Wall Street and the movies, each of which had their own pitfalls. In 1919 Joe put vaudeville comedian Fred Stone under contract, paying him an advance of $1,000 a week to make films through the summer when the theatres were shut. It was an advance, not a salary — to be paid back from his percentage of the net profits, which were calculated only after Joe had taken out every possible expense and cost. As the treasurer of Fred Stone Productions, Joe paid himself $100 a week and gave himself an expense account, but had to admit there wasn't any real money to be made this way. Wise to the power of celebrity, Kennedy bought an option on a film starring Babe Ruth of the Boston Red Sox but couldn't find anyone willing to make a movie with a star of what was considered only regional appeal, and Ruth cancelled the deal.

Joe also assembled a ragtag crew of businessmen to found a fairly shaky distribution business called Columbia Films.[2] He again put himself on salary and scored a minor coup when he negotiated a deal with Carl Laemmle to distribute Universal's films in New England, including Erich von Stroheim's debut, *Blind Husbands*. Joe made sure everyone at Hayden, Stone knew that any film-biz opportunities that came in were to go through him. At the turn of 1920 he snapped up the chance to invest $86,000 (around $1.3m today) into Hallmark Pictures Corporation, but the company almost immediately went into receivership.

When Joe's big chance in the movie business finally presented itself, it was a chastened, or at least circumspect, man who wrote, just eight days after the Wall Street bomb had knocked him off his feet: "[M]y experience in the picture business with my own money, and, in some instances, with that of my friends, has been very disastrous, due, very likely to our ignorance of the business and our childlike simplicity in taking stock in anybody in the motion picture business." The letter was to Rufus Cole, the American co-founder of small film company Robertson-Cole, which had been in business since 1918, first selling cars then distributing films, but now, after buying land in Hollywood to build a studio, it was operating at a loss. Cole approached Hayden, Stone hoping to sell the business, but Joe had a different strategy in mind. As usual, flattery was the first phase of his plan, telling Cole: "It has been a great pleasure to know you and I do want to have the satisfaction of having a motion picture deal with a man in whom I have the confidence I have in you."[3]

Cole was a hard nut to crack, but by the end of 1920 Joe had formed a new company, the Robertson-Cole Distributing Company of New England. By a complex reorganisation of his portfolio, which included using funds belonging to his mother and loans relying on collateral from his father-in-law, he had spent only $5,000 of his own money to start up a company worth $300,000. He asked the secretary to whom he entrusted these orders to "kindly destroy" the letter after she had done his bidding. In February 1921, Joe came home early from his annual Palm Beach vacation with his buddies to prepare for the Boston premiere of *Kismet*, the first film made at Robertson-Cole's Hollywood studio. It was the second screen adaptation of an exotic Edward Knoblock play from 1911 about a beggar who becomes Emir of Baghdad, and starred Otis Skinner, reprising the role he had taken on Broadway. *Kismet* was directed by the capable Louis J Gasnier, a Frenchman who had been making films since the turn of the century. In Europe he worked with stars such as French comedian

Max Linder and Italian diva Francesca Bertini, and after moving to the States in 1910 he scored a global hit with the action serial *Perils of Pauline*. Nothing else in his career would make such an impact, save one of his final films, the 1936 exploitation title *Tell Your Children*, better known as the cult favourite *Reefer Madness*.

Naturally, Joe was hoping for a hit, but he did more than hope. He asked his father-in-law to use his influence to persuade the Boston papers to give *Kismet* good coverage and to persuade the venue, the Majestic Theatre in Boston, to lower the rent. Through gritted teeth, he spent his own money to rent oil paintings to hang in the lobby and to print 20,000 black-and-gold programmes and hundreds of desk blotters to give away to customers. His team's publicity wheezes included the suggestion that cinema owners hire camels to parade down the street, and men "dressed as Arabs" to hand out the blotters. In the end, neither Otis Skinner nor Cole himself could attend the premiere, but the film was the success Joe wanted, and cinema owner friend Bill Gray admired it, which meant a lot to him.

It wasn't enough to save Robertson-Cole's business model. They didn't have enough money to keep making such films, and once Joe became a company director and looked at the books, he could see the accounts were in a shambles and debts were rising. There seemed no choice but to sell the company, but Joe wasn't going to give up his place in the movie industry just yet, even if it represented one of his poorer investments. He shopped around for a merger, with no success. For now, Robertson-Cole would struggle on, renamed Film Booking Offices of America (FBO), with Cole out, replaced by Pat Powers, formerly the co-founder of Universal, with Carl Laemmle.

Joe declined to put any of his money into the business—he never put any of his own funds into any of his movie ventures. At this time, Joe's personal wealth and social standing grew, along with the rising stock market. By the end of 1923 he had five children, had formed an investment company, bought his first Rolls-Royce, put his pal Eddie Moore on the payroll as "chief of staff", and was proud to have provided both the liquor and a movie show (boxing matches and a bathing scene from *Kismet*) for his ten-year Harvard reunion party. He was not yet a millionaire but was well on his way—and slowly breaking into America's hottest new industry.

1.   Quoted, Betty Lasky, *RKO: The Biggest Little Major of Them All* (Round-table, 1989), 12.
2.   Nothing to do with the studio later called Columbia Pictures.
3.   *Hostage to Fortune*, 25-6.

3
The Legend

Erich von Stroheim was also multitasking to get ahead, working on both sides of the camera and on both coasts. In addition to acting, he was assistant to both John Emerson and D. W. Griffith on films including *Intolerance*. Griffith impressed him with his perfectionism, his emphasis on costume and décor for character building, his sentiment and his sense of scale. In 1916 Von was married for a second time, to May Jones, with whom he had a son, Erich Jr. He was also engaged in an extended and extremely reckless off-screen performance. Von was a filmmaker, a husband and a father—but to America moviegoers, and the American authorities, he was a villain.

The outbreak of war made Von's Germanic name and appearance both a liability and a tricky kind of asset to his career. While his credit was dropped from the Douglas Fairbanks pictures he worked on, Von got plenty of screen time playing dastardly Huns in films that banked on anti-German feeling. His most notorious role was as the tyrannous rapist Lieutenant Eric von Eberhard in the Universal film *The Heart of Humanity* (1918). Here, Von rips the heroine's nurse uniform off with his teeth as he assaults her, and in the same scene, throws a baby through a window. Jaws fell to the floor, Von's monocle glistened, and a legend was born.

Von even peacocked off-set in his costume, which was a dangerous way to get attention. Anita Loos, who was married to Emerson, remembered that Von, "dressed in the Prussian uniform of the movie's villain, would stalk over to the Plaza Hotel, engage one of the fiacres [horse-drawn carriages] stationed there, and ride arrogantly through Central Park, accepting the jeers of American patriots along his way with an imperious twist of his monocle".[1]

Augmenting his persona as a man with German military connections, he continued to advise filmmakers on the details of enemy operations. When Von was working on the spy thriller *Sylvia of the Secret Service* (George Fitzmaurice, 1917) he did some practical research into the explosives that German soldiers might use to blow up an ammunition dump. When he inevitably was arrested, the studio blazed in to get him out of jail, which made for great publicity—especially as Von was also playing The Villain. But it wasn't a publicity stunt. In fact, the authorities had been keeping an eye on Von throughout the war because of such antics and repeated "unpatriotic" or anti-American remarks. Von continued to play this dangerous prank by maintaining his cover story as a titled officer in the Austrian army, and an arrogant one at that, even under questioning. A report from the *Sylvia* incident reads: "When asked why he had visited U.S. military sites as part of his research, he replied that 'he smoked cigarettes laying against the big guns and no one had the nerve to ask him his business.'"[2]

This was in the wake of the Black Tom Explosion of 1916, when German agents had blown up a munitions plant on Black Tom Island in New Jersey, killing several people and damaging the Statue of Liberty. It would be all too easy later for people in the film industry to scapegoat a man who so enthusiastically presented himself as the enemy in and out of costume. *Close-Up* magazine, a European journal devoted to serious cinema, saw through the pose as an artistic gesture: "He becomes the man you'll love to hate, and as Stroheim knows what he is about, he is the man whom Stroheim wants you to love to hate."[3]

This dual life as a German thug also took a toll on the Austrian, who was rapidly losing friends. In Germany he was considered a traitor and a warmonger, but when he went out to restaurants in Los Angeles fellow patrons threw their bread rolls at him. He asserted his Austrian identity, to no avail: "We on the Danube loved the Germans as the Irish loved the English." Among people who knew him better than the public, Von also failed to win hearts and minds. When *The Unbeliever* (Alan Crosland, 1918), a war film made with the support of the U.S. Marine Corps and shot at Quantico, was screened in San Francisco, Von's dentist, who counted him as a friend, contacted Naval Intelligence with his concern that the man playing the German officer on screen was an Austrian spy, citing a suspicious incident from back in 1913. The investigation was dropped when the war ended. Even Von's colleagues on the Griffith lot found him odd, to say the least. Lillian Gish remembered that he wept like a child after missing out on a role he expected to get. They also witnessed his messy breakup with May in 1919, before he married his third wife, Valerie Germonprez.

Von met Valerie on the set of *The Heart of Humanity*. She was playing an ambulance driver and Von smeared her white van with mud in the name of realism. He started taking her out on dates while he was still married to May. The Germonprez family took him in when he caught influenza and when he went looking for work again, Valerie drove him round the studios, as Von didn't have a licence. He was writing screenplays, and there was one in particular that had promise. *The Pinnacle* was a love story set in the Alpine resort of Croce Bianca, near the Austro-Italian border, in which an amoral Austrian officer seduces an American tourist on holiday with her husband, a doctor. Desperate to get the story to Carl Laemmle, the German-born boss of Universal, Von turned up on the executive's doorstep, begged a meeting and proceeded to energetically act out the whole story on the spot, including the mountain-top climax. His pitch was the deal of the decade: he would direct the film for free, asking only $200 a week to play the seducer, Lieutenant Eric von Steuben.

Laemmle agreed, though soon discovered this wasn't the bargain it had first appeared to be. Von promised to bring the film in on a $75,000 budget, but costs rapidly ran away from him. He kept adding to the film and extending the schedule; the longer shoot, as well as hand-sewn costumes and other details, pushed up the negative cost to $112,114 (with more than that yet to be spent on marketing). He was inexperienced when it came to working with actors, shooting take after take as he attempted to manipulate the atmosphere on set. His actors included former colleagues Sam de Grasse as the doctor and Francelia Billington as his wife, plus Gibson Gowland, in the crucial role of the mountain guide. Valerie took a small role as one half of a honeymooning couple in the same resort, a representation of Von's innocent, romantic ideal.

However, even while Laemmle lamented the over-running shoot and rising costs, he could see that Von was doing something very special; the psychological realism was intense, the visuals sumptuous. This was the work of an exceptional director, albeit a debut. Von spent the summer editing the film down to a more release-friendly length, while Universal ramped up the hype. First, public opinion had to be massaged. The "von" was dropped from his surname in the publicity, which stressed that he was a naturalised American citizen (not true—yet) and a well-liked jolly fellow whose new film satirised the German mindset. Further, Universal promoted this film as one might the work of an established auteur. "Carl Laemmle offers Stroheim," ran the full-page ads, "the genius who conceived the idea, wrote the story, directed the production and who plays the leading role in the most enthralling picture of modern times." Laemmle and Von even agreed to put their names to a little trade-press spat over the film's change of name, to *Blind Husbands*, with the director protesting over "a name in which there is no beauty—no sense of the artistic"[4] in one ad, while the exec responded, "Art is a glorious thing in pictures, but when it comes to the title, commercialism must come first. Otherwise there would not be enough money in it to pay for the art!"[5] It was an argument Von was to have many more times, but with genuine fury.

Talking of the bottom line, when *Blind Husbands* was released in December 1919 it was a hit, winning rave reviews and more than making back its costs. Critics enthused over both the film and a director of remarkable promise. Von is excellent on screen too. He creates a captivating, grinning villain; vigorous and charming until he is overwhelmed by fear in the final reel. At only five foot six, Von carries himself with straight-backed military hauteur and wears his tailored uniform well. When the wayward wife dreams of the Lieutenant, an isolated closeup of Von's face (scar, monocle, beaming smile, cigarette holder) expands to fill the frame. This brands the film a Stroheim picture through and through. The story draws on aspects of his own life history and the legend he had created for himself. Von was putting his whole self into his pictures from the very beginning and making a success of it.

The triumph of *Blind Husbands* not only launched his personal brand into the stratosphere, it was the ideal start for his career as a director. By the date of its premiere he had finished shooting his second film, *The Devil's Pass-Key*. Von decided not to appear in this Paris-set story of an American playwright, his extravagant wife and the military man who offers her a loan in return for sexual favours. As with *Blind Husbands* it's a story of suspected cuckolding, with an army officer as the presumed homewrecker and a European setting. But the film, which took a full five months to edit, wasn't nearly as well received when released in August 1920 and the negative was destroyed in 1941, after it had begun to decompose. It has since been considered a lost film, a mayfly project. It served a purpose for Von, though. The previews had been strong enough for him to negotiate a pay rise from Universal: $800 a week for directing plus $400 a week for acting, with "escalator clauses" pushing the figures up after the first six months. Laemmle threw a fit when he saw the numbers, but Von had already started building sets for his next, most lavish film yet, the most expensive Hollywood had ever seen. Joe may have dreamed of accumulating a million dollars for posterity; for Von the dream was to spend that much money on a movie. The movie was *Foolish Wives*, and it would turn the next two years of Von's life into a nightmare.

Foolish Wives is where Von really became known for his multiplying excesses, his prohibitively expensive perfectionism, and his self-promotion. The film is a grander, more spectacular version of the *Blind Husbands* story, set in the sunny French Riviera. Von plays a scheming seducer who arrives in Monte Carlo posing as Count Wladislaw Sergius Karamzin, setting out to woo the wealthy married women visiting the resort. Audaciously, one character is shown reading a book called *Foolish Wives* by Erich von Stroheim. The female cast is strong, featuring women who would become key members of Von's unofficial troupe. Karamzin

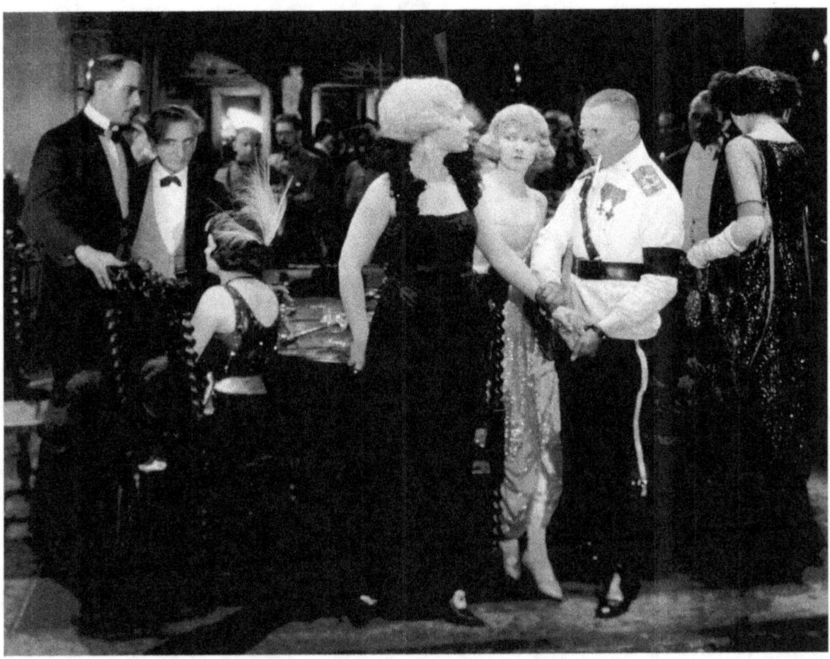

Erich von Stroheim as the scoundrel posing as Count Karamzin
in his film *Foolish Wives* (1922). San Francisco Film Preserve.

has two female accomplices, "Princess" Vera Petchnikoff and "Her
Highness" Olga Petchnikoff, played by Keystone alumna Mae Busch,
a former vaudevillian dubbed the "versatile vamp", who was in *The
Devil's Pass-Key*, and Universal stalwart Maude George, making her
second of four appearances for Von. His targets include the wife of an
American diplomat, played by an actress billed as Miss DuPont (real
name Patricia Hannon), but also Marietta, a young woman with devel-
opmental difficulties, played by Malvina Polo and most memorably
Maruschka, a hotel maid, played by the fantastic Dale Fuller. Fuller was
another former Keystone star, who worked with Von five times. Adding
villainy to his vice, Karamzin pursues the latter two women purely
because he considers them easy prey. The film contains some spectacular
set pieces. Maruschka, driven mad by Karamzin's ill-treatment, sets fire
to the hotel. Karamzin jumps out of a window to save his skin but dies at
the hand of Marietta's father, who dumps his body in the sewer.

Initially, Universal bought into the grandeur of Von's vision. Rival
studios had scored hits with epic melodramas such as Griffith's *Way
Down East* (1920) and Rex Ingram's *The Four Horsemen of the Apocalypse* (1921). *Foolish Wives* was slated as Universal's prestige money-
maker, which entailed concessions to Von's quest for authenticity—up to

a point. The set building began both in Culver City on the Universal lot, and also 300 miles north, on the Monterey peninsula, so that the replica facades of Monte Carlo could face on to a coastline. At one point storms razed the sets and construction had to begin all over again. Total cost: nearly $400,000, including $12,000 that went towards arranging the site so that the sets for the Casino and the Hotel de France would be reflected in the 48 huge windows of the Café de Paris—something on which Von insisted. The film was gorgeously art directed by Richard Day, a Von discovery who went on to design several more of his films and have an acclaimed four-decade career in Hollywood.

Laemmle installed a new wunderkind producer, Irving Thalberg, to do the impossible and rein Von in. But Von reacted badly to his interventions, threatening: "Remove me as the director and you remove me as the star, and you don't have a picture." When Thalberg stopped sending money, Von carried on shooting and sending Universal the bills. Universal, meanwhile, attempted to turn a negative (bank balance) into a positive. They linked the evil of Von's on-screen character to his famous extravagance as a director. "He's going to make you <u>hate him</u>, even if it takes a <u>million dollars</u> of our money to do it!" ran Universal's house ads. They called him "Von $troheim". The trades were fed stories like the one about Von being arrested for counterfeiting, after commissioning fake banknotes for the casino scenes. It was true that the U.S. Treasury was looking to make an example of someone but far better publicity to run with that than, say, the stories about Von bullying his crew so much that they all threatened to resign or Fuller being hospitalised with pneumonia; worse, Fuller losing two teeth after a scene required a struggle with Von in which he threw her against a dresser.[6] Following a subsequent shoot with Von, Fuller said to a reporter: "There is a society for prevention of cruelty to animals, a society for prevention of cruelty to children, but why are we character actresses left so unprotected?"[7]

The shoot was out of control. In June 1921, after eleven months of shooting, tragedy struck when the German actor playing the diplomat, Rudolph Christians, suddenly died. Although studio publicity claimed otherwise, Von still had sequences left to shoot with Christians and when his replacement proved far from a perfect match, he proposed a full reshoot of all the husband's scenes. That is the point at which Thalberg took action. Von arrived at the set one morning to find all the cameras had been returned to the studio.

Universal claimed that at this point the bill ran to $1,124,498, while Von maintained that it was only $750,000. One number was unarguable: Von had shot 326,000 feet of footage, of which 150,000 feet was "actual constructive action". Von presented a cut of 30 or 32 reels to the studio. He envisaged a film of maybe six to ten hours, to be split into two halves, shown over consecutive nights in the cinema. Universal knew that would be a nightmare to distribute. In August, the studio showed what was probably Von's 30-reel edit to a junket of censors from various state boards. The screening began at 9pm and ended at 3.30am. After this, Von was thrown out of the editing room.

Universal began to butcher *Foolish Wives*. To oversee the job, Laemmle hired his brother-in-law, Julius Stern, who later described Von's 30-reel version as "the most perfect and smooth picture I ever saw or hope to see."[8] He hired a team of people to trim the film down, even installing an edit suite on the train from Los Angeles to New York, so they could keep hacking away en route to the premiere. *Foolish Wives* made its debut on 11 January 1922 at three-and-a-half hours, riddled with continuity errors. The audience roared with laughter at an ending that now made no sense. So did some of the critics, with *Variety* opining: "Obviously intended to be a sensational sex melodrama, *Foolish Wives* is one of the funniest burlesque dramas ever screened."[9] *The New York Times* hedged its bets, deciding months later that the film offered. "Not a pleasant story and not always a good one, but in many of its scenes a strikingly expressive motion picture with some of the best and some of the worst of the direction and acting of Erich von Stroheim."[10]

Von called it "only the skeleton of my dead child",[11] but it was still far too long. Universal's team kept snipping. The film was shorter and shorter at each screening. As the decade wore on, a pattern formed in which Von's films were repeatedly slashed by the studio, though none suffered quite the same indignities as *Foolish Wives*. And to what end? Universal lost half a million dollars, the American critics hated the film (though Europe was kinder), and Von's reputation took a thrashing. Cinema owners across the country lost money on *Foolish Wives* and the industry lined up to throw mud at the man they blamed. An editorial in *Moving Picture World* called the film a "Darwinian Phantasy of Bad Manners and Sneers", attacking "the silly villain that shot the bank roll in an egotistic endeavor to glorify himself" and suggesting that Laemmle might "either shoot von Stroheim at sunrise, or step on him and squash him".[12]

Photoplay had hauled itself onto the moral high ground, devoting an entire page to calling the film "an insult to every American in the audience... Stroheim has made a film that is unfit for the family to see; that is an insult to American ideals and womanhood." The magazine lambasted the film's "continental morals and manners" and concluded that Von "has abused his directorial privileges". *Foolish Wives* "is not good, wholesome entertainment. It is not artistically great. It is really nothing."[13] This attack on the film's patriotism, outside the magazine's section devoted to film reviews, included criticism of the character of the

American Ambassador. In fact, during production, the authorities had once again been alerted to Von's lack of patriotism, talk that must have spread through Hollywood. A member of the Hollywood branch of the veterans' association the American Legion who worked on the film claimed that its depictions of the Ambassador and of American women were defamatory, and that it was produced by a German Jew (Carl Laemmle) with what he presumed (erroneously) was German financing. A spokesman for the American Legion said that Von had been heard to say "G-D—these dammed [sic] Americans anyway" on set and that the Legion was "much wrought up against this picture".[14] The Military Intelligence Division eventually recommended that the film be denied foreign export, advice that was not followed.

Von escaped punishment, but his cards were marked. He had played the villain too long to emerge from this mess unscathed. His face was attached to a succession of screen scoundrels and his name had been used as a byword for anti-Americanism and the kind of excess that could destroy the whole industry. He was out on a limb. What no one would have expected is that soon Gloria would find herself in a similar predicament, the scapegoat for a different kind of offence.

1. Anita Loos, *A Girl Like I* (Hamish Hamilton, 1967), 125.
2. Elliot Einzig Porter, "The two Vons: the World War I secret government investigation of Erich von Stroheim", *Film History,* Volume 22, 2010, 33.
3. H.A.M., "*Queen Kelly* and Queen Victoria", *Close-Up,* 1931, 137.
4. Erich Stroheim, "A Protest to the Trade", *Motion Picture News,* 27 September 1919, 2,304.
5. Carl Laemmle, "Carl Laemmle Answers Stroheim's Protest", *Motion Picture News,* 4 October 1919, 2,678.
6. "Actress Has Two Teeth Knocked Out", *Los Angeles Evening Express,* 2 June 1921, 23.
7. "No Charm in Skin Everybody Loves to Beat", *The Los Angeles Times,* 19 August 1923, 25.
8. Quoted, Koszarski, 93.
9. "Foolish Wives", *Variety,* 20 January 1922, 35.
10. "Screen; Pictures of 1922", *New York Times,* 2 July, 1922, 66.
11. Quoted, Koszarski, 93.
12. A.J., "A Millon! A Million!", *Moving Picture World,* 21 January 1922, 267.
13. "Foolish Wives", *Photoplay,* March 1922, 70.
14. "The two Vons", 344.

4
The Star

The Pinnacle was renamed *Blind Husbands* because of Gloria. At the dawn of the 1920s, Gloria was seated at the very top of Hollywood, a legitimate movie star, with all the attendant success and scandal. In childhood Gloria may have fretted over her teeth and ears but as a young woman she was blessed with a strikingly photogenic face: a brilliant smile, sharp jaw and cheekbones, clear blue eyes and dark, wavy hair. The beauty mark on her chin, accentuated with makeup, became her signature. On film she looked like a chic pen-and-ink drawing. She had a petite, trim figure and could carry off luxury designer fashions with ease, the image of a sleek glamourpuss. While other stars traded on girlishness, Gloria was elegant and expensive, chin aristocratically tilted upwards. This allure was key to her popular appeal, though as with Von and his Germanic associations she would soon come to resent it and try to shake off her fashion-plate persona as fast as she had earned it.

And boy had she earned it. Gloria recalled her early years in cinema as something of a trial, between the indignity of slapstick and the ordeal of performing stunts that involved great heights and cold water. The Essanay bosses quickly spotted her potential and paired her immediately with their new star, Charlie Chaplin, whom they signed at the end of 1914. This wasn't a match made in heaven. "I could not get a reaction out of her," said Chaplin. "She was so unsatisfactory that I gave up and dismissed her."[1] Gloria can just about be glimpsed in the background of the film-set farce *His New Job* (1915), after her scenes with Chaplin failed to make the cut. "All morning I felt like a cow trying to dance with a toy poodle," she remembered.[2] Nevertheless, Gloria's fastidiously funny Chaplin impersonation is a highlight in two of her best films, the silent comedy *Manhandled* (Allan Dwan, 1924) and Billy Wilder's ink-black Hollywood satire *Sunset Boulevard*.

The Essanay comic who did catch Gloria's eye was Wallace Beery, of the Sweedie franchise. Beery was a husky, rugged man, later to be renowned for memorable heavy roles on screen and some thuggish behaviour in real life. He was known to pursue underage girls, and when one girl's parents threatened to cause trouble Beery was sent west to Essanay's Hollywood studios. Teenage Swanson fell for him "in a schoolgirl way" and Beery reciprocated her crush. Gloria lost her job at the studio after a fellow actress complained about her dates with Beery, so in early 1916 she headed to Hollywood; Beery was waiting to show her around town. She joined the rough-and-tumble fun factory that was Keystone, presided over by Mack Sennett, where she made knockabout two-reelers, which weren't her preference, including the cross-dressing comedy *The Danger Girl* (Clarence Badger, 1916) and *Teddy at the Throttle* (Badger, 1917), a spoof on the melodramatic trope of a vulnerable girl tied to the railroad tracks; both still hold up well today. Gloria gamely did several of her own stunts.

Life off-screen was also perilous. On Gloria's 17th birthday she married 30-year-old Beery, a decision she regretted as soon as their wedding night, when he took her virginity by rape. In her own harrowing description she was "brutalized in pitch-blackness by a man who whispered filth in my ear while he ripped me almost in two."[2] Gloria's first marriage was short and grim. The nadir came when she fell pregnant; Beery gave Gloria medicine that he promised would assuage her morning sickness. It was, in fact, an abortifacient. After this betrayal, Gloria left him.

She left Keystone too, after enduring one more film shoot with Beery, and moved to the prestigious Triangle studio, but Famous Players-Lasky, and director Cecil B. DeMille, soon came courting. Gloria's collaboration with DeMille at the studio later known as Paramount would define her career forever. He, too, makes an appearance in *Sunset Boulevard*, calling her "Young Fellow", just as he did in 1918 when they embarked on a series of six hit films together, beginning with *Don't Change Your Husband*. DeMille was already one of Hollywood's most acclaimed and successful directors, part of Hollywood's origin myth because he was credited with the first feature film to be shot in the region, the 1914 Western called *The Squaw Man*, produced by Jesse Lasky and Samuel Goldwyn.

Not yet known for the Biblical epics that would come later in his silent and sound career, DeMille caught the public's attention with full-blooded even shocking dramas such as *Carmen* (1915), starring the opera singer Geraldine Farrar, and *The Cheat* (1915), a melodrama in which Japanese star Sessue Hayakawa plays a villain who gruesomely brands the heroine with a hot iron. Gloria's films with DeMille were lighter fare. They were "marriage films", or more bluntly sex films, suggestively titled dramas and comedies about sexually sophisticated men and women falling in and out of their wedding vows. Their success that persuaded Laemmle to retitle *The Pinnacle* as *Blind Husbands*, a name laden with the promise of adultery and an echo of DeMille and Gloria's films *Why Change Your Wife?* (1920) or *The Affairs of Anatol* (1921). A joke went around that the unpoetic Laemmle, mistaking "pinnacle" for "pinochle", said women wouldn't go to see a film about a game of cards.

Titles containing the words "wife", "husband" and "affair" were part of a trend that rippled around Hollywood, but at least DeMille's films, like Von's, could be counted on to be every bit as racy as their names. In *Male and Female* (1919), an adaptation of the J. M. Barrie play *The Admirable Crichton*, Gloria fearlessly played a scene with a lion. During a fantasy sequence set in Ancient Babylon, DeMille staged a reproduction of Gabriel von Max's painting "The Lion's Bride", with Gloria as the bride. First she confronted the beast in its den (the beast was Slats the Lion, later to find fame as the first MGM mascot). "He stared at me, I stared at him," she recalled. "In another second I was whisked off my feet, thrown up to the camera stand, and from there I was thrown to somebody else and somebody else and before I knew it they had me outside this enormous set."[4] Undaunted, Gloria steadied herself for a second take. After lunch, she posed with a sedated lion draped across her naked back with only a piece of canvas separating them. DeMille stood a few feet away with a gun in his hand. It was dangerous—but thrilling. "It was the most fantastic sensation, like hundreds of vibrators from the tips of your toes to the ends of each hair on your head," Gloria remembered. "Every atom of my body vibrated when the lion roared."[5] As a reward for her bravery, DeMille gave her a sapphire. That film also required her to appear soaked to the skin, her dress clinging to her figure in the shipwreck scene, and she was also shown undressed and stepping into a sunken bath. Although Gloria's modesty was preserved on set and only her décolletage exposed on film, the suggestion of nakedness was enough to titillate audiences—as was the luxurious bathroom, which became something of a trademark in DeMille's films of the period. As one prescient critic put it, DeMille "had dramatized the bathtub".[6]

DeMille spent and spent, frequently butting heads with studio boss Adolph Zukor. The Hungarian-born Zukor was a famously steely and ambitious man who had founded his Famous Players Company in New York in 1912. Four years later he merged his company with the Jesse L. Lasky Feature Play Company, where DeMille was already based, to form Famous Players-Lasky. Zukor was president and Lasky vice-president, so DeMille had a new boss, one less lenient about the director's fondness for lavish décor and elaborate costumes. But these elements were central to the appeal of the DeMille-Swanson titles. These are the films that made Gloria a star and forged her fashionista image, although she was paid modestly by the studio. "I kept her, so to speak, under wraps," remembered DeMille, "but they were gorgeous wraps, designed by

Alpharetta Hoffman and later by Mitchell Leisen, and worn in settings of Wilfred Buckland's best creation. Nothing was spared to bring out all the glamour that was Gloria."[7]

Her head turned by her film costumes, Gloria began spending beyond her means to wear similarly stylish outfits off-duty. "I have gone through enough of being a nobody," she said in 1922. "I have decided that when I am a star I will be every inch and every moment the star! Everybody from the studio gateman to the highest executive will know it."[8] After her time with DeMille she would make ten more films for the same studio with director Sam Wood. But what DeMille, Wood and Gloria thought was entertainingly risqué, others outside Hollywood would read as vulgar, with the capacity to corrupt public decency. A moral crusade was coming to the American film industry and Gloria was about to fall victim to a new wave of puritanism—and not just because of her films.

Until then, Swanson had played up to her screen image, entertaining the press with her modern ideas about love and sex. "Marriage is just a game... divorce should be made more easy, instead of more difficult," she trilled to *Motion Picture Magazine* in December 1919. That very same month Gloria was married for the second time, to Herbert K. Somborn, the president of struggling film distribution company Equity Pictures—and she would soon have more reason to wish that divorces were easier to come by. Gloria met Somborn when he passed on a flattering message from Equity star Clara Kimball Young, someone Gloria deeply admired, because she ran her own company.[9] Aged 39, Somborn was nearly twice Gloria's age but he was solicitous and kind, handsome and well-dressed. Gloria expected that life as Mrs Somborn would be restful, certainly in contrast to her first marriage. Joyfully, she became pregnant again, which enraged the studio bosses, who didn't want to see their money-making actress either unable to work or de-sexualised in the public imagination.

Meanwhile, Gloria became aware of her husband's inability to pay their bills. She took charge, playing hardball with the studio over her contract, leasing a more modest apartment and planning for a natural birth at home, in keeping with her equally modern ideas on health and wellness. Baby Gloria arrived in October 1920, not without a little medical intervention. Her mother, despite being an early enthusiast for breastfeeding, went back to work eight weeks later. She made the glamorous *Affairs of Anatol*, starring as a kittenish young wife whose undeniable charms win back her husband from three competing temptresses—including Bebe Daniels as an immoral devil dancer called Satan Synne. *Anatol* was a hit, proving Gloria's public image was still as hot as it was before she became a mother. All was not well between husband

and wife, however; in the spring of 1921, Gloria moved out and rented rooms near the studio. One day, when she stopped by the marital home, she found a letter from Somborn formally ending their union. But the studio was the third party in this marriage. Jesse Lasky had failed to stop Gloria having her baby, but this time he put his foot down. No way could its highest-profile leading lady rack up a second divorce in three years.

To tell the full story about the end of this miserable marriage, we need to focus to the rest of Hollywood; Gloria and Somborn's eventual divorce was part of a wider earthquake shaking the industry, with clear ramifications for *Queen Kelly*. Risqué dramas were one thing, but the nation's self-appointed moral guardians were more outraged by real-life scandal. Mary Pickford and Douglas Fairbanks had carefully managed the public reaction to their individual divorces and subsequent marriage in March 1920 with the help of the fan magazines, but Hollywood was rapidly earning an unhelpful reputation as a den of sin. A few months later, Pickford's brother Jack was in Paris with his wife, actress Olive Thomas, when she died after ingesting mercury bichloride solution. It has never been established whether she took the poison in error as an attempt to end her life or if it was fed to her.

In September 1921, a young actress called Virginia Rappe attended a boozy party in a San Francisco hotel room. She fell ill and died a few days later from a ruptured bladder. The comedian Roscoe Arbuckle, who was at the party, was arrested on suspicion of rape and murder. It took three very public trials before he was exonerated, but his credibility was destroyed—and Famous Players-Lasky cancelled his $3 million contract. The surname of Norma Desmond in *Sunset Boulevard* is a deliberate callback to a famously sordid Hollywood scandal. Film director William Desmond Taylor, another employee of Famous Players-Lasky, was found murdered in his bungalow in February 1922. He was shot in the back; the murderer was never identified. Gloria was well enough acquainted with Taylor to speculate on the possible motive. "When everything came out in the papers," she said, "I knew better than to ask."[10] In 1923, matinee idol Wallace Reid (one of Gloria's co-stars) died in the sanatorium where he was rehabbing from addiction to the morphine he had been prescribed after being injured in a train accident four years earlier. He had been caught in the wreck on the way to the set of *The Valley of the Giants* (James Cruze, 1919), a film he was making for Famous Players-Lasky.

All these scandals reached the newspapers, giving Hollywood the reputation of "Sodom on the Pacific", while stories of illicit drinking, drug use and the casting couch swirled through less formal networks. In response to this, plus a persistent thrust of antisemitism against a new, largely Jewish-run industry, state censorship boards were increasingly finding fault with the films themselves. A court case in 1915 had established that films, being a commercial product rather than artistic expression, were not covered by the protections of the First Amendment, which meant they could be censored. When states demanded cuts to films, or reworded intertitles, studios bore the cost of making and shipping alternative prints.

In 1921, Jesse Lasky had attempted to renovate his studio's reputation by drafting a 14-point list of "Don'ts", rules that his producers would follow, to ensure that their films were suitable for all the family. Top of the list: "No picture showing sex attraction in a suggestive or improper manner will be presented."[11] *The Affairs of Anatol* managed to escape cuts, although it was widely agreed to be pushing the limit of what was appropriate. More serious action was required for the whole industry, not just one studio. Just as Major League Baseball had appointed Kenesaw Mountain Landis as commissioner after the 1919 World Series gambling scandal, the studios called in Will H. Hays—a Republican, Presbyterian face of respectability—to clean up Hollywood. In early 1922 he resigned his office as Postmaster General in Warren G. Harding's new administration to become the first president of the Motion Picture Producers and Distributors of America, or MPPDA. His mission: to scrub the tarnish off Tinsel Town. His remuneration was very nice indeed, with a starting salary of $35,360 (around $680,000 today).

Hays pushed on with a proposal for centralised film censorship, with 32 states holding referenda on the Federal Film Board Bill in his first year in office. His Hollywood reforms would eventually include the establishment of the Central Casting bureau in 1925, building enlarged premises for the Hollywood Studio Club, a chaperoned dormitory for young women, in 1926, and the 1930 Production Code of "Don'ts and Be Carefuls", guidelines for studios. Before then, in 1924, Hays drew up "the Formula", a gentlemen's agreement over the 13 undesirable elements that should be avoided in studio pictures. It was very similar to Lasky's list. Numbers one to five were all to do with sex and sex work. Stories should be avoided that "dealt with sex in an improper manner"; "were based on white slavery" (sex trafficking); "made vice attractive"; "exhibited nakedness"; or "had prolonged passionate love scenes". Following six more rules about the presentation of crime, drunkenness, religion, gambling, violence and public officials, the final no-nos referred to "vulgar postures and gestures" and "salacious subtitles and advertising". To avoid the need for cuts or censorship, the Hays Office would require that producers share the plots of films before beginning production. As soon as Hays took up the job, Hollywood had become full of apprehension. Gloria, DeMille and Von, their pictures already frowned upon as "Continental", had every reason to be concerned that their kind of films were not long for this world.

Joe Kennedy was keen to ingratiate himself with Hays. Fortuitously for Joe, Massachusetts became the site of a key battle in Hays's campaign to wrest censorship from the states and keep it within the industry. The Massachusetts legislature had passed a censorship bill that was going to a statewide referendum, a vote Hays could not afford to lose. Hays and MPPDA lawyer Charles C. Pettijohn fought a strong campaign, and claimed a major victory when voters rejected the bill decisively. Although many more state censorship bills were drafted, none passed. Joe had written to Hays personally to offer his political assistance, reassuring him that there would be "little trouble" in the state, and it's very possible his contacts were of use to the cause. Increasingly, Joe was beginning to see himself as a potential saviour for the beleaguered film industry: the Harvard-educated, Christian financier and family man who could rescue the movie industry from its moral mire. Daydreams of glory aside, he was very aware of the prejudices he could exploit. This was just the start of his very special relationship with Hays.

But we must return to the messy end of the Somborn-Swanson marriage. Gloria may have been forced to delay her divorce, but the studio could not control her sex life—or so she thought. By day she was shooting the romance *Beyond the Rocks* (Sam Wood, 1922), co-starring her old friend the "Latin lover" heartthrob Rudolph Valentino, a story by steamy English novelist Elinor Glyn, with gorgeous European settings: the Dorset coast of England, Paris and the Swiss Alps, all simulated in California. By night she started seeing the film director Marshall "Mickey" Neilan, a recent divorcee and one of the hardest partiers in town, who had proposed, if only in jest, to Gloria the first night they met. This was on a nightclub dancefloor. Gloria called him a "wild, beautiful devil".[12] They had a fine old time together, but Neilan was not Gloria's only beau and Los Angeles not her only playground. Leaving the baby with a nanny, she embarked on an extended trip to Europe, where she juggled aristocratic lovers in different rooms at Claridge's in London then travelled to Paris and Berlin where she hooked up with Neilan again. They partied, drank (Neilan especially), fought and made up in style.

In the summer of 1922 Neilan married actress Blanche Sweet, whom he had been seeing while he was still married to his previous wife. But this did curtail his affair with Gloria; she boasted that he had breakfast with her on the morning of his wedding. Neilan bought Sweet a house but remained in his mother's home and continued to woo Gloria with gifts, letters and telegrams. He co-wrote "Wonderful One", a hit song of

1923, widely thought to be inspired by Gloria: "Just you, only you, in the shadowy twilight,/in silvery moonlight there's none like you."

Despite such a delightful distraction, Gloria turned her mind to her own domestic matters, buying herself a grand house at 904 North Crescent Drive, opposite the Beverly Hills Hotel, for $250,000. She had to borrow from Neilan for the deposit, but immediately embarked on renovations to make it a home fit for Hollywood's most fashionable star. By January 1923 Gloria was ready to entertain her movie friends in style and even allowed cameras inside; the lavish interiors were used as a set for her newest film, a flapper drama called *Prodigal Daughters* (Sam Wood, 1923). Newlywed Neilan installed a 12-seat home cinema for her in the basement as an early birthday present. Gloria was acquiring a taste for spending money on décor, fashion and cars. She wore shoes with diamonds in the heels and drove top-end imported motorcars. In his contentious history of early movie-making, *Hollywood Babylon*, first published in English in 1965, Kenneth Anger quoted Gloria as saying: "The public wanted us to live like kings and queens. So, we did… And why not? We were in love with life. We were making more money than we ever dreamed existed and there was no reason to believe it would ever stop."[13] (The book was subsequently banned for ten years and apparently Gloria did not see a copy until 1976 when, for this quote and other inaccuracies, she took Anger to court.[14])

In March, Gloria brought home the gift that she wanted most of all, adopting a baby boy from a San Francisco orphanage. She christened the child Joseph after her father but always called him Brother—giving her daughter the sibling she never had herself. Rumours flew around town that the baby was Gloria's own child, the adoption a cover story, and that the child's father was one of an alleged roster of men in the movie business. Gloria knew she was getting a bad reputation but laughed off such ridiculous claims. She was constantly being filmed and photographed— it's unlikely she could have concealed a pregnancy. Perhaps she didn't quite realise that Hollywood was going to make her confront the consequences of all her indiscretions.

Gloria's domestic comfort was shattered when Somborn finally sued for divorce, leaving her both stunned and offended. Somborn alleged that Gloria had committed adultery with fourteen different men, all of whom he named in the suit. Neilan was on the list, but also Zukor, Lasky, DeMille and Wood. Some Gloria had not even met. He wanted $150,000 from the divorce, as although Gloria had been dodging contract negotiations, she was bringing in a pretty penny. Naturally, Gloria was outraged by the false accusations, but the studio urged her to comply and avoid yet another scandal. Gloria resisted until DeMille showed a telegram from Hays himself arguing that she should settle the matter quietly, in the best interests of "the entire industry". Gloria took it like "a hammer between the eyes". With the entire business at stake, what could she do but give in? With the decision made, the studio intervened on her behalf, knocking Somborn down to $70,000, which it advanced to Gloria from her newly drawn-up contract.[15]

That new contract was not benevolent. It contained a new Hollywood invention, a morality clause, which meant Gloria could be dismissed if she were "charged with adulterous conduct or immoral relations with men other than her husband". Naturally, the studio wanted to have its cake and eat it too. While the morality clause forced her to be irreproachable in her private life, she was required to play the provocateur on screen. The next film Gloria made for Famous Players-Lasky was *Bluebeard's Eighth Wife* (Sam Wood, 1923), a risqué comedy about divorce.[16]

But that wasn't the worst of it. Shortly after the divorce, Gloria was seated next to Hays at a banquet and understandably gave him the cold shoulder. It was only when Hays politely asked what he had done to offend her that the scales fell from Gloria's eyes. He knew nothing of the telegram. It had been a cruel hoax, drafted by the man she considered her mentor, DeMille. Devastated by the betrayal but also angry beyond belief, Swanson created a furious scene with Lasky, who remained implacably unrepentant. After eight years in the lions' den, Gloria had finally reached her limit. She packed her bags. Who could blame her—a newly divorced single mother with bills to pay and a contract to fulfil—for wanting to get as far away from Hollywood as possible?

1. Charles Chaplin, *My Autobiography* (Simon & Schuster, 1964), 166.
2. *SoS*, 40.
3. *SoS*, 61.
4. Swanson's 1950s audio recordings, quoted in Tricia Welsch, *Gloria Swanson: Ready for My Close-Up* (University Press of Mississippi, 2013), 56.
5. Op cit, 57.
6. Daniel A. Lord S.J., *Played by Ear: The Autobiography of Daniel A. Lord S.J.* (Loyola University Press, 1955), 277.
7. Cecil B. DeMille, *The Autobiography of Cecil B. DeMille* (W.H. Allen, 1960), 201.
8. Cited widely, perhaps first in Alexander Walker, *The Celluloid Sacrifice: Sex in the Movies* (Penguin, 1968), 17.
9. In fact, Young would later accuse her lover Louis J. Selznick, who was the president of Clara Kimball Young Film Corporation, of taking her profits and blocking her input in the company.
10. Quoted, Axel Madsen, *The Sewing Circle: Female Stars Who Loved Other Women* (Robson Books, 1998), 127.

11. "Famous Players-Lasky Ban Sex Films By Fourteen Donts To Studio Officials", *Variety*, 18 February 1921, 46.
12. *SoS*, 218.
13. Quoted by Kenneth Anger in *Hollywood Babylon*, but never attributed.
14. Her suit was unsuccessful. For more detail, see Anne Helen Petersen, "What to do with a Coffin Full of Sugar: Gloria Swanson, Kenneth Anger, and Self-Authorship in the Star Collection", *The Moving Image: The Journal of the Association of Moving Image Arch*ivists, Vol. 13, No. 2 (Fall 2013), 81-98.
15. Keen fans of Hollywood lore will note that Somborn spent the settlement money on opening a Los Angeles restaurant, the first Brown Derby on Wilshire Boulevard, scene, like its sister restaurant on North Vine Street, Hollywood, of many a storied showbiz encounter, and a favoured watering hole of Wallace Beery.
16. A lost film, subsequently remade by Ernst Lubitsch in 1938 with Gary Cooper and Claudette Colbert, from the first screenplay written by Billy Wilder and Charles Brackett. Their last was *Sunset Boulevard*.

5
The Producers

Making money on the stock market in the mid-1920s was not so difficult. A rising tide was carrying canny investors to giddy heights. But to make money the way Joe did was not for amateurs or faint hearts. In an as-yet largely unregulated market he became a master of practices that are now illegal. He developed the skills not just to buy and sell stocks but to manoeuvre their value as he wished. It took meticulous planning, nerve, exhaustive effort—and of course he had to be comfortable working furtively and knowing that each cent of profit came at someone else's expense. It was a skill that could be used occasionally to help others, but most often to feather one's own nest.

A triumphant anecdote Joe would often share is the story of the Yellow Cab Company. In early 1924, one of Joe's friends, Hearst newspaper editor Walter Howey, asked him to help out another friend, Joseph D. Hertz, owner of the Chicago-based Yellow Cab Company. Hertz's business, newly listed on the stock exchange, was subject to a bear raid; malicious buyers were selling the stock short and driving down the price, then pocketing the profit. Joe knew exactly what to do. He and Eddie Moore holed themselves up in a room at the Waldorf with phones and a ticker tape machine for six weeks, buying stock with more borrowed money and pushing the price back up. Joe emerged several pounds lighter and many, many dollars up. He was given a $20,000 fee for his success in stabilising the stock price. However, Hertz would subsequently claim that Joe also made a shady personal profit from running a bear raid of his own on the stocks at the same time.

While the stock market lined Joe's pockets, the picture business remained his goal. By 1925 he was a millionaire and ready to make his big play for the movies. He had resigned from the board of Film Booking Offices of America (FBO) a couple of years earlier when Pat Powers was brought in to run the show but stayed in touch with the film industry, founding Columbia Advertising to sell ad space on cinema curtains. When he saw that FBO was really struggling, Joe put together a bid to take it over using money from investors gathered by Guy Currier. It was not a swift process, but at the beginning of 1926 Joe finally picked up FBO cheap, for $1.1 million, a price not much more than the tag on the company's Hollywood premises. The FBO purchase created a wave of publicity for Joe, the first outsider to buy a Hollywood studio.[1] Will Hays publicly welcomed this sign that bankers were backing the film business and rolled out the red carpet for Joe in particular. Swiftly, Joe befriended Hays, buttering him up and calling him "General". This was a lasting friendship of like minds, fellow operators. It was the "General" who taught Joe one of his favourite mottos: "Things don't just happen, they are made to happen."[2]

A couple of years later, a loving profile of Joe by Catholic journalist Terry Ramsaye in *Photoplay* explained that Hays wished "to endow the febrile motion picture industry with an atmosphere of Americanism and substantiality. Kennedy is a valuable personality from this point of view. He is exceedingly American."[3] Whichever way you squint at that final phrase, it means "not Jewish". In this entirely biased article, MGM's Marcus Loew was said to have joked, "A banker?—why I thought this business was just for furriers." The joke is a reference to Zukor's former trade, one firmly established in the public's mind as a Jewish business.

"When [Joe] went to Hollywood," wrote Rose in her memoir, framing it as the tale of a plucky underdog, "there were predictions that this Boston Irishman soon would be sadder and poorer."[4] It would be misleading, however, to map the Kennedys' experience of exclusion by the WASPs who ran Boston and its banks onto this portrait of a plucky Irishman taking on another industry ruled by men of a different faith. Joe was bolstering his position in Hollywood by forming a tactical friendship with the Protestant Hays. Further, his personal antisemitism was deeply ingrained and deadly serious. In later life, at the peak of his personal power and influence, when Joe was the U.S. Ambassador to Great Britain, he was an extreme isolationist. He saw the Nazis' victory as inevitable and chose appeasement over resistance.

Joe quickly settled into FBO, writing to a new colleague: "I am beginning to think I am a 'picture' man."[5] He hired Edward Bennett (E. B.) Derr and Charlie Sullivan, two brilliant accountants from Fore River, who would prove loyal but not sycophantic allies, to help him run the business. The trio carried themselves like gangsters, even styling themselves "the gang", with Derr and Sullivan referring to Joe as "Boss". Joe also set up a fund called the Cinema Credits Corporation, which generated cash from investors and the market to keep the FBO coffers full. As always Joe would avoid putting his own money into the venture, but he was keen to maximise profit, which meant slashing production costs. The gang instituted a new, rigorous ledger system, which meant FBO's producers in Hollywood would have to account for every dollar and cent they spent on each film.

In the spring of 1926 Joe, with Moore at his side, travelled to Hollywood for the first time. He wasn't just there to admire FBO's modest studio, where a minaret from the *Kismet* set still towered over the lot, but to make connections and deals. He befriended Hays's man in Los Angeles, Fred Beeston, and FBO reactivated its lapsed membership of the MPPDA. He made friends too with Martin J. Quigley, the editor of trade paper *Exhibitors Herald,* a fellow Catholic and a prominent campaigner for what would become the Production Code. They bonded over politics and their appreciation for Catholic author Hilaire Belloc, who had recently published his antisemitic book *The Jews* (1922). "[N]o one could have launched me more successfully on the waves of the film industry," Joe wrote to Quigley, promising to double his advertising spend in the *Herald.* "All I hope is that you will not be disappointed in your handiwork, and that you will stand by and help finish the job."[6] He also began to forge a friendship with James R. Quirk, another Catholic, the Boston Irish editor of leading fan magazine *Photoplay*, which had so thoroughly excoriated *Foolish Wives.* Joe's trip was timed to coincide with the FBO sales convention, where he presented himself as a benign, unthreatening novice slowly getting to grips with the movie business, and he appeared on stage with the studio's biggest star, cowboy sensation Fred Thomson. Thomson's films were big sellers but also had big budgets, which meant that under the new FBO regime he was to be given his own production unit and $10,000 a week.

Joe wasn't just frugal, he was ruthless, as Thomson would find out. The Western hero, with his trusty horse Silver King, became the second biggest star at the box office in 1926 and 1927, but Joe just couldn't stand the expense, so he negotiated a four-picture deal with Paramount on behalf of Fred Thomson Productions. FBO guaranteed $75,000 in financing for each new picture, but the deal stipulated that Paramount would return that, plus $100,000, to FBO—and the new studio would be responsible for paying Thomson's $15,000-a-week salary. This was a deal that generated profit for FBO while deleting its biggest payroll cost but left Thomson stranded. Paramount wanted to sign Thomson directly but Joe wouldn't agree to let him go. While Thomson was busy at Paramount, Joe had signed the number one cowboy star, Tom Mix, behind his back, so there was no place for Thomson back at FBO either—forcing him to tread water, while the films he made at Paramount mostly flopped. Thomson and his wife, the powerful screenwriter Frances Marion, never forgave Joe; they had genuinely believed he was their friend, inviting him and Rose into their home. Tragically, Thomson died the following year after contracting tetanus when he trod on a nail in a stable. He was just 38.

When he started at FBO, Joe was canny with his budget, hiring sports stars whose fame would guarantee a certain success at the box office. When female star Evelyn Brent complained about the reduced budgets for her pictures she was let go and replaced by Viola Dana—a newer, therefore less expensive leading lady. Let other studios make expensive prestige productions, argued Joe, who wanted to corner the lower end of the market. "In other words, we are trying to be the Woolworth and Ford of the motion picture industry, rather than the Tiffany,"[7] he told the *Boston Globe*.

Self-promotion, on the other hand, was free. FBO films hit the screen with "Joseph P. Kennedy presents" on the title card, and Joe loved to talk business to the trades. His soft spot was that he still craved the respect of the crowd back east, specifically his revered alma mater, so he concocted a plan to boost his reputation and that of the film industry with a little Ivy League credibility. With Hays's backing and in his role as self-appointed saviour of the film business, Joe suggested a series of lectures at Harvard, to be delivered by the great and the good of Hollywood on the art of motion pictures. A promised $30,000 donation to Harvard all but guaranteed the university's agreement. One forward-thinking suggestion was made and much-discussed but never finally put into action: Harvard's Fine Arts department would establish a film library, to contain a copy of the best films produced each year, as decided by a committee of Harvard academics,[8] as well as the best of the older films.

Joe tasked Hays with inviting the speakers, but he had plenty of suggestions, not least that he should himself take the podium. He did so on 14 March 1927, inaugurating the lecture series at Harvard's Graduate School of Business Administration by hyping up the other speakers and sharing his wisdom on the business. He chose examples from FBO and other studios, including "the Gloria Swanson picture that opened in Roxy's Theatre the other night"[9], *The Love of Sunya*. He was followed by Hays and a list of other luminaries, including Adolph Zukor and Jesse Lasky, William Fox, Robert H. Cochrane of Universal, Henry Warner (who discussed the Vitaphone sound system), Marcus Loew of MGM, and Cecil B. DeMille, on "the ideal formula which fuses art and efficiency in making a photoplay".[10] DeMille shared anecdotes from the Swanson pictures as well as describing how he produced his Biblical epics *The Ten Commandments* (1923) and *The King of Kings* (1927). Milton Sills, star of pirate blockbuster *The Sea Hawk* (Frank Lloyd, 1924), which topped the box office in 1924, and co-founder of Actors' Equity, also spoke, displaying a shrewd understanding of the studios business and the craft of acting. Joe could not have found a more effective way of currying favour with the biggest names in Hollywood. He was delighted with his new-found popularity and the publicity garnered by the lecture series.

Despite the failure to launch a film library, the event had a tangible legacy. Joe had the lectures published in a book, *The Story of the Films*. The preface praised Harvard's foresight in turning its attention to the cinema, characterised the speakers in political terms as "almost the entire inner cabinet of the film industry",[11] and emphasised Joe's efforts in initiating the series. The biographies at the back of the book flattered Hays generously as "the best known, the most picturesque, and the most many-sided figure in the business department of the industry".[12] James Seymour, Harvard's head of publicity and alumni affairs, who had been integral to the success of the series, was given a job in the FBO publicity department.13 Four years later, after several reminders, Joe actually paid his $30,000 pledge to Harvard.

When Joe returned to California he was on a high and he was even happier when he found he was able to replace his production chief, who had been doing a disappointing job, with his most high-profile hire yet. This was William LeBaron, who had been editing pictures and running Famous Players-Lasky's Astoria studios in New York. The very place to which Gloria had fled after DeMille's betrayal four years earlier.

o o o

A fortnight's break in the Big Apple turned into a semi-permanent relocation, and what Gloria called the "rebirth"[14] of her career. Back in Hollywood, Gloria had resisted her films' reliance on her glamorous outfits and the same saucy bedroom and boudoir scenes designed to titil-late the audience. "I don't want to be a clotheshorse. Let me out of this thing. I want to be an actress. I want to do character parts. I want to do fun things," she screamed.[15] New York was her chance to break the mould, albeit for the same studio. Gloria did not return to Los Angeles for the divorce hearing in September, where Somborn told the court that she had announced: "I must have my career; nothing can interfere."[16]

In New York she made some of her best silent features, including a romance, *Zaza* (1923), set in France, and a comedy, *Manhandled*, set in New York. These two were directed by Canadian-born Allan Dwan, whom she adored, and with whom she made eight films in total—Gloria had approached him on Neilan's recommendation. She was extending her emotional range, developing the ability to cry on cue and playing roles that had been originated on stage by legendary actresses. With Dwan, Swanson was beginning to think outside of the studio. In preparation for *Manhandled* she spent a couple of days working incognito in a New York department store and even braved the subway for a memorable comic sequence. For *A Society Scandal* (1924), the courtroom scenes were shot in a real Brooklyn courthouse; known socialites were cast in the party scenes.

Without abandoning her stylish image altogether, Gloria was expanding her range of characters she could play beyond the spoiled upper-class wives that typified her work with DeMille. In *The Humming Bird* (Sidney Olcott, 1924) she played an "Apache" thief in Paris who pickpockets the jewellery of café patrons disguised as a young man and escapes from jail during a Zeppelin raid on the city. In the comedy *Stage Struck* (Dwan, 1925), shot on location in New Martinville, West Virginia, Gloria played a rural waitress besotted with a man who loves actresses, her fantasy life presented in a spectacular sequence shot in two-strip Technicolor. One journalist wrote at the start of 1925: "Gloria Swanson has made the swiftest ascent of the feminine bevy. She has contrived with well-chosen roles to achieve a high prestige. Beneath those cuckoo coiffures at which we jeered there lurked a keen and determined mind."[17]

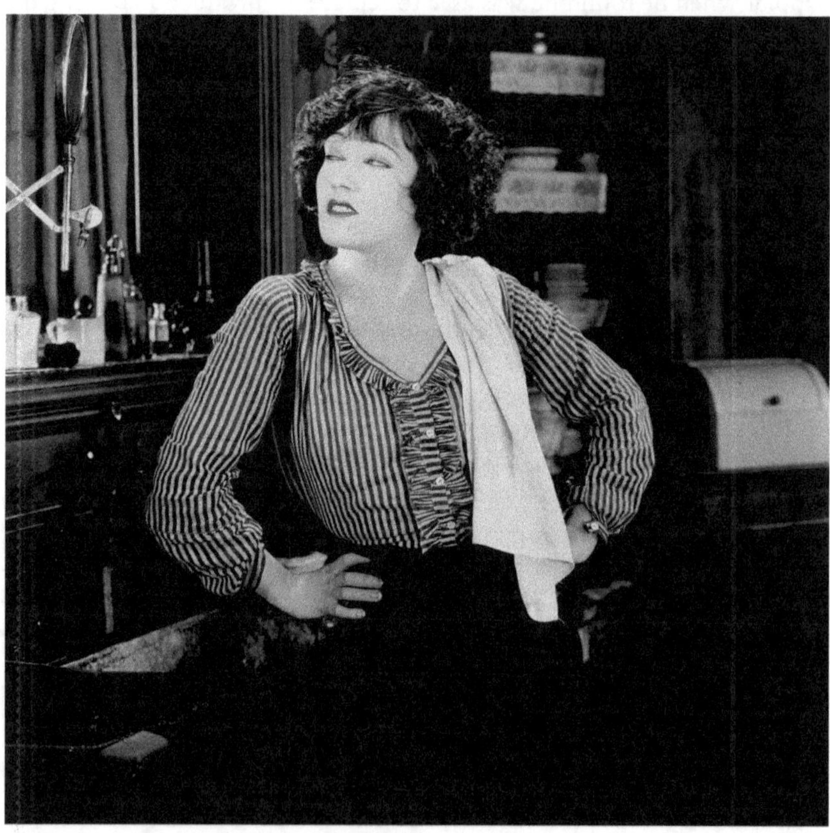

Gloria Swanson plays a Parisian thief in *The Humming Bird*.
Milestone Film & Video.

Looking back, Gloria told *Photoplay* that "in my life, the years 1924 and 1925 were a veritable Mt Everest. Those were the bonanza days for movie stars when public adoration ran high and star salaries, free from income tax, even higher."[18] Hitting her mid-twenties, Gloria was living it up, her life outside the studio a whirl of dates and parties and shopping sprees. She revelled in the cultural and social life of New York, attending and hosting parties with her new friends and boyfriends as her celebrity continued to soar. She gratified her every desire—morality clauses and bank balances be damned. But she was also growing up. She had new obligations as a mother and new sorrows (her father died in October 1923) to go alongside her new freedoms.

In 1924, photographer Edward Steichen shot Gloria for *Vanity Fair* through a veil of black lace. "She recognized the idea at once. Her eyes dilated, and her look was that of a leopardess lurking behind leafy shrubbery, watching her prey," said Steichen. "You don't have to explain things to a dynamic and intelligent personality like Miss Swanson. Her mind works swiftly and intuitively."[19] The image didn't appear in print for four years, but once published it became iconic, the height of Gloria's glamour aligned with a shade of mystery, and a new mature expression. Her glistening eyes dominate the image, her signature mole obscured behind the lace. Whatever the image meant to Gloria at the time, viewed in hindsight she appears to be encased by the monochrome of the silent screen, a modern face wrapped in antique lace. Gloria always photographed well but whether for Steichen in 1924, in Richard Avedon's *Vogue* portraits of her in 1980, or in her finest films, she looked her very best in black and white.

Gloria's elevated artistic vision expressed itself in *Madame Sans-Gêne* (Léonce Perret, 1925). Her screenwriter friend Forrest Halsey first suggested the story to Gloria and as they discussed it their plans grew grander. The source is a comedy-drama play written by Victorien Sardou and Émile Moreau about the life of Catherine Hübscher, an outspoken laundress who married a Duke and became the Duchess of Danzig. When she is presented at the court of Napoléon she is an outsider by birth and offends the sensibilities of many with her brazen talk. However, she reminds the Emperor of her contributions to the Revolutionary struggle, and in particular of the time she wrote off his laundry bill when he was a poor soldier. Napoléon welcomes Catherine into his inner circle. The role was first played on stage in 1893 by the acclaimed thespian Réjane—a performance that was recorded in two silent film adaptations, giving Gloria a daunting act to follow. But Gloria was not easily intimidated.

She travelled to Paris and persuaded Paramount's European chief, Adolphe Osso, that *Madame Sans-Gêne* should be shot on location, a trailblazing Franco-American co-production. In October 1924, Gloria sailed to France to shoot the film "like a diva",[20] with an extensive retinue of family, friends and staff. She was waved off by one large gathering in New York and greeted by a crowd so vast when her train arrived in Paris that the police were called in. The cast of her new film was mostly French, led by Émile Drain as Napoléon, and so was the director, Léonce Perret, a veteran with a taste for the avant garde who had worked on both sides of the Atlantic. For the first time Gloria had Swiss designer René Hubert create her wardrobe and she agreed to every expense he requested. Hubert had been recommended by her new French interpreter, a man Halsey described to Gloria as "one of a group of smart Paris swells who frequented the Ritz bar". According to the writer, he "spoke English like Bernard Shaw, had the body of an athlete and the face of a matinée idol, and carried the title of marquis".[21]

This miraculous man was Henri de La Falaise, and he was about to become Gloria's third husband. At 26, he was far closer to Gloria's age than her previous spouses and apparently had never seen any of her films. He was a World War I hero, having won the Croix de Guerre, a feat he would repeat in World War II. He was indeed a marquis, the eldest son of Louis Venant Gabriel Le Bailly de La Falaise and Henriette Lucie Frédérique Hennessy, whose family owned the famous cognac brand. He was sadly, perhaps inevitably, broke—bearing a name and a title but no family fortune. But he was lovely, tall and handsome with a moustache—and he was kind. Gloria remembered him as the best of her five husbands, "a more delightful companion than any I have known",[22] a truth worth holding on to through what happens between this romantic first meeting and their divorce in 1931.

They waited until Gloria's divorce from Somborn was final before marrying in Passy town hall on 28 January 1925, after filming on *Madame Sans-Gêne* had finished. This was the happiest day of Gloria's life, her "pinnacle of joy". The following day, she was "more wretched than she had ever been before".[23] Gloria kept an appointment at a hospital to abort their child. She would have welcomed another baby but such an early arrival would have been proof that she had broken Paramount's hateful morality clause. Complications sent Gloria to hospital for several days in a dangerous fever, and newspapers back home reported that she was at death's door. On her eventual return to the States with her new husband, the crowds were even bigger than when they left. Acknowledging the extent of the welcome parties, Dwan told Henri: "If Gloria were thirty-five instead of twenty-five, she could run for President."[24]

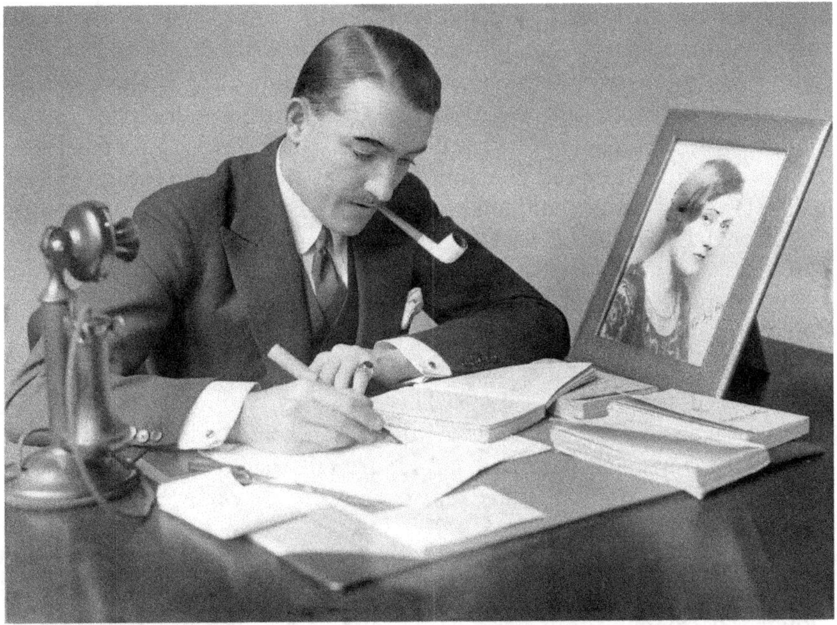

Henri de La Falaise, Gloria Swanson's third husband, whom she married in Paris in 1925 at the peak of her silent career. Milestone Film & Video.

Madame Sans-Gêne is now a lost film, but based on stills and the trailer it is all-too-easy to imagine its beauty and how enthusiastically Gloria inhabited her romantic, rags-to-riches heroine. She would always look back on its production as the high point of her career. She was devastated that the film could not be found, telling *Sight and Sound* magazine in 1969, "It's a crime that it's lost... The Cinémathèque française claim they don't have a print, but I don't BELIEVE them! Is [Cinémathèque director] Henri Langlois an old man? Is he older than I am? Because if he is, I'll outlive him and I'll see it yet. I would go down on my KNEES to this man... Just let me look at it, I'd say, I'll keep your secret..."[25] The trailer boasts of the film's views of Paris and the Fontainebleu, Malmaison and Compeigne palaces: "Staged on a scale of Napoleonic splendor in Paris and Versailles—amid the actual scenes of Imperial magnificence." Permission had never been granted for filming at these locations but Gloria's lobbying and Paramount's production budgets were persuasive.

The film was not entirely beloved by the critics; many felt the story and Swanson's performance didn't live up to the grandeur of the backdrops. They cottoned on to continuity errors, introduced when Paramount cut half an hour from the film before distribution. In *Photoplay*, though, Quirk raved: "Here is a motion picture answer to the croaking of the cynics. In it Gloria Swanson sets herself securely in motion picture history… the entire production is a credit to motion pictures and reflects unlimited credit on the organization that produced it."[26] These words should not be taken out of context. Elsewhere in the same issue of the magazine, Quirk also penned a puff piece about Gloria's hunky new *mari*, which romanticised his family's history during the revolution but also reassured readers that he was easily mistaken for an American, with plenty of Irish in his heritage via the Hennessy line. "Everybody calls him Henry. And Gloria is still Gloria."[27] Gloria's stardom, and Paramount's publicity funds, all but guaranteed success for the film. Even without the movie itself to review, we can measure the impact on Gloria's career, mostly in the shifting scale of her ambition. That was the message that reached the public in 1925. This was also an important achievement, a feather in the cap of both studio and star. And Gloria was the Queen of the Movies. After she and Henry returned to the US and those cheering crowds, they travelled across the country on a private train to Los Angeles, where more hoards of fans were waiting.

Gloria was also rehearsing a new role: producer. Even before she left for France Gloria had been talking to her friends Mary Pickford and Douglas Fairbanks about her dissatisfaction with Paramount, who had not even suggested her for the lead in a forthcoming adaptation of the J. M. Barrie play *Peter Pan*, a role coveted by almost every female star in Hollywood, including Pickford. Further, the studio had interfered with her life in the most obscene manner. Despite her successes, Gloria considered herself "a victim rather than a victor in the realm of pictures… the very thought of the Hays Office and morals clauses made me ill."[28] She attributed two bad marriages and two dead children to the movie business. She had seen her co-star Wallace Reid die before his time, destroyed by addiction, and her friend Rudolph Valentino hounded by the press as they pulled apart his sexuality. He too would die young in 1926, aged 31. Everything Gloria really valued, including her third marriage, her children and her health, she had achieved despite the studios, not because of them.

There was another option. Since 1919, Pickford and Fairbanks had been at United Artists, the company they co-founded with Charlie Chaplin and D. W. Griffith. The objective was to produce their own films, on their own terms, instead of being beholden to studio bosses. Richard A. Rowland of Metro Pictures famously freaked out: "The inmates are taking over the asylum." One early ambition was for each name to produce five pictures a year, but this was soon abandoned. By the time Gloria spoke to Pickford and Fairbanks in 1924, Chaplin, notoriously slow and perfectionist, had only made one, the sophisticated melodrama *A Woman of Paris* (1923), in which he barely appeared—although the following year he would release *The Gold Rush* (1925), one of his best films and a box-office hit. Also that year, Griffith had left the company, and Joe Schenck, an established Hollywood producer, had been brought in as chairman—in 1927, he would take charge of the company as president. Schenck took no prisoners. This Russian-born Jewish immigrant was a notoriously tough-as-nails character who had worked his way up from running amusement parks with his brother Nick in New York to becoming a movie producer, along the way marrying star Norma Talmadge. Now Nick worked for MGM.

Gloria was one of the most bankable stars in Hollywood and she had proven she could take charge of her own material, so of course United Artists wanted her. In 1925 Gloria was faced with the option of renewing her contract with Paramount at more than $1 million a year and remaining on the treadmill of making four pictures annually, or tasting artistic freedom with United Artists, making half as many films, and choosing her own projects. She signed a six-picture deal with UA. If there is one career choice that defined Gloria, it was this stone-cold audacity in turning down a $1 million salary from a Hollywood studio to go her own way.

In the summer of 1926, after completing her commitments to Paramount, Gloria chose her first UA project, a story even she admitted was familiar territory. The first (and last) film to roll out of The Swanson Producing Corporation would be an adaptation of a 1917 play called *The Eyes of Youth,* in which Sunya, a young girl struggling to choose her path in life, is shown visions of her future, should she either opt for fame as a singer in Europe or marry for money to suit her family. Both paths end in disaster, so Sunya follows her heart and marries for love, following her husband to start a new life in South America. Gloria hired Hubert to design the gowns and chose the director Albert Parker, who had made a film of the same play in 1919 starring Clara Kimball Young, distributed by Somborn's Equity Pictures and co-starring a young Valentino as the villain. Gloria had worked happily with Parker back at Triangle. Apparently, late one night Beery found the two of them getting cosy in a car together and punched the director squarely on the nose. Parker, in an unusual act of chivalry, drove his car into a tree on the way home, to create a cover story for his bloody nose so neither of their respective spouses would believe that Beery had caught them cheating before their divorces were final.

Against Schenck's advice, Gloria chose to make *The Love of Sunya* at a studio in New York instead of Hollywood. The production ran behind schedule and over budget, while Gloria exhausted herself working long days to keep on top of the work. When the film premiered in March 1927 at the brand new 6,200-seater Roxy Theatre in New York, it felt old-fashioned, a repeat of Gloria's umteen glossy romantic dramas. This was the film Joe referred to in his Harvard lecture. Gloria was disappointed in its quality and it just about broke even, but the reviews were largely favourable, with *The New York Times* hailing "an intriguing picture, with pardonable exaggerations".[29] *Photoplay* was especially keen, but not aware of any progression: "Good girl, Gloria Swanson!… Keep on playing ladies who are sharp, naughty and a little hard-boiled… and beautifully dressed."[30] However, Gloria was confident that next time she would do better. "I was hooked," she remembered. "I was thinking like a producer."[31]

That meant knowing when to listen to good advice from colleagues and when to follow her instinct. Gloria conceded Schenck's point that Hollywood was the most convenient place to make films, but what she wanted was "a challenging script and an exciting director".[32] Raoul Walsh had played John Wilkes Booth in *The Birth of a Nation* but had also been making some of Hollywood's best and most ambitious silent films, from urban crime drama *Regeneration* (1915) to the exotic spectacle *The Thief of Bagdad* (1924), starring Fairbanks. His biggest hit yet was 1926's *What Price Glory*, in which Victor McLaglen and Edmund Lowe play U.S. Marines during World War I, rivals for the charms of a French girl played by Delores del Rio. Walsh was a macho guy who bred racehorses in his spare time and would later be renowned for gangster films and Westerns, starring John Wayne, James Cagney and especially Humphrey Bogart. He was also under contract to Fox but Gloria wanted him. Dwan recommended him too, which carried a lot of weight, and she was impressed that he had brought *What Price Glory* to the screen at all, because its source play was based on was filled with language that would horrify the Hays Office.[33] She was swayed by war veteran Henri's estimation of the film as a "masterpiece", and she admired "its frankness, its naturalness".[34]

When Gloria and Walsh started talking about potential projects, they couldn't shake the thought of another controversial play: *Rain*, written by John Colton and Clemence Randolph, based on Somerset Maugham's emotionally devastating short story. *Rain* was on Hays's list of banned sources but Maugham's story was not. It was first published in a magazine in 1921 as "Miss Thompson". In the original story, set in tropical, rain-lashed Pago Pago, American Samoa, a missionary attempts to reform a "harlot", Sadie Thompson, browbeating her into repentance. When the missionary's body is found, his throat cut with a razor, it becomes apparent that in the process of trying to save Sadie's soul, he succumbed to temptation—and so killed himself out of shame. "You men!" Sadie jeers. "You filthy, dirty pigs! You're all the same, all of you." Every step of the way, the story flouts the edicts of the Hays Formula.

"Filming *Rain* in 1927 was the maddest idea in the world, but every other idea suddenly seemed dull,"[35] confessed Gloria.

Gloria intended *Sadie Thompson* to be her equivalent to Chaplin's *The Gold Rush*, using the freedoms offered by UA to make a statement of artistic value, and in her case to defy the industry's moral hypocrisy. Just like the missionary in the story, Hollywood bosses preached virtue but craved vice. As Gloria wasn't the head of a studio, she hadn't signed up to the Hays Formula pledge and had a little leeway: "Henri and Raoul and I sat around a table under the trees and conspired about how best to break the Hays Code."[36] Some changes were easy to make, especially in a silent film. First, no profane language; second, the missionary, called Reverend Kelly in the play, wouldn't be a clergyman, simply a "reformer". Things got a little fuzzier when it came to prostitution and kissing, matters that had to be handled with "taste". It helped that Maugham's literary pedigree conferred a certain prestige. But diplomacy was still required. Gloria invited Hays to lunch where she flattered him by asking to drop his name when asking Maugham for permission to make the necessary changes. While Walsh and Gloria worked on the screenplay, Schenck bought the rights to both story and play.

Opposition came not from the Hays Office itself but producers who had signed the pledge. No fewer than fifteen studio heads, including Joe, signed a letter to Schenck, forwarded in a telegram to Hays, urging UA to cancel production, claiming it would "IN OUR OPINION BE AN ACTION UNFORGIVABLE AND UNWARRANTED AND A DIRECT VIOLATION OF PROMISES WE HAVE MADE THE PUBLIC THAT MATERIAL OF THIS KIND WOULD NOT BE MADE."[37] Their motivation was partly jealousy; if someone else was filming salacious plays, why couldn't they? As it turned out later, the Fox studio was trying to buy *Rain* itself, a revelation that made Gloria channel the spirit of Sadie herself: "Those hypocritical sons of bitches!" She explained in her memoir: "All of them being so high and mighty, so prim and proper, so protective of the industry and the American family. And all of them dying to get rich without getting caught."[38] Undeterred, Gloria wrote to each of the studio heads to argue her case. FBO's Charlie Sullivan replied on behalf of Joe, offering the equivalent of an out-of-office autoreply, which Gloria dismissed as "useless".[39] The original telegram had been the first time she ever saw Joe's name. But Marcus Loew of MGM helpfully broke rank. This much-loved figurehead was seriously ill. He had raised himself from his sickbed to give one of Joe's Harvard lectures and would die in his sleep just three months later. He graciously wrote that if Hays agreed to the film's production so would he, and would do his best to assist.

Gloria persisted. The making of *Sadie Thompson* was a case of fortune favouring the brave. Production took place on Santa Catalina Island, near Long Beach, California, and, as with *Sunya*, the production ran over schedule and over budget, climbing to $650,000. This time Gloria was forced to sell one of her homes, a farm in Croton-on-Hudson, 40 miles north of New York. Lionel Barrymore played Davidson, the reformer, and Walsh returned to screen acting for the first time in 15 years to play "Handsome" O'Hara, Sadie's love interest. The kisses continued off-camera; Walsh, whose divorce from actress Miriam Cooper was imminent, fell in love with his star. When his divorce was finalised, Gloria threw him a party. Elsewhere in Hollywood, on the same night, Von and actor Norman Kerry threw a matching soiree for Cooper.

Gloria is magnificent in *Sadie Thompson*, playfully comic at the start of the film and soulful in the love scenes, but first bold, then distraught as Davidson tries to break her down. She collapses while praying. When Sadie is at her lowest ebb, fearful for her future and tormented by the endless rain, Gloria's performance bears comparison to the tour-de-force emoting of Lillian Gish in *The Wind* (Victor Sjöström, 1928). In those love scenes, Gloria and Walsh smoke cigarettes in the dark just like Greta Garbo and John Gilbert in *Flesh and the Devil* (Clarence Brown, 1926)—and sparks fly. She looks great too, her hair tucked into a low bob with a kiss-curl in the middle of her forehead or worn loose to her shoulders, with the heavy eye-makeup that suits her strong features, and in one scene with white orchids pinned next to her ear. She has several costume changes, sundresses and negligées, a chic take on cheap, though a world away from the aspirational high-end glamour of her Paramount roles. She glows, too, having recently taken up the healthy diet that she would stick to for the rest of her life, on the recommendation of a health quack called Dr Bieler: a regime of vegetables and brown rice, bolstered by stints consuming only puréed greens. What today we would call a detox diet.

There's more to the film than may meet the eye. Sadie arrives in Pago Pago in natural makeup, wearing a collar and tie and a sun visor, before changing her costume into something more overtly feminine and street-walker-coded: a feathered hat and fur collar. In her first modern outfit, as she signs a ship worker's autograph book ("Smile, Bozo, smile"), she looks like Gloria Swanson the beaming movie star, swiftly ushered ashore to meet and greet the soldiers stationed at the nearby base. That's one dangerous comparison, between the star and the sex worker. Davidson signs the book too, with a motto about the "knife of reform" curing a "sin-sick world". Censorship has unforeseen consequences. Barrymore's character has been twisted into a "professional reformer", not a cleric but someone who intimidates politicians and acts as if he owns

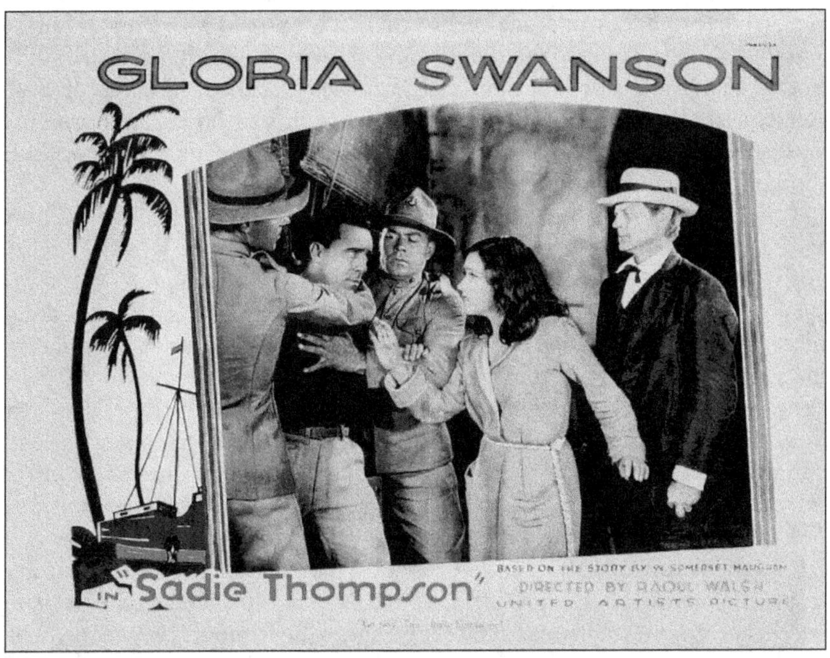

"Suddenly every other idea seemed dull." Gloria provoked the industry by making *Sadie Thompson*. Milestone Film & Video.

the island, who is vocally determined to clean up the island but who is seen as powerless. This now invites a subversive reading: the movie star vs the reformer. Gloria is re-enacting her battles with if not the Hays Office itself then the Hollywood hypocrites she despised. In one confrontation Handsome clasps his hand over Sadie's mouth to silence her stream of profanity while Davidson raises his hand to shield his eyes and two watching women clap their hands over their ears. See no evil, hear no evil, speak no evil. A mocking parody of censorship. Davidson tells Sadie she is wicked but he is tortured by dreams about her, dreams that one character suspects are "not altogether unpleasant". And in *Sadie Thompson*, the hypocrite meets a grisly end.

The film wasn't released until early 1928, an event *Vanity Fair* marked by printing Steichen's lace-veiled portrait of Gloria. The Hays Office had scrutinised the film, an exasperating process that delayed its release. Its changes included deleting the word "rain" from all the intertitles, to deny all link with the play. The reviews were enthusiastic, praising the dank, tropical atmosphere, and Swanson's performance especially, but also Barrymore's villain turn, as well as the film's delicacy in leaving something to the imagination. "While this actress may have given clever performances in some of her pictures," wrote Mordaunt Hall in *The New York Times,* "she displays more genuine ability and imagination in this present production."[40] Gloria was Oscar-nominated for Best Actress, at the very first ceremony. She lost out to Janet Gaynor, who was garlanded for three films—in two of them she plays a streetwalker, though much more coyly.[41]

Sadie Thompson became a hit too, making more than $1 million at the US box office, and seven times that around the world. Yet, as events transpired, Gloria was not to benefit financially. *Sadie Thompson* survives to this day, albeit with the final reel missing. It is a tremendous film, a testament to Walsh but also Gloria's vision, her craft, and audacity in facing moral double standards head on. Joan Crawford would play the role in 1932's *Rain,* directed by Lewis Milestone, and Rita Hayworth in *Miss Sadie Thompson* (Curtis Bernhardt, 1953), but Swanson's is the definitive screen Sadie, her finest performance in silent cinema, both as star and producer. She was also beginning to master Hollywood politics. "I had outsmarted Will Hays along with the whole pinochle club."[42]

In the autumn of 1927, *Sadie* went down a treat at a preview screening in San Bernardino, giving Gloria confidence in a job well done, but she had other worries. She was concerned about how much had been spent on this film, and she still didn't have her next project lined up. She had tried to take on too much herself and rarely listened to advice. She had personal debts, was struggling to pay her staff, and had borrowed from friends already. She planned to look for investors on her next trip to New York and was considering selling her house in Malibu. Robert Kane, a friendly producer from Paramount, counselled caution, telling her that movie producers are always in debt. Gloria didn't need to sell off any assets, just wait for the money to come in. He recommended someone she could talk to about finding investors. Gloria thought the man was a film distributor, but Kane assured her he was also a banker. So in November 1927, Gloria made a date to have lunch with Joe.

1. Occasionally misnamed as Joseph B. Kennedy.
2.   Rose Fitzgerald Kennedy, *Times to Remember* (Doubleday, 1974), 289.
3.   Terry Ramsaye, "Intimate visits to the Homes of Famous Film Magnates", *Photoplay,* September 1927, 125. Ramsaye would go on to work for Kennedy at Pathé, and to write one of the first Hollywood histories, *A Million and One Nights: A History of the Motion Picture* (Simon & Schuster, 1926).
4.   *Times to Remember,* 171.
5.   *Hostage to Fortune,* 46.
6.   Letter from JPK to Martin Quigley, 20 August 1926, Georgetown University Special Collections.
7.   Quoted, Doris Kearns Goodwin, *The Fitzgeralds and the Kennedys* (Simon & Schuster, 1987), 347.

8. This could have resulted in a kind of critics' awards ceremony, like those run by various regional Critics' Circles, or even the Golden Globes, run by the Hollywood Foreign Press Association, alongside the annual Academy Awards, voted on by industry members, which was inaugurated in 1929. More presciently, it would have been the world's first film archive by several years. MoMA's Film Library was founded in 1935; the Harvard Film Archive in 1979.

9. Joseph P. Kennedy (Ed), *The Story of the Films: as told by leaders of the industry to the students of the Graduate school of business administration, George F. Baker Foundation, Harvard University* (A.W. Shaw Company, 1927), 16.

10. Ibid, 124.

11. Ibid, IX-X.

12. Ibid, 340.

13. Seymour went on to work as a screenwriter at Warner Bros. in the 1930s, before returning to work for Joe as secretary and press attaché when he was the US Ambassador to Great Britain.

14. *SoS*, 196.

15. *Hollywood, Episode 6: Swanson and Valentino* (dir. Kevin Brownlow and David Gill, TX 1980).

16. "Gloria Swanson Divorced", *New York Times*, 20 September 1923, 5.

17. Herbert Howe, "Close-ups and Long Shots", *Photoplay*, January 1925, 47.

18. Gloria Swanson, "My Most Wonderful Experience", *Photoplay*, April 1951, 90.

19. Edward Steichen, *A Life in Photography* (Bonanza Books, 1984), 146.

20. *SoS*, 221.

21. *SoS*, 224.

22. Quoted, Welsch, 379.

23. *SoS*, 3.

24. *SoS*, 7.

25. Rui Nogueira, "I am Not Going to Write my Memoirs!", *Sight and Sound*, Spring 1969, 60.

26. J.R.Q., "The Shadow Stage", *Photoplay*, June 1925, 48.

27. James R. Quirk, "Everybody Calls Him 'Henry'", *Photoplay*, June 1925, 108.

28. *SOS*, 261.

29. Mordaunt Hall, "New Roxy Theatre Has Gala Opening", *New York Times*, 12 March 1927, 1.

30. "The Shadow Stage", *Photoplay*, May 1927, 53.

31. *SOS*, 287.

32. *SoS*, 296.

33. Infamously, lipreaders in the audience were all too aware of the profanities uttered by the two lead actors, which were not duplicated in the sanitised intertitles.

34. *SoS*, 296.

35. *SoS*, 298.

36. *SoS*, 298-9.

37. *Hostage to Fortune*, 52.

38. *SoS*, 323.
39. *SoS*, 311.
40. Mordaunt Hall, "The Screen", *New York Times*, 6 February 1928, 12.
41. *7th Heaven* and *Street Angel* (1927 and 1928, both Frank Borzage). She also won for *Sunrise: A Song of Two Humans* (F. W. Murnau, 1927).
42. *SoS*, 330.

6
The Genius

Von had been bruised by the experience of making *Foolish Wives*, but Hollywood had far worse in store for him. Between the release of that film and starting production on *Queen Kelly*, Von made three, four or five films, depending on how you cut it. Each one of them was a bitter ordeal—both for Von and his colleagues. Not one exists in the form that he planned. One no longer exists at all. You might call Von a great auteur of the unfinished film, a master of incompleteness. He has this in common with Orson Welles, who similarly saw several of his films diminished by studio interference or otherwise left unfinished. Out of all the films Von directed, only two were presented to the public as he wished, and one (*The Devil's Pass Key*) no longer survives. Watching Von's work requires leaps of imagination, and should you be so inclined, leaps of sympathy too.

In 1922, although his relations with Universal were fraught, Von owed the studio one more film. What could be a better subject than a tale of Old Vienna? *Merry-Go-Round* is a multi-plotted romance in which a count (Norman Kerry) falls in love with an organ-grinder (Mary Philbin) at the city's famous Prater amusement park. It should have been a surefire hit and a happy experience. Von and Valerie Germonprez had been married during the *Foolish Wives* shoot and she gave birth to a baby boy, Josef, during the production of *Merry-Go-Round*. While Von was still directing it, that is.

Filming began in August, and Thalberg installed a production manager, James Winnard Hum, to keep the shoot to schedule, an inter-ference heavily resented by Von. Between Von's improvisational directing style and Kerry's persistent heavy drinking, the schedule soon became a fantasy. Von and Hum went to war. Von "raved", wrote Hum in his diary, threatening to have both him and Thalberg sacked. Von loved to delay shooting until nighttime, when the crew were forced to use vast quantities of electric light, overloading the circuits, and causing a blackout, which put work back yet further. One night, when at 1am an exhausted Hum left the set, Von announced: "Now that the stool pigeons have gone home we will go to work."[1] What Von shot, and how he shot it, was enough to give the studio conniptions, including a naked Kerry stepping out of his bath and an orgy scene in which the extras were boozed up on real champagne and whiskey, charged to the production budget. After eight weeks, Thalberg had had enough. Von was fired, to be immediately replaced by Rupert Julian, who completed the film. *Merry-Go-Round* was officially no longer Von's movie, but when it was released, a year later, fans and journalists contested the film's authorship, seeing his talent throughout this otherwise compromised work. *Screenland* went to bat for Von: "In justice to a much maligned man of rare directorial ability… the obvious fact is manifest that *Merry-Go-Round* is his in every essential sense of the word. The story was shifted and abbreviated—but the spirit of Von Stroheim remained. And that spirit made *Merry-Go-Round* one of the best pictures of the past film year."[2]

Von was not unemployed for long. He had been courted by other studios even before Thalberg kicked him off *Merry-Go-Round* and in November he was hired by the Goldwyn Company on a three-picture deal, which turned out to be anything but. Von's first project was an adaptation of Frank Norris's 1899 novel *McTeague*, the story of a San Francisco dentist, his wife and his best friend, their lives destroyed by rivalry and avarice after the wife wins the lottery. Von saw it as pure Greek tragedy. What happened next has become a Hollywood legend, the painstaking creation of a classic out of blood, sweat, tears and time, and its subsequent undoing by the forces of commercialism. Von's screenplay for *Greed* was a meticulous adaptation of Norris's novel. The performances he drew from his actors, led by Gibson Gowland, ZaSu Pitts and Jean Hersholt, reached new peaks of psychological realism.

Von would harangue and even bully his cast, even threatening violence. Reporters invited to observe the filming of *Greed* in San Francisco witnessed an exasperated Von harassing and belittling an actor. The reporter for the *San Francisco Chronicle* noted how Von "has much to try his patience; the long waits that sometimes seem endless; the stupidity of actors; annoyance from technicians; interruptions; a hundred and one little things that come up to get on one's nerves". After eight takes with actor Cesare Gravina, who plays Zerkow the junkman, "it wasn't surprising to hear him say, sotto voce: 'I'll kill him! I can't help it!'… On the ninth trial it was accepted, although Von Stroheim shrugged his shoulders and muttered: 'It's the best I can get, I suppose.'"[3] Other writers variously reported how Von berated Gravina, acted out his part for him, and announced that the actor was clearly scared of the scene they were shooting later, which would entail jumping into the bay. That scene is not in Norris's novel, nor did it make it to the theatrical cut of *Greed*.

The actors' painful efforts to create naturalism were matched by the authenticity of the interior sets and location shooting both in San Francisco and, for several sweltering weeks, in Death Valley. Realism was Von's chief preoccupation, which elsewhere expressed itself in glamorous, if absurd, gestures, notably his insistence that there had to be real caviar on the banquet table in *Queen Kelly* and hand-embroidered silk underwear for the extras in *Merry-Go-Round*. The realism of *Greed*, the unflinching scrutiny of humanity in all its lowest moments, was different. Von employed a popular 1920s phrase, one with a moralist implication, arguing that the screen should be "life's mirror", and also, in a more modern expression, saying the film should appear as if it were shot by hidden cameras, capturing the actors unawares. All this grim reality was impressively photographed by William H. Daniels with stencil colouring in key frames, particularly bright yellow for the dangerous lure of gold, the love of which, the Bible tells us, is the root of all evil.

Von and his remarkable team shot the film from March to October 1923, resulting in 85 hours of footage and a bill of $632,079. The legend of *Greed* insists that Von presented the studio with an edit of some 40 or more reels, nine or ten hours, in January 1924. Journalist Harry Carr, who saw this presentation, wrote: "For stark, terrible realism and marvelous artistry, it is the greatest picture I have ever seen. But I don't know what it will be like when it shrinks from 45 to eight reels."[4] The long-cut screenings were a kind of publicity stunt on Von's part to establish his preferred version in the minds of journalists, however the film turned out on release. June Mathis, the studio's editorial director, was already working her way towards a 12-reel cut.

Von slashed *Greed* to 22 reels himself and editor Grant Whytock cut it further—to 15 reels. During this process, Goldwyn merged with Metro to form Metro-Goldwyn-Mayer which meant, distressingly for Von, that Thalberg was once again in charge of his new film, as was Louis B. Mayer, who had a natural distaste for anything grim, realist or uncheerful. Von was removed from the editing room, once again. The film was stripped down to 10 reels, running two hours and 20 minutes. Von disowned it. What else could he do? In all that hacking, the studio had failed to sanitise *Greed* completely—the censors made further snips too. The critics were dismayed by either the extent of the cutting or the sordidness of the subject, but could only admire the undeniable quality of the direction. Mordaunt Hall began by sneering at Von's "audacity" then went on to tie himself up in knots: "Mr. von Stroheim has not missed a vulgar point, but on the other hand his direction of the effort is cunningly dramatic."[5] Others went out of their way to praise Von's vision and his personal integrity, with *Photoplay* hailing him as "the artist, living in the garret of the motion picture Latin Quarter"[6], although the same magazine's review was lukewarm. *Motion Picture Magazine* asked: "Why should the cutters have butchered it?… That it remains a splendid thriller in spite of all is due to the talents of the director, who is incapable of shooting a single reel that is not interesting."[7] That is a copper-bottomed truth about Von. In *Picture-Play*, Agnes Smith argued that "The only thing to do with the picture is to force all the movie people — director, actors, writers — to look at it once a week and study it. If they want to consider it the work of a spendthrift madman, they are free to do so, but there isn't a person in the business who couldn't learn something from it." Also true. *Harrison's Reports,* which took a moralist stance on all pictures, called it "the filthiest, vilest, most putrid picture in the history of the motion picture business" one that would "turn inside-out even the stomach of a street cleaner".[8]

Audiences largely stayed away. The original, uncut *Greed* is lost forever, although valiant attempts to reconstruct the film, using stills to cover missing scenes, give us a glimpse of what might have been. It's enough to take one's breath away. *Greed* is a heart-harrowing study of human corruption, with one of the strongest and bleakest endings in film history: Gowland and Hersholt trapped in a deadlock, roasting alive in Death Valley. Pitts, usually cast as a quirky comedienne, is a revelation as the dentist's wife, driven to insanity by wealth. Von, who had blown the budget several times over, knew that his film was always going to be criticised by the censors and that the original length was unrealistic for exhibitors. But the fact remains that Von made a masterpiece that was destroyed before his eyes — and everyone in Hollywood knew about it.

Von's image was shifting. No longer playing the villain with a wink, he was now a more complicated character: Hollywood's pet visionary — a credit and a pest at the same time. Louella Parsons called him "film-land's greatest luxury". To the public he could be marketed as a master, but to the industry he presented a problem: a loose cannon incapable of sticking to a budget, or honouring the Hays Formula. He was a "true artist", as Welles would later put it, but obliged to work in a commercial industry within clear constraints, which most of his peers accepted. The wit Robert E. Sherwood called him "a genius… but he is badly in need of a stop watch".[9] It would become a point of pride with Hollywood producers to show that they had the strength to control the DeMilles and Stroheims — to reap the glory of their brilliance without paying too high a price. This was a key strategy in asserting the primacy of the producer protecting the efficiencies of the studio system. Their hypocritical approach to Von's brilliance was similar to the way that they wanted Gloria to be provocative on screen, but demure in her private life. This

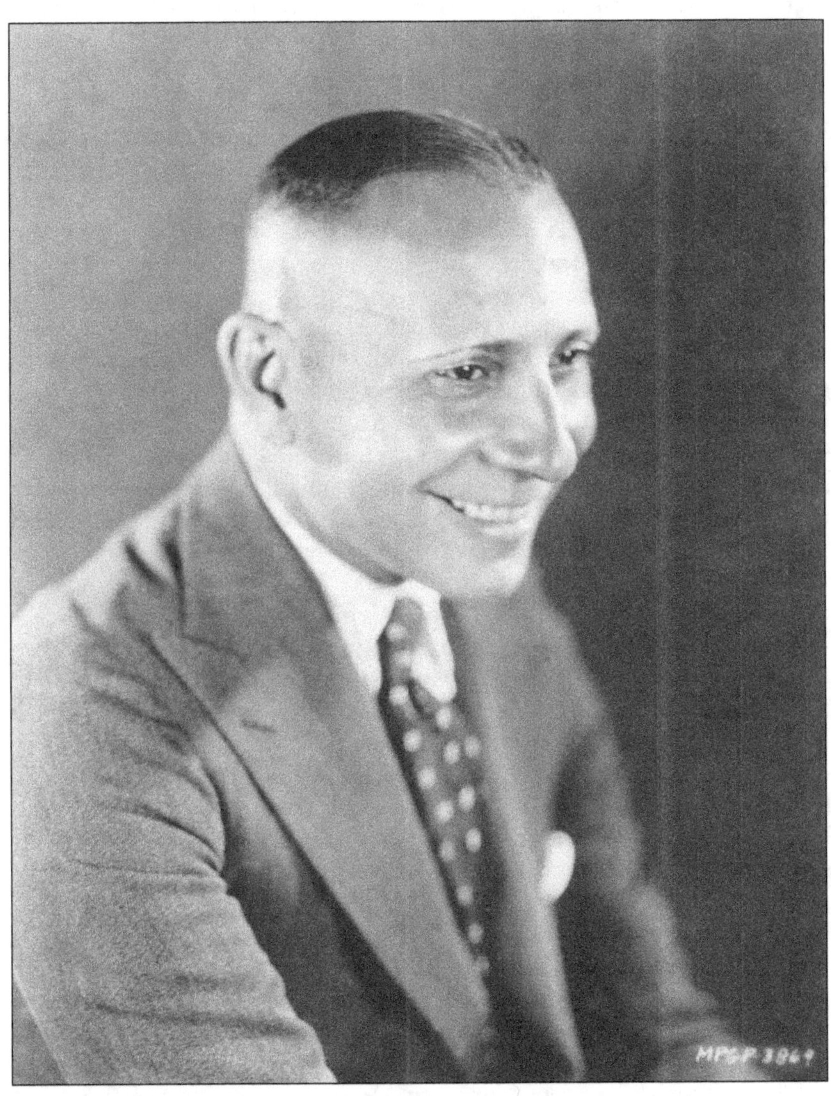

"Filmland's greatest luxury": Erich von Stroheim in 1925.
Author's collection.

paradoxical treatment could only encourage perversity in Von. There were those who felt he was purposefully trying to provoke the studios, spending thousands and thousands of their dollars in order to make films that were not commercial but asserted his own brilliance—their only real value as testament to his genius.

While his darlings were being murdered in the editing room, Von got back to work. Looking back, he would claim that the experience of making *Greed* had forced him to drop all his fine ideas about art and realism; he was now a hack for hire. Yet his next film for MGM had his signature all over it: an adaption of a Viennese favourite, the Franz Lehár operetta *The Merry Widow* from 1905. The first clue that Von would not have his way was the casting of two stars, John Gilbert and Mae Murray, "the girl with the bee-stung lips". Gilbert and Roy D'Arcy played two lascivious Crown Princes, both familiar Von characters—Euro aristocrats in uniform. They both lust after Murray's Sally, a frisky Irish-American vaudeville dancer from New York who is passing through the sleepy Ruritanian idyll of Monteblanco. Here, the quintessential Von character, the aristocratic, uniformed European seducer, is split into two halves; Gilbert's handsome, smiling lover (who wishes to be known as "just plain Danilo Petrovich"), and Mirko, the monocled brute who bares his teeth and clenches his jaw.

MGM attempted to encourage good behaviour by offering Von bonuses for finishing on time, a plan which almost worked. It was a fraught 12-week shoot, with Von openly hostile to the stars who had been foisted upon him. He and Murray, who was imperious, prone to temper tantrums, and demanded her own special lighting, were often at each other's throats. Von didn't dare attack a star like Murray physically, but he did his best to tear her down mentally. She in turn complained to Mayer about the "filth" in the story, and even called Von "You dirty Hun" to his face. On the filth front, Von had made sure to spice up the story with a feather-strewn orgy, plenty of ripe innuendo, even nudity. A sickly and depraved Baron, played by a leering Tully Marshall lurching erratically on two walking sticks, clearly demonstrates a foot fetish, which the film shamelessly indulges, a fact that gave rise to an apocryphal anecdote. After Von explained to Thalberg why the Baron was eyeing up Sally's shoes, the producer supposedly responded: "And you have a fetish for footage." Von's excesses were perceived as pathological.

MGM tried to replace Von with Monta Bell during the shoot but the extras and crew rebelled. He finished the film but his relationship with MGM was dead and buried. *The Merry Widow* impressed critics and audiences alike, the biggest box-office hit of Von's directorial career, although not, he considered, his film at all. Yet its structure, narrative, even individual lines and shots carry over directly to *Queen Kelly*.

The Merry Widow was good for many people, if not for Von. Between this and *The Big Parade* (King Vidor, 1925), Gilbert made it to the big leagues of Hollywood stardom, and Murray had never been better, as critics breathlessly noted. Von's mastery was also acclaimed in glowing reviews, which frequently acknowledged just how much he had ramped up the "sex angle", with Mordaunt Hall archly noting Von's "Emile Zola-Elinor Glyn complex".[10] But the director, who had two families to support, never saw a penny of the film's considerable profits.

It was Pat Powers, formerly of Universal and Robertson-Cole, who hired Von next. Powers was a gruff Irishman, something of an operator, who clearly felt he was tough enough to handle Hollywood's "spend-thrift madman". Von, who had several simpatico working relationships with Irish Americans, found Powers an appealing colleague. Fay Wray, who starred in the picture they made together, wrote in her memoirs: "I believe he thought his business acumen would guide him to know how to cope with von Stroheim's extravagances, but it was probably their mutual Catholicism that brought them together."[11] It is not clear entirely whether Von ever officially converted to Catholicism, however, the Catholic church features heavily in many of his films, he was very close friends with a Father John O'Donnell in Culver City, and he was known to attend mass. Although the film Von and Powers made depicts several varieties of moral degeneracy, it is firmly set in the Catholic world, revolving around Vienna's St Stephen's Cathedral and opening on Corpus Christi, providing Von with an opportunity to stage a mounted military parade and a High Mass. Powers partnered with Paramount for financial backing and distribution of what was to become *The Wedding March*, more or less.

The Wedding March revisits Von's interest in Cinderella romances between a Prince and a commoner, and picks up motifs from earlier films, such as the pigs in *The Merry Widow* and the Viennese setting of *Merry-Go-Round*, as well as developing some ideas we will see again in *Queen Kelly*. In *The Wedding March*, Von plays the romantic lead, impoverished Prince Nicki ("Let's make it—just Nicki") who falls in love with Wray's humble Mitzi in prewar Vienna. There are complications beyond the class divide: Mitzi is engaged to a gross butcher (Matthew Betz) whom Nicki packs off to jail, but he is soon released and Nicki is unwillingly betrothed to a disabled heiress, Cecilia (ZaSu Pitts). Several sumptuous scenes, including the wedding of Nicki and Cecilia, are set in St Stephen's Cathedral, which naturally Von had rebuilt at enormous cost, along with the surrounding streets, trees laden with apple blossom, palatial suites and a picturesque Austrian wine garden. He borrowed a royal coach from the Vienna State Museum.

"Von Stroheim, notwithstanding his reputation for the spirit of ruthless realism in his pictures, is of the Romantic pre-Raphaelite school so far as concerns infinitude of detail,"[12] marvelled *The New York Times*. The paper listed such examples as painting the horses' hooves black, spending three days shooting a sneeze, and warning his crew that he was willing to film 24,000 takes of one scene. Wray wrote: "There was never any sense of having to compete with time. Time was his, he owned it. He used it as it should be used by an artist. He ignored it."[13] Defending himself yet again to a fan magazine reporter who came to the set, Von referred to the horror that greeted *Greed*: "They say I give them sewers—and dead cats! This time I am giving them beauty. Beauty—and apple blossoms! More than they can stand!"[14] The blossoms drift into almost every frame, as if it is snowing in summer. And yes, there is beauty, masses of it. The material Von shot for *The Wedding March* includes much that is deeply romantic, frames filled with grand architecture, mythical imagery, and embellished with Technicolor sequences. Then there is the *Greed* model of realism, in the brawls, the crowds and an extended orgy scene in a brothel, with copious amounts of naked, oiled skin on display. The orgy was achieved over a month of shooting, lubricated by bootleg gin and assisted by employees of Hollywood brothels run by the madam Lee Francis. This notorious figure, real name Beverly Davis, wrote proudly in her memoir that she had "waxed rich if not fat on the bounty of the moguls and the beauty of the maidens".[15] All of this, as Von well knew, was more than the studio could stand.

Von filmed from June 1926 to January 1927, when Powers finally pulled the plug. He had 200,000 feet of film and had spent upwards of $1,250,000 on a $300,000 budget. Von planned a two-part film and began to cut, but after he produced a four-and-a-half hour first instalment, Powers took charge. Austrian-American director Josef von Sternberg, a choice Von initially approved, was to make the necessary cuts. After a poor preview, Paramount opted for a 12-reel cut of *The Wedding March* and an eight-reel sequel, *The Honeymoon*.

Released in October 1928, *The Wedding March* was a flop. Critics found it too ponderous to compete with the talkies that were stealing the audience's favour, even though it had a synchronised musical effects score, plus colour sequences. "Because of what they are called upon to do and not because of the performances of the players the characters are not much more human than a troupe of Robots," wrote Mordaunt Hall.[16] Trade ads featuring a portrait of Von stated: "In addition to being a good picture, it is an important picture," which seems like a desperate argument, although it *is* a good picture. Fay Wray makes for a sweet but substantial heroine, one who bites her lip distractedly when she first sees Nicki in his dress uniform. The young actress, just 19 when the film was made, was besotted with Von, which is plainly apparent in her scenes with him as Prince Nicki. The Prince's parents, played by George Fawcett and Maude George, are excellent comic grotesques, a contrast to the prettiness of the love story. While the lead storyline tends towards the sentimental, the film is perked up with humour and biting dialogue. Like *Greed*, it also has a first-rate, unhappy ending, one that pre-empts the dejected newlyweds of *The Graduate* (Mike Nichols, 1967) by four decades and borrows something from the *Old Heidelberg* story in which Von appeared in 1915 and had been recently filmed by Ernst Lubitsch as *The Student Prince in Old Heidelberg* (1927). At Von's request, *The Honeymoon* was never released in the US and was destroyed in a nitrate fire at the Cinémathèque française on 10 July 1959, two years after Von's death. Curiously, Henri Langlois chose to describe this loss as a kind of suicide, declaring that the film *"est mort voluntairement"*.[17] The cause was more prosaic: reels were left out in the hot sun under a glass canopy. Nitrate film is even more combustible than Von's temper was.

While *The Wedding March* was awaiting release, Von was exploring his options. The genius had burned his bridges at Paramount, but his plan of returning to Universal was scuppered by his association with Powers. By the time the film opened, Universal was re-editing *Foolish Wives* yet again for a potential release with a Movietone score. Von viewed the edit and vetoed the reissue. More excitingly, though, he was preparing to shoot *Queen Kelly*.

1.   Quoted, Koszarski, 122.
2.   "Von Stroheim We Hand it to You", *Screenland*, November 1923, 100.
3.   "Von Stroheim Making Film In Heart Of Busy San Francisco", *San Francisco Chronicle*, 15 April 1923, 39.
4.   Quoted, Koszarski, 161.
5.   Mordaunt Hall, "The Screen; Frank Norris's McTeague", *New York Times*, 5 December 1924, 28.
6.   James R. Quirk, "My estimate of Eric von Stroheim", *Photoplay*, January 1925, 27.
7.   W. Adolphe Roberts, "Confidences Off-Screen", *Motion Picture Magazine*, March 1925, 27.
8.   Quoted, Koszarski, 166.
9.   Robert E. Sherwood, "The Silent Drama: Greed", *Life*, 1 January 1925, 24.
10.   Mordaunt Hall, "The Screen", *New York Times*, 27 August 1925, 14.
11.   Fay Wray, *On the Other Hand: A Life Story* (St Martin's Press, 1989), 65.
12.   "Von Stroheim's New Film", *New York Times*, 8 January 1928, 113.
13.   Wray, 70.
14.   Dorothy Bay, "First the Artist, then the Human Being, that's Von!", *Motion Picture Classic*, December 1927, 23.

15. Serge G Wolsey, *Call House Madam: the story of the career of Beverly Davis* (Martin Tudordale Company, 1945), 128.
16. Mordaunt Hall, "Mr Stroheim's Picture", *New York Times*, 15 October 1928, 16.
17. David Robinson, "Stroheim's Lost Masterpiece", *The Times*, 24 January 1975, 9.

7
The White Knight

Gloria had money on her mind when she met Joe but only $65 in the bank. That didn't mean she couldn't be the director of this scene. She had booked into the Barclay hotel on East 48th Street—her concession to frugality—and arranged for Joe to meet her there. The maître d' would call her when Joe arrived in the dining room so she wouldn't be left waiting, and the bill would go on her tab. Gloria made her entrance in style, turning heads as she approached Joe's corner table. But she was surprised by Joe's unprepossessing appearance; his suit was too baggy and his tie too tight. He was boyish and animated, in his late thirties, with sandy hair, spectacles and soft hands unburdened by heavy work, but he looked nothing like a mogul or a banker. As Gloria and Joe made small talk they found more differences than similarities. Gloria marvelled that Rose was expecting their eighth child; Joe was surprised that Gloria's adopted five-year-old son Brother had not yet been christened. She stuck to her new regime of string beans, celery and courgette; he had three courses, finishing with pie and ice cream. When she brandished a cigarette, Joe was embarrassed that he didn't have a light. He asked her how she had got *Sadie Thompson* past the censors, but when she explained he guffawed, implying that she had merely used her feminine charms on Hays. Gloria was deeply offended and not about to take that from a man who produced shoestring Westerns and the formulaic adventures of Ranger the Wonder Dog. She asked him why he had joined the campaign against the film. It was no more than a favour to his peers he said, backtracking on a touchy subject.

When time came to talk business, things got worse. She presented two financing plans she had been offered for her next film. Joe didn't offer one of his own, just asked her questions she was unable to answer and sighed over the fact that Hollywood types neither understood money nor a more important concept, that the financial value of a film was entirely theoretical until the audiences were queuing at the box office. Despite all this, Gloria could tell that he was taken by her beauty and impressed by her fame. For her part, she appreciated his lack of formality, his hearty laughter. When he really let rip, he smacked his thighs in delight. Yet she was confused. It wasn't really a business meeting—Joe hadn't offered her any financing, suggesting only that she stay with Schenck and UA—and it certainly hadn't been a date either. He didn't even offer to pay for the lunch. Even stranger, later that day he reappeared at the hotel, asking her to do a favour for a mutual friend. Gloria's lawyer Milton Cohen was representing a Paramount executive's wife in their divorce. Could she persuade him to be more amenable? And could she call him now, this afternoon? Joe insisted—and he waited while she made the call. Then, finally, he asked her to dinner.

The dinner was a date. A spruced-up Joe collected Gloria from her hotel in his chauffeur-driven, heated Rolls-Royce, presented her with an orchid corsage (Gloria's "unfavorite flowers"[1]), and whisked her out of the city, across the Queensboro Bridge, to a restaurant in Long Island, a discreet distance from the new Kennedy family home in Riverdale. During the journey, Joe asked Gloria questions about the film industry and why she had turned down Paramount's million-dollar contract. She imitated his accent and he whooped with laughter. In the restaurant, Joe was clearly overawed—not by his surroundings but by his glamorous companion. Misjudging his audience, he intimated that he could arrange for Gloria to have wine in a teacup if she liked. At least this faux pas meant they could bond over their shared teetotalism. Over dinner, he regaled her with the story of the Harvard lectures. They both giggled unkindly over the idea of Zukor addressing the scholars in his rich Hungarian accent. Joe gave Gloria a copy of the Harvard lectures, with her name stamped in gold on the cover. She berated him for not inviting any female lecturers—he should have asked Charlotte Pickford, Mary's mother, she argued, who understood the movie business better than anyone. Joe agreed, but said Gloria would have been a better choice. That's quite the chat-up line from a man who had bemoaned her lack of financial literacy just hours before. How could Gloria fail to be smitten by someone trying this hard to impress her? This time he even had a light for her cigarette.

In the Rolls on the way back to Manhattan, Joe pounced... on Gloria's future. His proposal: let me manage every aspect of your career. "Together we would make millions,"[2] he said. He saw her star value, her worth at the box office, but he was also impressed, perhaps even seduced, by her artistic aspirations. Joe argued that they should make an "important" picture, to continue the leap forward she had made with *Sadie Thompson*: "A great story *and* a great director. Isn't that what you turned down a million dollars to be able to do, Gloria?"[3] It was certainly what Joe wanted to do next. His plan to take Hollywood entailed thinking bigger than FBO and its small-budget films. His biggest hit so far had been *The Gorilla Hunt* (Ben Burbridge, 1926), a semi-staged documentary about big game hunting in "the fever-ridden jungles of Africa"[4], which he confessed that he couldn't bear to watch. His Harvard scheme had turned his head and he told Gloria that night that one of his former colleagues was currently making an important picture, like the one they should attempt, a prestige drama led by a genius director. The colleague was Pat Powers, the film was *The Wedding March*, and the genius was Von.

Joe wanted Gloria, but she wanted him too. Gloria was convinced she had spent a "significant evening" and "stumbled on the right business partner to straighten out my career".[5] Henri had been her saviour when it came to making arrangements in Paris, but he knew nothing about business and even less about the movies. Joe presented himself as the capable adviser she sorely needed. Their mutual attraction was, at this point, unspoken. A couple of days later two men arrived at her office to requisition her accounts. Gloria's secretary Grace Crossman rang her in a panic, wanting to be reassured they weren't what they looked like: mobsters. "The man they work for is a Harvard graduate with seven children and his father-in-law used to be the Mayor of Boston,"[6] replied Gloria. All good reasons to have faith in Joe.

Joe and Gloria kept in touch by phone as he made plans to disentangle her financial affairs. His assessment of Gloria's situation was dire. In his opinion, her earning potential was still high but her finances were in a mess: she had been badly advised and taken on too much borrowing. After he prescribed "emergency surgery", his team set to work. They were the "four horsemen" who had been with Joe since the shipyards: Eddie Moore, his righthand man, E. B. Derr and Charlie Sullivan, the numbers whizzes, plus Ted O'Leary, who was, to put it bluntly, the muscle. She liked them, these working-class Irish "Catholics and devoted family men"[7] who were attentive and kind to her children. Their stated goal was to liberate Gloria of all her debts, her "deadwood" advisers, her obligations and her ties to other organisations, so she could start afresh. They were horrified by the number of people she employed, including servants, a dressmaker and a stenographer, and by Henri's habit of buying paintings. Their plan was to dissolve Gloria Swanson Productions and establish new company, Gloria Productions, in its stead. "My only job," remembered Gloria, "was to forget everything and let them set up a proper company for me once and for all."[8] She signed her power of attorney over to Derr. At this point, a lot of things started happening all at once, often in unorthodox fashion. It would take a mind as busy as Joe's to really keep it all straight.

Joe's ruthless interventions had driven a wedge between Gloria and Joe Schenck, the formidable exec at UA whom she now no longer believed to have been working in her best interest. Joe's bold suggestion was that Gloria should get out of her current deal and sell all the rights to *The Love of Sunya* and *Sadie Thompson* (still unreleased) to UA. Gloria reluctantly agreed, and so did Schenck, who offered to write off everything she owed them in exchange for the rights to both films, but agreed that she could still be part of UA, which would distribute her next film, whatever it was. Schenck was happy with this agreement. UA was riding high and he had found Gloria difficult to work with, or so he said. He signed the papers, telling Derr, "I'll do anything to help somebody I like, and I like Joe Kennedy."

The horsemen worked fast, albeit warily and in secret, communicating in code. Those gangster comparisons were no mystery. "If I don't go to jail on this deal, I never will," joked Pat Scollard, another of Joe's associates dating back to the Fore River days, as he described how he had filed papers for Gloria Productions in Delaware. Derr was named president and Scollard vice-president; the papers drawn up for Fred Thomson Productions were used as a template. The Corporation Trust of Delaware required a lawyer to approve the papers before they were filed, but Scollard and Joe didn't want any outsiders to see any of the paperwork. The FBO counsel was persuaded to make the necessary phone call without anything in writing. "Five minutes later, I had a man in an automobile going over the road from Wilmington Delaware to Dover to file the charter," bragged Scollard, "and I want to tell you that there was never a corporation formed with the speed that this one was formed."[9] It wasn't illegal, just not entirely above board.

While all this was happening, Joe was celebrating success (FBO had made $1 million more this year than the last) and making more deals. Warner Bros.' *The Jazz Singer* (Alan Crosland, 1927) had been released in October and the sound revolution was looking more inevitable every day. The success of that film proved that audiences would pay extra for talking and singing—if it was done well. While other studios installed Western Electric equipment, Joe negotiated with David Sarnoff to put his system, RCA Photophone, into the FBO studios and start using it to make talkies. He was also in the process of taking control of a second studio, Pathé. A man with two studios who was freshly wired for sound could afford to be ambitious and spend serious money on a serious film—with a serious star.

In typewritten notes for Swanson's 1980 memoir, the phrase "complete surrender to white Irish knight"[10] sits next to the date 25 January 1928. That's the day Gloria remembered[11] that she and Henri gave in to Joe's "wild telephone calls" and boarded a train to Palm Beach to join him and his friends on holiday. En route, she received a telegram from Cohen. "Regret your attitude exceedingly. Wish always to be your friend but never your lawyer." Cohen had been strongly encouraged to resign without her knowledge, having clearly outlived his usefulness to Joe. Gloria understood well enough to respond to Derr, instead of Cohen, writing: "Can't see what I have done that is so terrible. Advise whether I am to cut my throat or not."[12] The day they arrived, *Film Daily*'s front-page headline read "Gloria Swanson-Kennedy Deal?",[13] with a report speculating on the negotiations. Joe, the article stated, was unavailable for comment. One reason was that he was already in Florida, waiting at the station for Gloria, ready to make his next power play—albeit a clumsy one.

Joe, always a man to act fast, leapt on the train as soon as it slowed down. While Henri stepped onto the platform to take care of the luggage, Joe raced down the aisle and into Gloria's suite. With "a few excited words" he stooped down to embrace her and kissed her twice. Just as swiftly, he stood up straight, bumping his head on the luggage rack and sending his spectacles flying. Gloria laughed, first at the sight of him on his hands and knees hunting for his glasses, again when he stood up with dusty knees and lipstick smeared across his face. What could have been a love scene was instead a burst of Mack Sennett slapstick.

Gloria rode with Joe to the hotel, where the manager greeted her with orchids on arrival and more in her suite. During their stay in Palm Beach, Joe had arranged a round of social occasions where he could show off the movie star and the Marquis to the smart set, led by the Stotesburys, an elderly investment banker and his wife worth a cool $100 million. Five years later, Joe would buy his family their own Palm Beach mansion, La Querida,[14] which would serve as the Winter White House once JFK achieved his father's highest ambition for his children and was elected President of the United States. (It is six miles north of the Mar-a-Lago Club, which at the time of writing fulfils the same function for the current president.) Gloria found Joe's obvious pride in his success and his elevated social status endearing. She admired him for using his intelligence and determination to improve his situation, which was certainly something she could identify with. He, or his men, took care of everything. Gloria never really romanticised what happened between her and Joe, but she did romanticise his background, this idea of the working-class boy who made good in defiance of anti-Irish prejudice. It was in Palm Beach, as Gloria recalled, that she signed away the rights to her last two films and Joe offered Henri a job. As European director of Pathé, Henri would be gainfully employed, but not by Gloria, and conveniently out of the way, commuting between California and Paris. "In a few brief sessions," said Gloria. "We had rearranged the world."[15]

There was one more card to play. One day Henri was invited to go fishing with the horsemen, while Gloria relaxed in the resort. Joe made his way to Gloria's suite, where he overheard her telling the hotel florist she hated orchids and would prefer red carnations. If the revelation threw him off his stride, he recovered rapidly. "He was like a roped horse," wrote Gloria, "rough, arduous, racing to be free." He moaned, "No longer, no longer. Now," as he pulled open her kimono. "After a hasty climax he lay beside me, stroking my hair. Apart from his guilty, passionate mutterings, he had still said nothing cogent." This is not the same as Gloria's horrifying account of her wedding night with Beery, but it also doesn't sound like an account of consensual sex. Just as he had forced Gloria's hand in business matters, Joe seems to have also taken what he wanted in the bedroom without asking. The testimony of many women over the years suggests that such brief, mechanical sex, without kisses or foreplay, was Joe's regular modus operandi—and that of his philandering sons too. If Gloria had entertained the idea that an alliance with Joe promised her power, true independence from the strictures of the studio system, this joyless first encounter was Joe's demonstration that power resided with him alone. By the time Henri came back from his fishing trip, Joe had claimed Gloria as he would a new business. First by stealth he would acquire the leverage he needed, then publicly announce his takeover. "All arguments were useless," she said. "The strange man beside me, more than my husband, owned me."[16] At Mrs Stotesbury's party that night Gloria carried a red carnation and Joe and Henri each wore another on their lapels. Carnations would always be Gloria's signature flower. Orchids would be Queen Kelly's.

Gloria and Joe's affair would last for three years, and have lasting consequences. Joe found Gloria sexually exciting, while she found him a disappointing lover, but he had other redeeming features: he worshipped her, he had a head for business, able to plot moves far in advance, and he made her laugh. She also believed that he had her best interests at heart. They made a clashing couple, one tall and conspiratorial, the other petite and charismatic. Gloria was on her third marriage at the age of 28 and her love affairs were widely known among her Hollywood circle, if not her fans. Almost as soon she said "I do" to Henri, the gossips started predicting the end of the marriage, not to mention that she had had two abortions, one by choice. The films she had made ranged from saucy to scandalous—even before the quite deliberate provocations of *Sadie Thompson*.

Outwardly, at least, Joe was a very different character. Although his friends knew he was an inveterate womaniser, he was careful to be discreet and no one looked twice at a banker or movie exec squiring a chorus girl or starlet around town in any case. He was careful to spend just enough time at home with Rose and the children, visibly providing them a life of luxury and ease. His public image was embedded in his Catholicism: the Irish-American *paterfamilias*, supporting a wife and many children while making wholesome, family-friendly movies. It had only been a couple of months since Terry Ramsaye in *Photoplay* described Joe as "exceedingly American", explaining that he brought with him "an atmosphere of much home and family life and all those fireside virtues which the public never hears in the current news from Hollywood".[17] The article printed pictures of Joe, Rose and each of their children. "Which proves Joseph P. of F.B.O. to be the most thoroughly family man in all the great industry of the motion picture."[18] The clash of values was part of the attraction for Joe. Gloria and Rose were both alike to look at: beautiful, dark and petite. But while his wife's Catholic faith made her reject sex unless it was for the purpose of having children, Gloria was a liberated woman who had no such hangups. She liked sex, the company of men, and wasn't monogamous by nature.

Joe's reputation as a good Catholic family man, however, made his intention to hire Von frankly bizarre. Von's Catholicism was at best newly adopted, if not as fraudulent as his claim to aristocratic blood and his military record. He was not devout, had been divorced twice, and his films were a riot of immorality, filled with religious imagery, but not without reverence for the teachings of any faith. His characters are motivated by lust and materialism. *The Wedding March*, in particular, flagrantly disrespects the institutions of marriage and the church. As one critic noted, Von "does not hesitate to show crucifixes during inopportune moments".[19] Still, Joe had secured Von's services almost as soon as he had propositioned Gloria in his car on the journey home from Long Island. What Pat Powers had, he wanted as well. He wanted a masterpiece, and so he wanted Von.

1. *SoS*, 334.
2. *SoS*, 339.
3. *SoS*, 340.
4. "Record runs on 'Gorilla Hunt' prove power of exploitation", *Exhibitors Daily Review*, 25 February 1927, 10.
5. *SoS*, 340.
6. *SoS*, 341.
7. *SoS*, 343.
8. *SoS*, 343.
9. Quoted, Beauchamp, 134.
10. GSA.
11. She also remembered that it was a Sunday, but 25 January was a Wednesday.
12. *SoS*, 351.
13. *Film Daily*, 25 January 1928, 1.
14. Bought for $120,000 on 30 June 1933.
15. *SoS*, 355.

16. *SoS*, 356-7.
17. Terry Ramsaye, "Intimate Visits to the Homes of Famous Film Magnates", *Photoplay*, September 1927, 125.
18. Ibid, 123.
19. Mordaunt Hall, "Mr Stroheim's Picture", *New York Times*, 15 October 1928, 16.

8
The Swamp

Gloria was thrilled by the thought of working with Von. He had the swagger to match Walsh, another actor-director overflowing with masculine oomph. He was another DeMille in terms of scope and ambition—for good or ill. For Gloria, Von's films were unique, always with "a savor of delicate, authentic decadence about them, like the smell of cut gardenias at the end of a party".[1] Their collaboration offered her a chance to work once again with a director of exceptional gifts and epic vision, not as a wet-behind-the-ears girl but as an actress of acclaimed talent and comparable aspiration. Gloria had now starred in a lavish production of her own, *Madame Sans-Gêne* (which Von admired), had pushed Hollywood's taste and decency boundaries with *Sadie Thompson*, and knew what it was like to go toe-to-toe with executives. Gloria and Von were able to commiserate other over their shared experience of studio interference; they were almost kindred spirits. Although Joe found it distasteful, Gloria knew *Sadie Thompson* was "sort of a masterpiece" and that she could do it again. The dream she had when she joined UA was still alive. Gloria wanted to make her *Gold Rush*.

Gloria described Von and Joe as alike—"Catholic, political and ambitious". Yet Von's appeal to Joe, the family man, who cosied up to the advocates of censorship and always put the bottom line first, was less clear. In retrospect, Gloria was perceptive and scathing. "Much as I cared for Joseph Kennedy, he was a classic example of that person in the arts with lots of brains and drive but little taste or talent. I knew that he wanted more than anything in the world to produce a successful picture and have his name on it."[2] Von was Hollywood's resident genius and, more attractively for Joe, he was forbidden fruit, still under contract to Powers. This meant that the deal had to begin as a covert operation, which was always Joe's preference. Should the plan come off—and Joe's plans invariably did—they would be ready to release their film hot on the heels of the surefire success of *The Wedding March*. The difference is that their film would star Hollywood heavyweight Gloria Swanson, box-office dynamite. For Joe, hiring Von was something akin to orchestrating a heist.

Romantically inclined readers may recall that in the 17th century a Mughal emperor built the Taj Mahal in tribute to his late wife, and in the 19th century the Russian Tsars commissioned jewel-encrusted Fabergé eggs for their empresses. In the winter of 1928, Joe filled his prospective lover's Florida hotel suite with orchids. Did he also intend to lavish Gloria with the most expensive director in town—"filmland's greatest luxury"—as a grand gesture of his affections? That may be true, but as will become apparent, the gifts that Joe bestowed upon Gloria were always charged to her business account, including the services of Erich von Stroheim.

As for Von, he was chasing the dream of directing without studio interference. This new film, an essentially independent production, could be everything he had ever wanted. There was no movie mogul to throw his weight around and curtail Von's artistic freedom. It's true that he was wary of working with established stars, and Mae Murray had done nothing to change his mind, but it was obvious that Gloria was no ordinary star. She was up for a fight and prepared to challenge the orthodoxy, so he would write her a film that only a true Hollywood rebel would countenance appearing in.

Von arrived at Gloria's Hollywood home in March 1928 to take coffee on the patio with her and Joe and to sell them the story he had written: *The Swamp*. Von was a little cocky yet effusive in his praise for Gloria, and very charming. This story was designed to make even the least refined listener choke on their coffee. In it, Von built a world of filth and cruelty, deliberately provocative, and yet, against all odds, drew out a tale of pure love, with a happy ending.[3] According to Gloria's memoirs, Von had not yet seen *Sadie Thompson*, but in bringing this story to Gloria it is abundantly clear he was aware of its content and intended to script a similarly controversial character. Either he was aware that Joe had been gifting her orchids or he picked up that detail from *Sadie Thompson*. The earliest typescript that survives of Von's scenario gives us a good idea of the story he told on that day—compelling, outrageous. But we can only guess at the live performance element. Von was hypnotic, exhibiting an excess of passion and charisma as he enacted a tale to his rapt audience. Just as he had acted out every scene of *Blind Husbands* to Laemmle in his study all those years before, now he transported Joe and Gloria to Dar Es Salaam in German East Africa (now Tanzania) and spun a story of larger-than-life characters in a debauched, far-off milieu, surrounded by lethal danger. A commanding woman is reduced to a chattel bride, married to a monster, then rescued in dramatic circumstances by a foreign prince, culminating in a moment of dramatic peril. As with *Sadie Thompson*, it offered considerable difficulties, especially when it came to appeasing the Hays Office. But once again, every other story would seem dull in comparison.

The scene is set in a "seaport dive" known as The Swamp in the district of Poto-Poto,[4] Dar Es Salaam. This establishment has German bartenders and is frequented by drunken sailors and "girls" (or "tarts") of all ethnicities who are selling sex—as the screenplay just stops short of saying. Macaws scattered around the saloon squawk "Pay as you enter," recalling the signs in the brothel in *Greed* that read "Buy a drink and help yourself." The script was littered with racial stereotypes, racialised insults, and many uses of the N-word to describe the locals. A repulsive, drunken and amoral white man called Jan, Poto-Poto Jan, or the King of Poto-Poto, enters the venue and is thronged by the girls as he flashes his cash around the bar and spits out tobacco juice. "They say he is worth half a million but he is a crazy old lunatic and the tales about him are darker than Africa itself," says one barfly. "He is some humdinger—filthy as a pigsty."

Jan is enthralled by the entrance of the owner of the establishment, Queen Kelly, AKA Kitty Cold Cash Lady Kelly. Von's description of Gloria's role took the bravado and glamour of Sadie and amplified it: "A gorgeous looking creature, exotic and bizarre". She is beautiful and imperious, with a braided hairstyle "like the Empress Elizabeth of Austria", dressed in a tailored black outfit, which clings to her figure, accessorised with simple but expensive jewellery and white orchids pinned to her chest. "All in all, she looks more like a Viennese comtesse than an inmate of Poto Poto." Kelly, who was educated in an elite convent before inheriting Poto-Poto from her aunt, presides over this place, but is a virgin, "clean as a whistle," who refuses to sleep with any man no matter what the price and dreams of marriage and children. She closes the place every Sunday morning to go to Mass.

Jan immediately wants Kelly, but she does not reciprocate. As they drink together, she disposes of the contents of each glass. Understanding that she will not sleep with him, he proposes marriage and claims he loves her. "Love—in your hat—Love, me eye," scoffs Kelly in her Irish accent. She sets an extortionately high price (250,000 Marks) and refuses a cheque. He must pay cash. While Jan writes to his banker for the money, Kelly learns quite how wealthy he really is ("They say he has passed the hundred million mark"), that he lives in a house on the other side of the swamp, and that he is horribly sick and won't live much longer. Meanwhile The Swamp is at risk, down to its last two hundred bottles of champagne and reliant on the arrival of a big ship full of sailors the next day to stay in the black. Kelly oversees the strip-search of a sailor who refuses to pay his bill, and a moment later she hands the money he was hiding to a sick old woman who needs charity. Jan returns with the full price of Kelly's hand in marriage.

Jan and Kelly are married "by an American negro, and ordained minister" whom they bribe to overlook the drunkenness of the wedding party. It is a crude parody of a cathedral wedding, witnessed by Jan's "bozo friends". Kelly takes Jan's diamond ring as her wedding band. Travelling to their remote, marital home, Kelly learns how impassable and mosquito-riddled the swamp is, and Jan is bitten by a tsetse fly. He now has "a month—perhaps two years" to live, and breaks down in tears.

Cut to Germany and "the imperial palace in Potsdam", where our romantic hero, Count Wolfram von Eschelburg, is being raked over the coals by the Emperor: "This is the third time and the last time that you ballsed things up with your damned love affairs. You have your choice. Either leave the service—or Africa." The Count chooses the latter and his friends throw him a farewell banquet, teasing him about the horrors he will face in Dar Es Salaam.

Two years later we return to Poto-Poto, where Jan is paralysed from the waist down and close to death. Kelly is regretting her choice to spend the best years of her life in the solitude of the swamp and beginning to suffer the first effects of malaria herself. "One pleasure she derives indirectly thru Poto-Poto. She that loves orchids has never less than a hundred blossoms in vases and baskets in her room, brought by negroes from the swamp expressly for her."

The Count arrives at his new post, in command of a hundred Black men ("what a come-down!"), and quickly realises that being in Poto-Poto is "almost like being buried alive". He asks a lieutenant what there is to do for entertainment in this place and is told: "Smoke, drink—poker—or 'mammy-palava'." Desperate for white company, the Count dresses in his "light gray uniform with silver embroidery, silver belt, and his Schuttestruppe hat" to visit Jan and Kelly at their remote home. When Kelly and the Count meet, they exchange meaningful gazes, a love-at-first sight moment. "Then their eyes falter in the instinctive knowledge of the male and female that fate had written down the meeting as a main event in their lives and that they could play star parts in each other's future." Jan's arrival barely interrupts him and the Count is determined that "There is no husband in the world, especially not one in a wheel chair, that will stop him." Jan falls asleep after dinner but before the Count leaves he and Kelly share a passionate kiss. Kelly prays before going to bed.

When the Count returns to visit again, he is told that they are not at home. This provokes a row with Kelly that culminates in Jan smashing a vase of orchids then whipping the Black servants, who arrive to clear up the mess. Kelly sneaks out to see the Count ("We have a very interesting, intimate love scene, into the detail of which I cannot go in short synopsis form.") but Jan spies on them as they spend the night together. When Kelly returns in the morning, Jan makes it clear he knows what has happened and she breaks down sobbing.

The Count, alerted to the situation by a note from Kelly's maid, arrives to rescue his lover, who has decided to leave Jan on her own. He insists on going with her and she tells him that the only possible route is to cross the swamp. Jan eavesdrops when they confess their love for each other. At midnight the Count and Kelly set out on their perilous journey. Jan has sent a band of dozens of drummers to torment them with a monotonous drumbeat as they pass. In the morning they are hindered by the onset of the "equatorial rain", which thunders down for months at a time. At home, Jan is "smiling diabolically" as he realises the lovers are destined to fail in their escape attempt and that Kelly will not now inherit his wealth. The lovers take shelter under a dead tree stump overgrown with orchids as the water rises around them. The end is surely nigh.

Back at the house Jan collapses and dies. Should she know it, Kelly is "the undisputed heir of One Hundred Millions—had they waited they could have lived happily ever after, with no sacrifices or hardships". Kelly also drops the package containing the 250,000 Marks Jan gave her for their wedding—crocodiles fight over it as it sinks into the swamp water. "Nothing is left to them but their love for each other—strong, clean, death-defying love, that has come to them out of the swamp."

At this moment, the German army surgeon, who has passed out from drinking, wakes up and reads the Count's letter of resignation, which explains that he has fallen in love and is escaping with Kelly through the swamp. The surgeon sends out a search party of "one hundred black soldiers in slickers". Crosscutting between the party and the lovers raises the suspense until the film climaxes with one of two endings. Just as all hope of survival has gone, either the lovers see the approaching flashlight and realise they are saved, or they mistake the flashlights for fireflies or men sent by Jan. The Count, to save Kelly from a fate worse than death, puts his gun to her heart ready to shoot, but as they share a final kiss he hears his name called out and realises they are saved. Either way, they are taken to safety at Lake Victoria where, having been informed of Kelly's inheritance, the lovers "board a German gunboat which brings them to safety and the promise of marriage and happiness".

It was a promising scenario in many ways: a love story between two gorgeous young people in a richly imagined, exotic locale, albeit a seedy one. Our lovers must overcome peril and embrace the better part of their natures, foregoing material wealth to be together. Gloria would be as wonderful as the strong-willed, confident Cash Lady Kelly as she was in *Sadie Thompson*. The recurring orchid imagery could work as effectively as the apple blossom in *The Wedding March*. A recent Mary Pickford picture, *Sparrows* (William Beaudine, 1926), had been a great success with a sequence involving an escape through a swamp (innocent children, not lovers, braving the mud). That screenplay was by C. Gardner Sullivan, who had worked on *Sadie Thompson* as title writer and editor. Von had recently done some uncredited rewrites on Sullivan's script for *Tempest* (Sam Taylor, 1928), a romance starring John Barrymore and Camilla Horn, set during the Russian Revolution. That film, and *The Wedding March*, both had soundtracks of sorts. This screenplay required, if not full synchronised sound, then at least audio effects, especially during the swamp sequence with the drumbeat. The music played in the bar, the bird calls and the rain would all be very effectively rendered in sound, poising the film to take advantage of the talkie revolution.

However, the red flags were unmissable. The story as written was certainly likely to fall foul of the Hays Formula; it contained depictions of sex work, a suggestion of sex between Kelly and the Count, several uses of profane language, disrespect to the institution of the church and of marriage, and there was a suggestion that Jan has a pre-existing relationship with a Black woman. All these things might be worked out if immense care was taken not to offend, to be euphemistic, and to sanitise the dialogue. However, the story was almost entirely populated by Black people, hugely unusual in 1920s American cinema. They were generally described in vile, offensive terms as "stinking" or "squirming", with the beating of the "tom-toms" figured as an oppressive sound. But it is also a Black regiment that rescues our heroes, so the film seemed destined to offend both Black people *and* racists. One senses very strongly Von was trying to shock. Of the three white leads, one is the out-and-out villain, another has a disreputable past, and the third, the virginal romantic heroine, is a brothel madam. Even in the most determinedly innocent reading she is a mercenary owner of a dive bar.

Could this story be contorted into a film palatable for American audiences? Possibly, if great pains were taken and compromises made, but there was a warning note attached to the end of the scenario that should have checked Joe and Gloria's hopes of pacifying the Hays Office. "All of the sequences thru the swamp, including the rescue, will of course be worked out in great detail in the continuity, and great care will be taken through the entire story to develop and emphasize the theme that nothing clean and good and healthy can come from or be based on surroundings and conditions which are base and unhealthy or foul."

Gloria remembered that she had several worries about the story but that Joe was impatient to get started, so they greenlit Von's screenplay straight away. In her account, she didn't voice her concerns "because something told me that this was the film that would change my life".[5] She also seems to be talking about a different screenplay, possibly recalling an amalgam of both a later version that includes all the scenes that were eventually shot, but also the chase across the swamp, which occurs in none of the later versions used in production. They shook on the deal. Gloria recalls asking Joe whether he knew that "the man of his choice had a growing reputation for being an undisciplined spendthrift, a hopeless egotist, and a temperamental perfectionist". Joe was undaunted. "I also know he's our man. I can handle him."[6]

The likely truth is that Joe and/or Gloria had several changes to suggest to Von. And then there were more. Subsequent versions of the screenplay are quite different from the first draft. Later drafts opened in Germany and show Wolfram meeting Kelly as a convent girl and the two of them falling in love, long before they meet again in Poto-Poto. The adventures in the swamp itself were sidelined in favour of scenes set inside the saloon bar and its rooms. Kelly is threatened by a Chinese sailor who tries to rape her. Distraught that she has lost the Count's love, she tries to commit suicide, but he breaks down the door to rescue her and the film ends with their wedding. The mad queen is introduced to be Wolfram's fiancée, adding a fourth point to what had been a love triangle (Wolfram and the Queen, Kelly and Jan), and that on her death he ascends to the throne. The racist caricatures, especially of the Black Africans, are diminished in number with each redraft, as one Black woman, Kali Sana, emerges as a distinct character. Somewhat present but not emphasised in all versions of the story is a critique of imperialism in the comparison between the very obvious flesh trade in Tanzania and the aristocrats carousing with courtesans in Germany—with the Mad Queen and Poto-Poto Jan as degenerate symbols of malignant white rule. Every subsequent version also finishes with a variant of one of Von's favourite lines. When the happy couple are married, Kelly is addressed as "Your Majesty", to which she responds, "'Majesty', me foot. Just 'Queen' Kelly!"[7]

One lesson that all involved should have learned from Von's first draft is that it's all too easy to walk into a swamp but a hell of a lot harder to pull yourself out of it.

Von had the go-ahead, however, so while Joe overhauled Gloria's life, he went away to redraft the screenplay and begin pre-production. As he was under contract to Powers still, he did so via a proxy. Enter Wilhelm von Brincken, a German of many names and careers. The son of a baron, born in Berlin, von Brincken was exactly the kind of person you would expect Von to hire, the kind of person he was in many ways impersonating. He bore a scar on his face that he claimed to have won in a youthful sword duel and he was a university graduate, a former officer in the German army, a knight of the Teutonic Order — and an enemy spy.

Von Brincken moved to America in the 1910s to be the military attaché to San Francisco's German Consulate, and while living in California he dabbled in movie acting under the stage name William Vaughn, making his debut in *The Redemption of David Corson* (1914), in the role of "Gypsy Chief". Shortly after the outbreak of World War I he was arrested as a spy and sentenced to two years in prison for his role in two plots: the Hindu-German Conspiracy to overthrow British colonial rule in India, and schemes to blow up sections of the Canadian Pacific railway. The trial for the former charge was infamous; one defendant shot the other dead in court. Even before his release, von Brincken's name was frequently in the papers. He had sold his life story, exploiting the notoriety of his crimes and his gossip-column fame, which arose from his second marriage to American beauty queen Milo Abercrombie and their ensuing divorce. He returned to the movie industry in the 1920s as a technical assistant to Von and played a small role in *The Merry Widow*. He worked for MGM as a researcher on films such as *Flesh and the Devil*, which required German military uniforms. According to press reports, he was just plain Wilhelm at this point, having renounced his Barony to become an American citizen — briefly he had gone by the name Roger Beckwith. He also expressed an interest in movie producing.

In March 1928, von Brincken was working for the Goldwyn studios on the Alsace-set romance *The Awakening* (Victor Fleming, 1928), starring Vilma Banky. He placed an advert in the *Staats-Zeitung*, a newspaper for German immigrants in California, calling for any German cavalry veterans to contact him at the Goldwyn Studios to take part in a new film. The thousands of available cowboy extras may have been good enough for Fleming but wouldn't satisfy Von's demand for realism. He was working on *The Swamp* by stealth, while Joe helped him extricate himself from Powers. The male lead of *The Awakening*, English actor Walter Byron, would go on to play Count Wolfram in the new film. Byron, under the name Walter Butler, was already a success in British cinema, "the greatest discovery in British leading men since the war" according to *Picturegoer*.[8] Von initially intended the role to be taken by either Norman Kerry from *Merry-Go-Round* or Edmund Lowe, a handsome leading man who would go on to be best known as Sergeant Harry Quirt in the Quirt and Flagg army comedies, opposite Victor McLaglen, characters that originated in the film that so impressed Henri, Walsh's *What Price Glory*. The next choice was Harry Reinhardt, son of

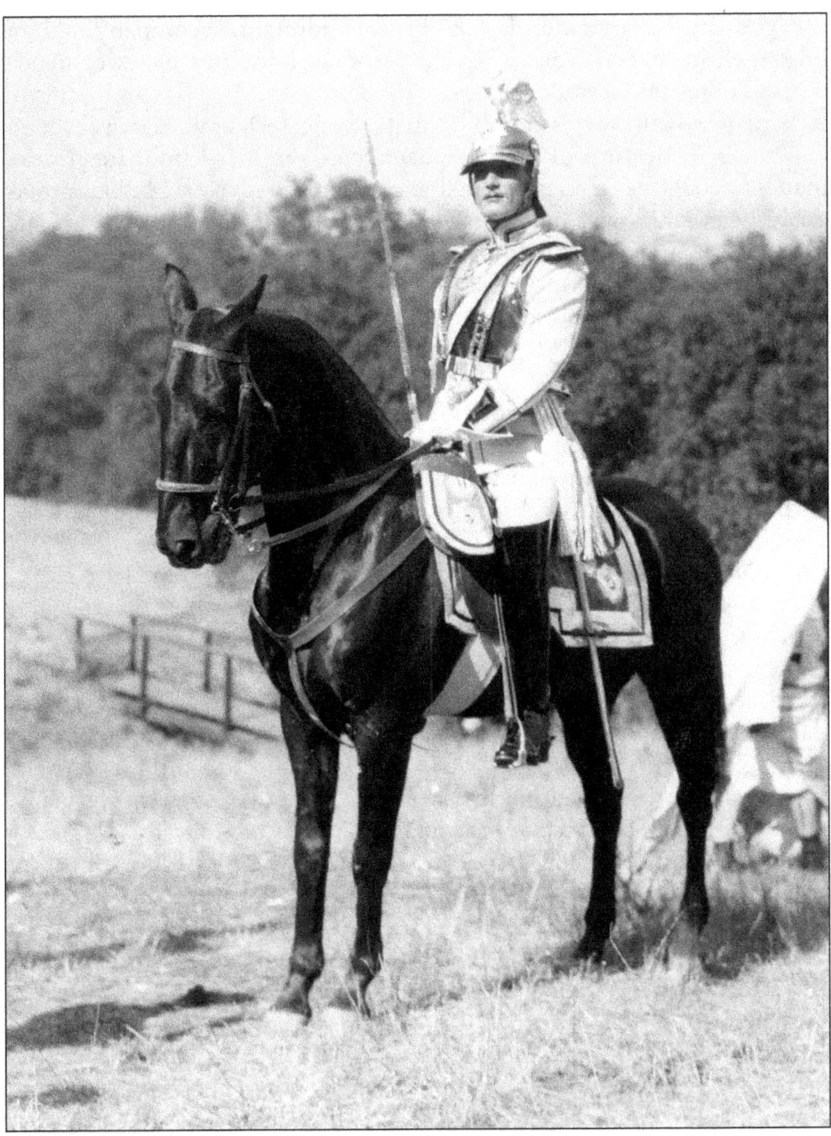

'The greatest discovery in British leading men.' Walter Byron as Prince Wolfram.
Harry Ransom Center/Milestone Film & Video.

composer Heinrich Reinhard and a veteran of the Austrian cavalry, an
obscure actor under contract to Von who had been working behind the
scenes in Hollywood for some years and had an uncredited role in *The
Wedding March*. Von considered him a "find". Reinhardt was announced
in the lead role in July 1928 but was dropped in favour of Byron.

Von Brincken would play the Prince's adjutant, accompanying him on screen in several scenes. He also produced copious pages of hand-written notes on German Imperial military uniforms, titles and phrases. A British Royal Navy veteran, Donald Robert Overall Hatswell, who had a vast collection of picture postcards of military uniforms (more than 720,000), was also employed as a technical advisor. He had previously been employed on *The Wedding March* and would have a long working relationship with John Ford—his final credit was on *Beau Geste* (Douglas Heyes, 1966). All this scholarship was required only for the early sequences of the picture, the scenes at court and Wolfram's first meeting with Kitty. But for Von, there was no such thing as too much detail.

Von officially started work on the film in May, after Joe managed to get him to sign a contract and negotiate a release from Powers. Joe's team were cautious enough to ensure they had an exit strategy from a potentially problematic relationship with Von. They paid a low fee for the story idea, "SO THAT AFTER SCRIPT IS COMPLETED IF TOO EXPENSIVE TO SHOOT YOU ARE NOT LEFT WITH EXPEN-SIVE STORY ON YOUR HANDS WHICH ONLY VON STRO-HEIM CAN SHOOT".[9]

Around this time Von produced a second version of the story, which contained much less provocative language, a more thrilling ending, and the marriage coda. This version was published by the Court Press for copyright reasons on October 1928 and is likely the text submitted to the Hays Office for approval, hence its delicacy. This story opens in Germany, or in "Reginenberg, capital of the imaginary state of Cobourg-Nassau in the German Empire" where the "roistering… Prince Wolfram-Ehrhardt von Honenberg-Felsenberg" and convent girl Patricia Kelly, "a most charming, beautiful and impudent-nosed girl of Irish attraction [sic]" fall in love at first sight. The Prince, however, is duly betrothed to the "spinster queen" of the region, Regina V, a matter of expedience for him and unrequited passion for her. In order to see Patricia again, the Prince stars a "fake fire" in the convent, which gets all the girls out of bed. He drapes his coat over Patricia's nightdress and they share a supper and mutual professions of love. Then "he picks her up bodily and carries her back into the apartment". The queen discovers them and attacks Patricia with a riding crop, whipping her out of the palace.

The German story ends on the third of nine pages. Patricia is distraught and attempts suicide by jumping into the river but is rescued by a policeman who returns her to the convent. There she is informed that her aunt in Dar Es Salaam is dying and wishes to see her. Kali-Sana, one of her aunt's employees, greets her and brings her to The Swamp, where she finds her dying aunt, who tells her that the place really belongs to local multimillionaire Poto-Poto Jan. He has been paying for Patricia's schooling as well, and when he learns of her "virginal loveliness" he demands her hand in marriage. A shocked Patricia consents to the wedding but is then horrified by the situation she has got herself into and tells Jan she will never consummate the marriage and will kill herself if he touches her.

Eight months pass, and Patrica is now Queen Kelly, respected proprietress of The Swamp. She reads in the paper that Wolfram is coming to Africa and runs out to see him arrive on his ship. She drinks heavily that night, and when Wolfram, on a wild night out, visits The Swamp, he sees her sliding off the bar. He asks how she got there. Fired up by drunken bravado she tells him to "Go to hell and stay there." But of course she collapses in tears when he leaves. Jan, who has been watching, surmises that maybe she isn't a virgin after all and drags her home with him. Patricia refuses to stay in his filthy home, but he too attacks her with a whip and "brings her sobbing, crushed and defeated down onto the bed".

Waking up dreadfully hungover, Wolfram asks two of the women in the bar where Patricia has gone and sets off to rescue her. He arrives late at night and has a fight with Jan, who has a revolver, and fires it. When the Prince falls to the ground, Patricia thinks he has died and rushes to him, trying to staunch the blood and kissing him passionately. Jan taunts Patricia: "I'll give you a chance to kiss him for the rest of your life." He orders his men to tie the lovers face to face, row them out to the middle of the swamp, and lash them to an ebony tree, where they are surrounded by crocodiles, to perish. As the rain falls, Jan tells them, the crocodiles will come inexorably closer. Wolfram revives and he and Patricia spend what they think will be their last hours together. He tells her how he broke his engagement and got transferred to Africa to be close to her. She tells him how she has saved herself for him.

Meanwhile the Governor of Dar Es Salaam receives a wireless message telling him that Wolfram is missing. His men trace his steps to Poto-Poto, where they question the girls of The Swamp, who lead them to Jan, whom they force at gunpoint to take them to where he abandoned the lovers. The Governor's men save the couple. As Wolfram and Patricia are stretchered away, Jan mistakenly believes they are dead, laughs heartily, loses his footing, and slips into the water, where the crocodiles devour him.

As the lovers recover in hospital, the Prince's adjutant informs Wolfram that Queen Regina is dead, making him King. Wolfram declares that he will give up the throne of Cobourg-Nassau, which now falls to him unless his people accept Patricia as his queen. They are married quietly in the Garrison at Poto-Poto. Cut to Reginenburg and the new

King and Queen leaving their coronation ceremonies. "The King looks at his bride and says 'Well, Your Majesty!' She, poking her nose impudently in the air, replies 'Majesty', me foot. Just 'Queen' Kelly!"[10]

This version presented many problems for the Hays Office, not least as it appears, despite all the talk of virginity, that Wolfram seduces Patricia on their first night together and that Jan rapes her. There are some plot holes too. How does Wolfram ascend to the throne if he is not even engaged to the Queen? But this was a snappy and exciting version of the *Queen Kelly* story, with a small cast of characters, set mostly in Dar Es Salaam, far closer to Von's original idea for The Swamp than what eventually got made. If you believed that Von would stick to this scenario and could be tempted to tone down some of the sex, you could just about see how this could be produced in a few months and be cleared by the Hays Office.

Gloria was in the mood to believe in contradictory ideas. She was at this point living two lives in Hollywood. When Henri was in Los Angeles they lived together, but while he was working in Paris she moved into Joe's home on Rodeo Drive. At Joe's insistence Gloria finally had her son Joseph baptised, with him as godfather and Patrick as his new middle name. The Hollywood Irish community, including the horsemen, turned out for the party. Although the dates don't line up, rumours persisted for decades that Joseph was Gloria and Joe's lovechild. "As time passed, Joe spoke less and less of our separate families," recalled Gloria,[11] and their love affair was an open secret in Hollywood. "That doesn't mean they went around walking openly on the boulevards holding hands or linking arms," said George Cukor. "But if anyone saw the look on Joe's face when he was with Gloria, it was clear that he was infatuated."[12] Gloria's friend Sport Ward would joke: "You have to take your hex off that man." Rose Kennedy must have known; she probably always knew. Henri must have known too, but he was too discreet to mention it, just as Gloria failed to ask him about the lady he was seen dining with at a Russian café on Sunset Boulevard.

Joe was corresponding with Henri at length over business matters and Gloria's health, but he didn't tell him about *The Swamp* until the last minute. That March, Joe gave Gloria a complete copy of the screenplay after dinner with the demeanour of "a college boy wanting to jump for joy, but compelled to be serious", assuring her that Robert E. Sherwood had acclaimed it "the best film story ever written", adding to plaudits from "other significant literary people". He told her that he had hired two producers to keep Von in line. They were familiar faces: editor and studio manager William LeBaron and Benjamin Glazer, a brilliant screenwriter who had previously led the story department at Paramount and co-written *The Merry Widow*. They would be the least effective supervisors Von ever

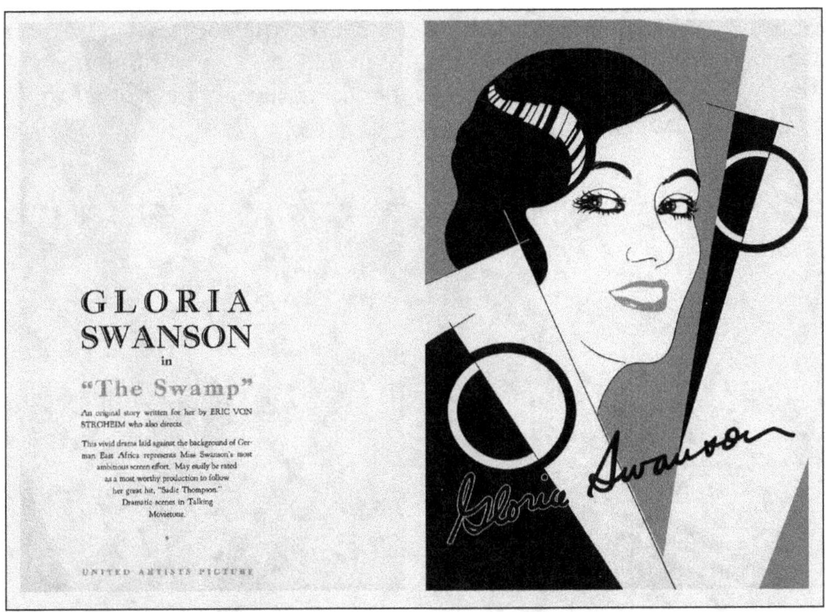

A trade advertisement for *The Swamp*, 'in talking Movietone', from 1928.
Harry Ransom Center/Milestone Film & Video.

had. For decades, most people had no idea they were involved in the film at all. Still, Joe was fully confident that "this is going to be a major, *major* motion picture".[13]

By May, Louella Parsons was excitedly telling her readers, "Here, there and everywhere one hears whispers that Eric [sic] von Stroheim will direct Gloria Swanson in her next picture."[14] Other reports speculated that Von was working with Gloria on either a film based on the life of Protestant celebrity preacher Aimee Semple McPherson, or his original story *The Swamp*, which was swiftly confirmed. Regina Crewe wrote that Gloria was making her home in a "seven-room bungalow" on the FBO lot and that Joe "appears vitally interested" in the new film, but did not name him as producer. She simply joked about the usefulness of "a hard-hearted banker to keep Von Stroheim from shooting all the film that Mr Eastman makes".[15] Von was still focused on the later stages of the film as he told *The New York Times* about his new project *The Swamp*, set in East Africa, in which Gloria would play a Queen Kelly. All this talk capitalised nicely on the continuing success of *Sadie Thompson*, released in January, which, despite Joe's predictions, was garnering lots of acclaim for Gloria and lots of money for UA. The Steichen portrait had taken up a full-page in the February issue of *Vanity Fair* with the caption "A Much Screened Lady".[16] To a lesser extent, the news was part of the anticipation for *The Wedding March*. Soon Von was building the Royal Palace on the FBO lot and supervising the stitching of all those well-researched costumes.

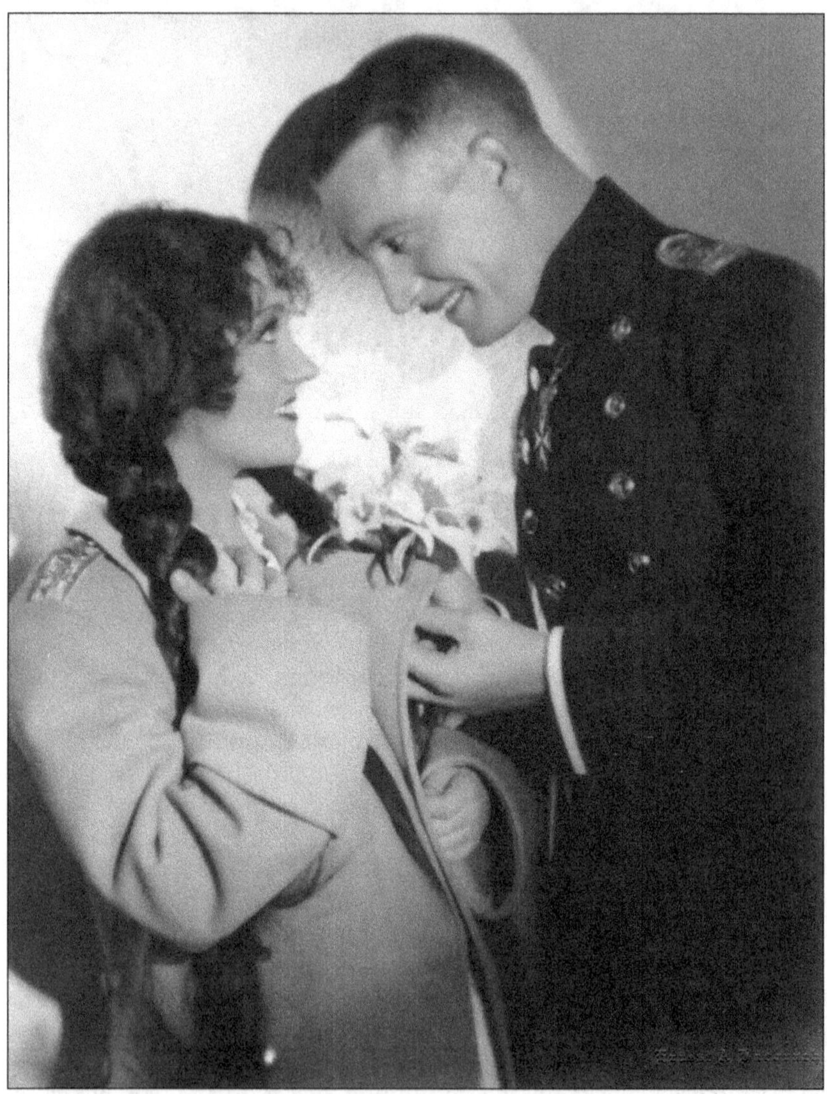

Gloria Swanson and Walter Byron in costume as Patricia and Wolfram, with the orchids that symbolised their love. Milestone Film & Video.

Joe wrote to Louis B. Mayer to request the loan of a camera operator for the shoot, and confessed his folly. "I have arranged to get Von Stroheim to direct, and I can already hear you saying: 'You have had no troubles in the picture business yet—they have just started.'"[17] Mayer couldn't spare the cameraman but was keen to reassure the less experienced producer. "I hope your results with Von Stroheim will be all that you wish them to be—and I have no doubt that they will. With your intelligent handling, I believe he can be made an asset in the direction of this particular picture. At least, if you weather the storm you will have something worth talking about."[18] Which was gracious of Mayer, considering that he, a veteran of the business, had gone through hell and high water with Von during the arduous production of *The Merry Widow*.

In June, Gloria Productions took out a loan of $500,000 from Bank of America, with Joe as guarantor, to finance the production, which was insured for $400,000. The policy was tweaked to ensure the film was covered in the event of Gloria falling pregnant—because she was a married woman, so that might happen, but also because Joe had recklessly said he wanted to have a baby with her. "For years," said Gloria, "I was constantly terrified I would get pregnant with Joe Kennedy—which he wanted in the worst way—but I didn't."[19] As their affair became more and more serious, the film became more and more romantic. What was once a short sequence set in far-off Germany became the first half of the film, a love story in itself. Joe was increasingly indiscreet about being seen with Gloria in a social context. He told her that he was "faithful" to her and invited her and her children to spend time with his family in Bronxville. Gloria agreed to the latter request but warned Joe that the public couldn't be manipulated as easily as stocks and shares. The only thing that the press were informed of that summer was that filming would begin in the middle of August, on a picture now titled *Queen Kelly*.

1. *SoS*, 345.
2. *SoS*, 397.
3. This synopsis is based on what appears to be the earliest draft of the scenario in Kennedy's papers.
4. An echo of *Sadie Thompson*'s and Maugham's Pago Pago. It means mud or dirty water in many African languages. There is a Poto-Poto district in Brazzaville, Congo.
5. *SoS*, 347.
6. *SoS*, 347.
7. Erich von Stroheim, *Queen Kelly*, Court Press, 1928, 9.
8. "Walter Butler", *Picturegoer*, June 1927, 21.
9. Telegram, E.B. Derr to C.E. Sullivan, 4 May 1928, JPK Papers.

10. *Queen Kelly*, 1928.
11. *SoS*, 360.
12. *The Fitzgeralds and the Kennedys*, 393.
13. *SoS*, 359.
14. Louella O. Parsons, "Stroheim May Direct Gloria Swanson's Next", *The San Francisco Examiner*, 1 May 1928, 15.
15. Regina Crewe, "Eric Von Stroheim May Direct Gloria Swanson in Film Story, 'The Swamp,' Which He Wrote", *The Pittsburgh Sun-Telegraph*, 2 May 1928, 25.
16. "A Much Screened Lady", *Vanity Fair*, February 1928, 49.
17. Letter from JPK to Louis B. Mayer, 25 May 1928, JPK Papers.
18. Letter from Louis B. Mayer to JPK, 5 June 1928, JPK Papers.
19. *SoS*, 414.

9
The Queen

United Artists, still signed up to distribute the new film, had made an important intervention by objecting to Von's original title. *The Swamp* was unappealing and decidedly unsavoury. It also obscured the film's strongest selling point, its glamorous leading lady. *Sadie Thompson's* title reminded everyone of the film's main attraction: Gloria, its stunning, expressive star, playing a knockout of a character. Suggestions for a new title for *The Swamp* included *The Scarlet Saint*, *The Saint in Scarlet* and *The Orchid Lady*, but audiences had all seen these in some form or another. Even *The Swamp* had been used before, by Robertson-Cole no less, for a 1921 film starring Sessue Hayakawa. Eventually, *Queen Kelly* was chosen, partly because, as far as the FBO staff could tell, it had never been used before. *Queen Kelly* was original, unique, and Joe was convinced it was a winner.

Nothing is entirely original. There was certainly a precedent for films with Kelly in the title in the silent era. It was a shorthand for Irishness, for melodramas and comedies about Celtic immigrants in big cities: underdogs, fighters, drinkers, boxers and sweet, green-eyed colleens. Two years previously at FBO, Joe had made *Kosher Kitty Kelly* (James W. Horne, 1926) starring Viola Dana and adapted from the musical of the same name. Earlier that year, Universal released *The Cohens and the Kellys* (Harry A. Pollard, 1926), the first of a series of seven films about two warring immigrant families from New York, one Jewish, one Irish, and the love affair between two teenagers. Broad stereotypes were the order of the day in such movies. The author of a 1922 stage play, *Abie's Irish Rose*, even sued Universal for copyright infringement, but the suit failed as the judge ruled that copyright protection could not be extended to stock characters. Hence, one supposes, *Kosher Kitty Kelly*.

Von's story proposes not a Jewish Kelly but a regal one: a brothel madam ironically called Queen, due to her status and imperious bearing, "like a Viennese comtesse", but who, in the final versions of the screenplay, actually becomes a queen when she marries Wolfram, who has just been crowned King. Gloria herself was Hollywood royalty before she became a genuine aristocrat on marrying Henri, entitled to call herself Marquise de La Falaise. Indeed, Gloria chose to be referred to as The Marquise, a title that she had printed on her business card (with no mention of Henri's name). Like the character she was about to play, Gloria's identity in 1928 encapsulated both old-world nobility, via Henri, and new-world vulgarity, via Hollywood. When, at the end of the film, the heroine refuses the title of Your Majesty, preferring "just plain Queen Kelly", she is choosing her brothel identity over her new marital and social status—a perverse choice. There is a shade of *Sadie Thompson* here, also of *Madame Sans-Gêne*, in which Swanson's laundress is elevated to a lady, and when she is presented at court wins the esteem of the Emperor for her past behaviour and her common touch, not her newfound rank. Despite a consensus of disapproval, all three women are unembarrassedly, defiantly themselves.

Von's leading men, if not his ladies, had used Kelly's line before. Playing Prince Nicki in *The Wedding March*, he proffers "plain Nicki" to the peasant girl he is trying to seduce. In *The Merry Widow*, John Gilbert introduces himself as "just plain Danilo Petrovich" to Mae Murray's vaudeville dancer. It is a gesture of humility and courtship. Is Queen Kelly, aware of the moral degeneracy of her new kingdom, attempting to appeal to her new, dissipated subjects? Interestingly, when promoting *The Wedding March*, Von claimed to have made the same gesture himself, with the papers reporting that he identified with Nicki's decision to drop his title: "When Erich Von Stroheim became an American citizen a few months ago he dropped several names which he had borne in Austria, and became plain Erich Von Stroheim. Apparently he had put behind him all the superfluous nomenclature of his fatherland… Erich Oswald Hans Carl Maria Von Stroheim."[1] This is transparently Von's gesture of mass ingratiation, an attempt to appeal to the domestic audience on the release of his latest film, to play the American hero rather than the Germanic villain. The show of humility is undercut by the knowledge that Von was indeed born plain Erich Oswald Stroheim, with neither a "von" nor a string of fancy middle monikers.

Von's European films, including *Queen Kelly*, were all set before World War I, when dropping one's royal title could be merely an optional affectation. However, the German and Austrian monarchies had been abolished in 1918, so in the 1920s such titles and ranks were rapidly becoming more antiquated than merely quaint. King and commoners were theoretically equal. A French marquis could marry an American movie star. Sex has a way of flattening the social hierarchies and formally stripping a person of their pomp. Famously, in 1936, King Edward VIII gave up his title for love. He became merely a duke after he abdicated the British throne so that he could marry the woman he loved, American divorcée Wallis Simpson.

Other causes are less romantic. While I was writing this book, King Charles III formally stripped another member of the British Royal Family, Andrew Mountbatten-Windsor, of what the Letters Patent call "the style, title or attribute of 'Royal Highness' and the titular dignity of 'Prince'." This followed the posthumous publication of a memoir by Virginia Giuffre which alleged that Mountbatten-Windsor had sexually abused her after she was trafficked by financier and sex offender Jeffrey Epstein. Such vile behaviour undermines the romanticisation of the "playboy prince" archetype—and finds an uncomfortable echo in *Queen Kelly*'s plot, in which a schoolgirl is seduced by an older man and ends up in a brothel. King Charles' decision was a popular one. Members of the British public interviewed by the BBC and even columnists in royalist papers *The Times* and *The Daily Telegraph* were supportive of the decision to relieve his brother of his dukedom, his military rank and his royal dwelling. "Well, karma comes to us all, and it has come with particular ferocity to Randy Andy, the playboy prince, and now plain old Mr Andrew Windsor," wrote one historian in the *Telegraph*, referring to Mountbatten-Windsor's tabloid nicknames from the 1980s.[2] Even in a country still clinging to its monarchy, accusations of lechery and rape were deemed incompatible with regal status, and one man's demotion from divinely ordained duke to "just plain Andrew"[3] was judged a suitable punishment for his crime.

Queen Kelly is a story of its time, about monarchy in decline. Wolfram is drawn to women from outside his aristocratic realm and, like Edward VIII, will marry a commoner. But it is Queen Regina V who strikes the tragic pose of a dynasty in decay. She is debauched, jealous, morbid and cruel—her madness is the symptom of the "blood mania" that runs in her family. We turn to gothic literature to find such characters, weakened and diseased by generations of in-breeding and hereditary syphilis, like the fragile twins in Edgar Allan Poe's 1839 story "The Fall of the House of the Usher". Regina is engaged to a prince who appears to be her cousin and lives in the same palace, clearly an insinuation of incest. She cannot contain her emotions, her appetites or her libido. She relies on sleeping pills and booze to get through the day and is confined to the palace and her bed. Queen Regina meets her maker off screen—the last of her line, assassinated by someone who presumably questions the divine right of kings. When her successor scoffs at the idea of majesty, her branch of the European monarchy withers and dies.

o o o

As soon as audiences heard the title of the new film they wanted to know: who is Queen Kelly? In the middle of August 1928, with the title chosen, Joe decided to get the public on side, ordering Gloria's publicist Lance Heath "TO GIVE BEST PUBLICITY HE EVER GAVE IN HIS LIFE"[4] and hastily commissioned shots of Gloria in costume, taken by her favourite stills photographer Ernest Bachrach. These photos are all of the character that was ever captured on film. Frustratingly, Gloria never got to play Queen Kelly. All the scenes that were shot of the film feature Gloria as Patricia "Kitty" Kelly, the convent girl who falls for Count Wolfram and is then sent to her aunt's brothel in Dar Es Salaam. We see her get married to Poto-Poto Jan, but not in her element as Queen Kelly, proprietress of The Swamp. Therefore, these press shots are tantalising to say the least. In a high-necked, tight, black satin dress accessorised with a string of pearls, matching earrings and a corsage of white orchids, Gloria smoulders in smoky-eyed makeup, her long hair pinned up on top of her head. In some shots she wears a picture hat and a cascading black feather boa, or waves a cigarette. She stands, or half-reclines, a hand or two on her hips; her gaze is always cool and distant. Gloria called it her "Mae West outfit". *Motion Picture* printed a full-page portrait, headlined "Fitting Apparel", with the caption: "Gloria's dress may not be the glass of fashion. But none can deny it is the mold of form."[5] As she put it, "To accentuate the vulgarity of the locale I wore an enormous ring and big earrings, and two orchids as big as cabbages on my shoulder."[6] There is certainly a cheapness to the tightness of the dress and the tacky boa, but the overall impression is of untouchable haughtiness: the contradictions of a virginal brothel keeper. Critic Herman G. Weinberg, diligent keeper of the Stroheim flame, floridly described these shots as "a sardonic commentary on all the Madames of history".[7]

In May 1928, Von embraced the contradictions when he told Mordaunt Hall about the role Gloria would play in his new film: "A beautiful young creature of Irish extraction, gorgeous and graceful as a peacock, but cold, calm, calculating and mercenary. Most of the time she has all the grace, charm, haughtiness and deportment of a born aristocrat, but on provocation she flies into the most unreasonable rage."[8] He says almost exactly the same in his own typewritten character notes, which use colourful, but unmistakeable language to describe the nature of Queen Kelly's business: "It caters varied and colorful entertainment to the natives, sailors of all nations, soldiers, cinnamon mahogany rubber ivory and ebony barons and other butter-and-egg men who have extracted the wherewithal for feminine entertainment from the bowels of Africa." They describe Kelly as dressing "in the austere manner of a lady-in-waiting according to Spanish court etiquette, with deep court décolleté front and back, trainer, sixteen-button gloves, dog-collar and

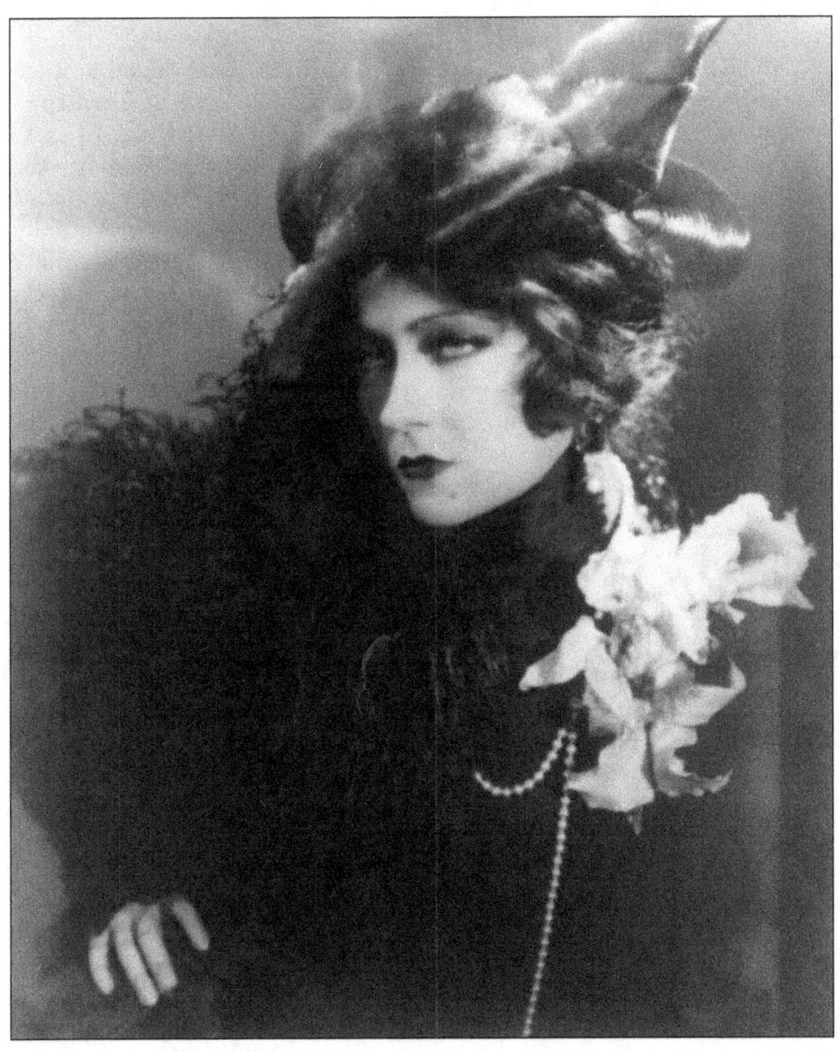

Gloria Swanson as hot-tempered Queen Kelly, the role she was never to play.
Milestone Film & Video.

meticulously marcelled pompadour". We will see that look softened slightly in the publicity images. Kelly is a "hothouse flower" often referred to as the "orchid", who believes only in money and has no faith in love, which we are told is an inherent trait, and not the result of a romantic disillusionment. Her virginity has been maintained despite her "lurid surroundings".[9]

Yet Kelly is a product of those surroundings. The original idea for the film was that it would be set in Germany and in one of Germany's African colonies, Tanzania. As the production progressed, one of these locations became more geographically vague, but they would still be very clear in the minds of the audience. Germany was swapped for a slice of Ruritania, the fictional Mittel-European setting invented by Anthony Hope for his 1894 novel *The Prisoner of Zenda* and its sequels—familiar to filmgoers from their several adaptations. The adjective Ruritanian was swiftly adopted for such fictional Germanic lands, defined by bucolic countryside and feudal power structures, like the setting chosen here: Kronberg, the capital of "an ancient Kingdom of Middle Europe", "the country of Cobourg-Nassau, before the Great War". Von, with his fictional Germanic persona of military rank and aristocratic blood, was in many ways the embodiment of Ruritania. Typically, Ruritanian romances involved doppelgangers, as well as swashbuckling action and evil aristocrats hellbent on separating young lovers. The last element is clearly in place here, and there is an implicit doubling of the two locations: the so-called "civilised" European kingdom, which is really degenerate, and the "uncivilised" African colony, ruled by the same powers and therefore just as morally corrupt, but more visibly so.

The African location, which is where we find Queen Kelly herself, was increasingly familiar to movie audiences. A little, also, to our filmmakers, thanks to the tropical setting of *Sadie Thompson*, and to a lesser extent the jungle scenes of Kennedy's shock-doc *The Gorilla Hunt*. In 1926, Walter Huston starred in a play on Broadway called *Kongo*, written by Chester De Vonde and Kilbourn Gordon, which MGM adapted into a 1928 film with a synchronised musical score, starring Lon Chaney, *West of Zanzibar* (Tod Browning, 1928). Huston later starred in a talkie version also called *Kongo* (William J. Cowen, 1932). Just as with *Sadie Thompson*, the makers of the 1928 version changed the name to get around the fact that the Hays Office had banned the play from adaptation. The plot of *The Swamp* and the African section of *Queen Kelly* are very similar to that of *Kongo*. The setting is Congo and the story revolves around "Dead-legs" Flint, a bitter, cruel paraplegic and his dreams of revenge against Gregg, the man who stole his wife and abandoned her before she died. To enact this revenge, he has paid for the education of their daughter Ann at a Cape Town convent. When Ann comes of age, Flint has her brought to Congo, where she becomes an alcoholic and is forced into prostitution. Flint's drug-addicted doctor falls in love with Ann, but Flint has him killed by tying him to a tree in the swamp where he will be attacked by parasites. When Gregg returns to Congo, Flint proudly shows him how degraded his daughter Ann has become at his hands. But Gregg reveals that Ann was really Flint's daughter all along and he has merely brought about his own punishment. In the background of this story of white settlers and traders is the presence of vicious natives, who practise voodoo—they ultimately kill Flint and burn his remains on a sacrificial fire. This racist depiction of African life as lawless and violent provides a hospitable setting for sensationalist, provocative melodrama.

When *West of Zanzibar* was released, an editorial in the moralistic publication *Harrison's Reports* described it as "an outpouring of the Cesspools of Hollywood!" and asked: "How any normal person could have thought this horrible syphilitic play could have made an entertaining picture?"[10] And yet, *West of Zanzibar* was a hit with critics and audiences, despite having changed the names and some aspects of the plot, removing references to venereal disease, drug abuse, abortion and miscegenation. It has remained a cult favourite, especially since it appeared on TV in the 1970s. The more explicit pre-Code talkie version was nothing like as successful. These films were not one-offs—there was a turn-of-the-decade vogue for such grisly and offensive African-set melodramas. You can see this trend spoofed in *Flames of Passion*, the film that the lovers watch in Noël Coward and David Lean's otherwise decorous romance *Brief Encounter*, released in 1945 but set in 1938. As Celia Johnson says to Trevor Howard: "I believe we should all behave quite differently if we lived in a warm, sunny climate all the time. We shouldn't be so withdrawn and shy and difficult." These films take advantage of prejudicial associations of primitive sexuality, mysticism and violence—including cannibalism—with African people. They make villains of some of the colonialists who strip the land of its resources and mistreat the local population, like Flint and Jan, but also heroes of others, like Wolfram and Queen Kelly, and in the film of *Zanzibar*, the character of Crane, played by Lionel Barrymore.

Von was obviously inspired by these contemporary fictions, but in his own fashion approached the task of recreating East Africa on screen with the same rigour that he did representing the Austria of his youth, or early 20th-century California. Realism meant research, and lots of it. While preparing his screenplay, Von bought up more than a hundred photographs and 19 books on the subject, including Martin Johnson's *Safari*, Henry Aloysius Gogarty's *Kilima-njaro*, M. Aline Buxton's *Kenya Days*, Stella Court Treatt's *Cape to Cairo* and Richard Francis Burton's *East Africa: An Exploration*. In this way, Von hoped to transcend the conventions of *Kongo* et al, which necessarily meant presenting something less palatable to American audiences. He sought to compare as well as contrast the two territories, finding an equivalent for every element of his European story in his African narrative, and vice versa. Each place has a raving despot: Poto-Poto Jan and the mad queen. The hallways of the brothel recall the dormitory corridors of the convent, and the girl carried aloft by two sailors recalls the image of Patricia carried to safety in Wolfram's arms.

Queen Kelly also shifts the balance of the narrative from the men to the young woman at the heart of *Kongo*'s sadistic plot. Queen Kelly is a woman with an immigrant background, defined by her job and independence of mind, body and finances, usually strong and self-possessed but given to fits of rage and bouts of heavy drinking. She is in the vein of Gloria's best roles: Catherine, Sadie and Norma Desmond. She has something in common too with her hot-tempered creations in the DeMille comedies. Gloria is at her most impressive when throwing her head back and laughing derisively. In many ways she was an old-fashioned actress, harking back to a style of the 1910s. She wasn't a waif like Lillian Gish or Mary Pickford, nor a vamp like Theda Bara. Gloria embodied a style of performance popular in European cinema, especially in Italy, but also in the Scandinavian films that she claimed bored her as a teenager. Gloria was the last of the divas.

The Italian diva actresses, including Lyda Borelli and Francesca Bertini, played passionate, powerful women in dramatic scenarios. They could be peasant characters who worked for a living or aristocratic women—but in either case their costumes would be as dramatic as their postures, shawls and gowns draped and pulled around their figures. These actresses also very often wrote or produced, and even directed their own films. Outside Italy, Danish star Asta Nielsen was a Nordic diva who rose to fame after a performance of intense raw emotion in a film called *The Abyss* (Urban Gad, 1910), which also included a censor-baiting raunchy Gaucho dance. She went on to spend most of her career in Germany, achieving such grand heights as starring in *Hamlet* (Svend Gade & Heinz Schall, 1921) as the Prince, who is secretly a Princess. In *La Perla del Cinema* (Giuseppe de Liguoro, 1916) and *The Film Prima-donna* (Urban Gad, 1913), Bertini and Nielsen respectively dramatised their lives as star-producers on screen. The diva dominates her films, on camera and off.

In Hollywood, the chief diva was Alla Nazimova, a Russian-born actress who made her debut on the American screen around the same time as Gloria, with *War Brides* (Herbert Brenon, 1916). Her Hollywood career came to an end shortly after the box-office failure of her Oscar Wilde adaptation *Salomé* (1922), which she starred in, wrote, produced and effectively directed. Too beautiful, too queer for the box office, *Salomé* is now considered a gay cult classic—embraced by the audience it was always intended for. And, of course, in *Sunset Boulevard*, Gloria's comeback film, Norma Desmond longs to play Salomé, and to write and produce the film as well. Billy Wilder saw that Gloria was a diva, as Von did before him, when he was writing *Queen Kelly* for her. It's worth noting that as a child, Gloria lived in tropical climates, in Puerto Rico and Florida, and briefly attended convent school, though this hardly qualifies *Queen Kelly* as a work of honest realism.

There is an element of wishful thinking in this characterisation. It takes little imagination to suppose why Joe would want his lover Gloria to appear on screen as an Irishwoman, and a Catholic too—a more suitable object of his affections. Or why he would wish to see her presented as the heroine of a grand love story, one who remains innocent despite a sordid milieu. Equally, it is all too easy to project Joe and Gloria's own clandestine romance on to the story of the film they fought to make together. In *Queen Kelly* the lovers are both married or promised to others, both of whom are monsters, thereby winning the audience's sympathy for the extramarital romance and even, in the eyes of some moralists, excusing the implied premarital sex on the night of the convent fire. Sex was very important to both of them. Joe boasted about giving Gloria multiple orgasms, relishing the chance to be with a woman who viewed sex as a pleasure, not a duty—so why wouldn't they make a film that tended to the explicit? One way to look at this is that Joe and Gloria had simply got carried away with the excitement of their affair. Viewed from another angle, you have to wonder how Henri, and especially Rose, could tolerate it: this portrayal adds insult to the injury of their infidelity.

The upshot of all their romancing, as well as Von's snail's-pace shooting speed, is that Gloria spent so long playing the starry-eyed convent girl that she never got to play the fiery, enthralling Queen Kelly at all.

1. "Changed His Name and It's No Wonder", *The Washington Herald*, 6 October 1928, 7
2. Alexander Larman, "The King's actions against the former Prince Andrew are just and proper", *The Telegraph*, 30 October 2025.
3. Sarah Laing, "King Charles strips Andrew of his prince title, royal residence", *Toronto Star*, 31 October 2025.
4. Telegram EB Derr to Charles Sullivan, 13 August 1928, JPK Papers.
5. "Fitting Apparel", *Motion Picture*, April 1929, 66.
6. *SoS*, 372.
7. Herman G. Weinberg, *Saint Cinema: Writings on the Film 1929–1970* (Dover, 1970), 161.

8. Mordaunt Hall, "Half an Hour with Von Stroheim", *New York Times*, 27 May 1928, 8.
9. "Characterization of Kitty Kelly—Cold Cash Lady Queen Kelly", JPK Papers.
10. Quoted, Brian Darr, "West of Zanzibar", San Francisco Silent Film Festival Screening Notes, Winter 2009.

10
The Palace

In August 1928, three days after the pictures of Gloria in costume were commissioned, work on *Queen Kelly* came to a halt, with Sullivan letting Derr know that the shoot would not begin for almost a month: "JUST RECEIVED TENTATIVE SCRIPT FIRST PART BELIEVE IMPRACTICAL."[1] This was just the first of many such messages that would be sent back and forth fretting over Von's extravagant and impractical plans. Joe was beginning to realise just how much *Queen Kelly* was going to cost. The official budget of $325,000 had already been revised up to $391,000. Joe's fear that the final tally could be as much as $800,000 was uncannily prescient.

Von wasn't the only person likely to bust the budget. Joe was dead set on adding to the expense by making *Queen Kelly* a talkie, hoping to reap subsequent financial rewards. In 1928 there were a few different ways of making a sound film, even putting aside the various technical systems for recording and synchronising sound, and Joe had already committed to one: the RCA Photophone sound-on-film system. You could make a complete talking picture, with synch dialogue in each scene and a musical score, like Warner Bros.' *The Lights of New York* (Bryan Foy, 1928), which was released that July. You could make a silent film and add a musical score and sound effects to it—like Fox's *Sunrise: A Song of Two Humans* (F. W. Murnau, 1927), or *7th Heaven* (Frank Borzage, 1927), both of which used the Movietone system and were in cinemas around the time that Joe and Gloria first met. Or William Wellman's *Beggars of Life* (1928), released a year later, as the final preparations were made for shooting *Queen Kelly*. Or you could make a hybrid film, known as a "goat-gland" picture, named after a dubious remedy for male impotence that involved injections of animal hormones. Inserting sound scenes or sequences into an otherwise silent film, as in Universal's *Lonesome* (Paul Fejos, 1928), was one way to cash in on the novelty of sound while still making the most of the studio personnel's talents. Silent pictures were at a pinnacle of professionalism and artistry, while most filmmakers and crew were still struggling to adapt to sound, which resulted in some static, awkward movies.

It seems that Joe was considering releasing Queen Kelly in both silent and sound versions. He told Al Lichtman, United Artists' vice-president in charge of domestic distribution, that Glazer, Pathé's resident sound expert, who had written the screenplay for *Beggars of Life* and the story for *7th Heaven*, would "work on sound in this picture".[2] He was tasked with writing a "talking ending", while a voice director, actress Laura Hope Crews, was hired at $100 a week to coach Gloria. Awkwardly, Gloria seemed to take against Glazer; Joe told Henri that she "hates, loathes and despises"[3] him. At the same time, Sullivan and Derr arranged a "supplemental agreement" to Von's contract, "under which we would get the rights to sound, music synchronization and talking", with Sullivan asserting: "I will most assuredly have this before the picture goes into production."[4] It looks like another hijack. Von will direct the picture silent and then Joe will walk off with the rights to the more lucrative sound version—made right under his nose.

Von and Gloria didn't want to make a talkie at this point. Gloria had made a sound film as a stunt in New York in 1925 at the behest of inventor Lee De Forest, who had devised a sound-on-film process. "He got Allan Dwan and Tommy Meighan and Henri and me into a little studio in Manhattan and had us talk to one another while a cameraman photographed us and another technician waved a microphone around on a pole. We all sounded terrible; none of us could believe our own voices."[5] For Gloria, sound was nothing more than a novelty, which did not flatter the performer. She recalled that even the acclaimed operatic tenor Giovanni Martinelli sounded awful in a Vitaphone short shown at the premiere of *The Love of Sunya*. For Von, introducing microphones and soundproofing meant compromising the fluidity and excellence of his silent film technique, and preventing him from filming in the open air. Both were convinced that their masterpiece should be made in the traditional style. The man at the top of UA was inclined to agree. That summer, Schenck told the papers that "talking doesn't belong in pictures. Pictures are on a silent ground… I don't think people will want talking pictures long."[6] Only sound effects and music were suitable additions in his view, and Von did place cues for sound effects in his new screenplay—though nothing quite as emphatic as the idea of the relentless drumbeats in his early draft.

Nevertheless, as early as August, the trade press reported that Gloria was going to use the Photophone system on *Queen Kelly*, which would be released in both silent and sound versions, and even that Gloria had her own home cinema wired up by RCA Photophone so she could see and hear herself in comfortable isolation. *Motion Picture News* confirmed that Gloria's voice would be heard. "'Queen Kelly' will not be an all-talkie picture, though much dialogue is planned for it. The climactic scene in the final reel will have a combination of voice, orchestral music, sound effects and visual spectacle."[7] The high-brows at *Close-Up* magazine were most amused by the prospect at any rate—in the light of Von's pace of work and Gloria's racy reputation. "Gloria's voice will be heard in her next. But as that is a Stroheim, we shall probably all be having three-dimensional colour television by the time it is shown, and will she be able to say what we are all sure she does say in her parts?"[8] Von and Gloria must have known that sound was going to be a part of *Queen Kelly,* even if they didn't appreciate quite how that would come about.

The FBO lot was already wired for sound, should anyone need it. But it wasn't going to be the FBO lot much longer. In March, Joe had fully taken over Pathé, which included laying down the law with the likes of DeMille, its most important director, who had been spending vast sums on *The King of Kings* and *The Godless Girl* (1928). DeMille had moved to Producers Distributing Corporation after finally breaking with Paramount, but PDC then merged with Pathé Exchange under the ownership of the Keith-Albee-Orpheum Corporation, a chain of vaudeville theatres and cinemas. By the end of April, DeMille had left with a generous pay out, leaving him free to sign with MGM—although Joe sounded him out about directing a film for Swanson, possibly very soon. In May, Joe bought a controlling stake in K-A-O. He did this via the holding company Blair & Co run by investment banker Elisha Walker, but it was Joe who raised the capital—$4 million in 48 hours—and who was made chairman of the board of K-A-O. He had no thought of the vaudeville business; he was in it for the cinema screens.

Over the summer, Joe began talks to start running a fourth studio, First National. Although First National was doing well, Joe moved in his usual swift fashion, assuring employees that "there is no danger of a good man… ever being let go,"[9] then firing vast numbers of staff. No one could have failed to miss Joe's corporate adventures. His friends in the press gave him glowing coverage, including full credit for all those deals. *Exhibitors Herald* called him "a figure of commanding interest and importance".[10] *The New York Times* profiled him in June under the headline "Movie Chief's Rapid Rise" and praising him for having "brought together the two industries—film and radio—which would necessarily be concerned in the production and exhibition of talking pictures".[11]

After two months at First National, however, Joe was abruptly dismissed. Hollywood gossip had it that he had bragged to a beautiful woman at a studio dinner that he was "the new ruler of one of the largest motion picture companies, having wrested control from a dumb and ignorant Jew".[12] The lady in question was the mistress of the studio president, Irving D. Rossheim, and she repeated Joe's sentiments to her Jewish lover. In truth, it was probably more to do with Joe biting off more than he could chew, but this story is nevertheless telling—about Joe's prejudices, how freely he expressed them, and how widely they were known. Shortly afterwards, First National would be snapped up by Warner Bros.

Joe characterised this failure as a mere setback, and in October, after returning from his six-week European vacation, made his really big deal of 1928. He sold his stake in K-A-O, along with FBO, to David Sarnoff's Radio Corporation of America. Sarnoff then established RKO Pictures, which became one of the big five Hollywood studios during its golden age, renowned for classics such as *King Kong* (Merian C. Cooper & Ernest B. Schoedsack, 1933), the Fred and Ginger musicals, and even *Citizen Kane* (Orson Welles, 1941). "One of the sure ways of making money in pictures," said Joe, "is to sell at a time when some one wants to buy."[13] This was a gigantic payday for Joe, who made $5 million ($94 million today), selling his stake in K-A-O for double what he had paid in the spring. He kept control of Pathé but as the *Queen Kelly* crew arrived on the FBO lot to start work, the RKO team were already taking over. As if anyone needed any more portents of doom, *Queen Kelly*'s producer appeared to be on his way out of the film industry before the first scene was in the can.

Von was certainly all in on the project, as Gloria recalled: "For the first time in his career absolutely nothing was wrong; everything worked."[14] He was building his dream world, with art direction by Harold Miles, who had worked on *The King of Kings* and *The Ten Commandments* for DeMille and later designed for Walt Disney. The six sets for the European section were vast; the palace featured a gigantic staircase, and the bedrooms and parlours were decorated with marble statues, made in a special plaster, with oil paintings and crystal chandeliers. Prince Wolfram sleeps next to a reproduction of Auguste Rodin's "The Kiss". Even the convent was impressive, with beamed ceilings and a stunning candlelit chapel. Von's aesthetic was never more maximalist. The frames are over-stuffed with extras, boughs of blossom, oil paintings and silverware— and most of all, innumerable flickering candles, often crowded into the foreground. The film almost appears to catch fire.

As for the swamp sequences, Von announced that he would be importing livestock from Africa because American animals "wouldn't have the right vibrations". He spent $81,000 on sets and props and more or less the same again on costumes, some of which went to waste after duplicates were accidentally ordered. The costumes, including some eye-catching looks worn by the Queen, are for the most part fantastic. They were designed by Max Rée, a Dane who had worked for years with Max Reinhardt in the German theatre before moving to the States and transferring his skills to ritzy and risqué burlesque shows on Broadway.

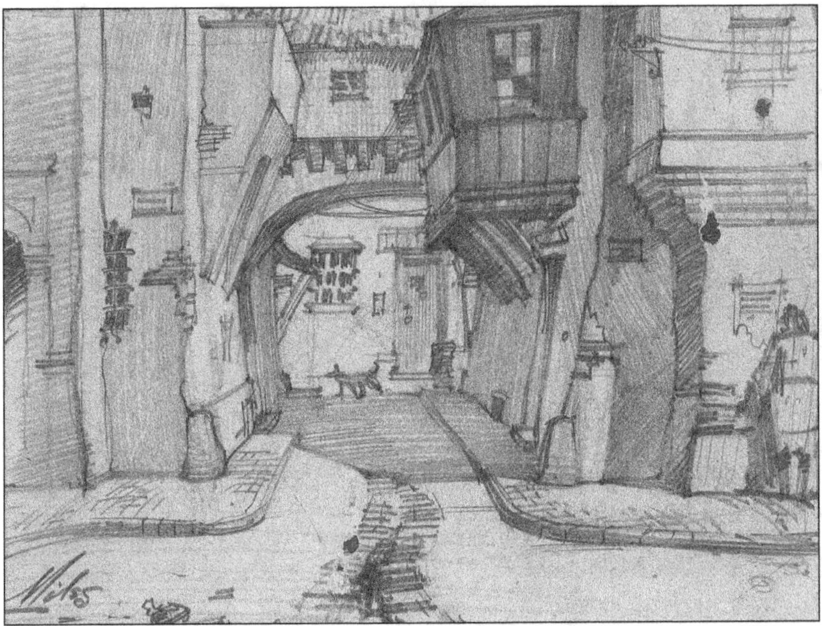

Production sketch by Harold Miles for Poto-Poto Gasse, home of The Swamp.
Milestone Film & Video.

In Hollywood he designed costumes for Constance Talmadge, Lillian Gish and Greta Garbo before moving to First National, where he worked with Billie Dove, Corinne Griffith and Colleen Moore. Rée stayed on at RKO to run the wardrobe department. The script supervisor was Viola Lawrence, who was to take on a key role in editing *Queen Kelly*. Von's assistant director was, as usual, his brother-in-law Louis Germonprez.

Von had signed on for a ten-week shoot and his contract said he would be sacked if he took too long or spent too much, so he wouldn't start shooting until he was confident he had the screenplay just right. He pulled an all-nighter with LeBaron to whittle it down from 735 scenes to 510, although that unwieldy number would rise again. He delivered those pages in provocative style, carried on a silver platter, hoisted aloft on two poles by Black actors wearing lion skins. He was also assembling his cast. Veteran villain specialist Tully Marshall, star of *Intolerance*, *The Covered Wagon* (James Cruze, 1923) and *The Merry Widow*, signed on as Jan. Byron was to play Wolfram, with Von Brincken, his adjutant, and Sidney Bracey and Wilson Benge, who both specialised in butler roles, playing his lackey and his valet, respectively.

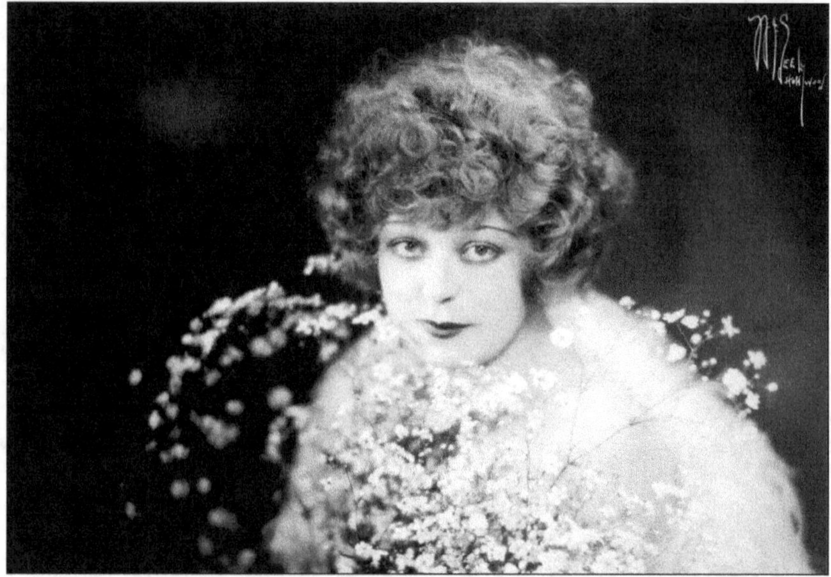

Seena Owen, pictured here in 1920, took on the showstopping role of
Queen Regina. Milestone Film & Video.

Seena Owen, the Danish-American actress who played the Princess
Beloved in the Babylon section of *Intolerance*, took on the showstopping
part of the unhinged Queen Regina. She proved a remarkably uninhibited performer, as anyone who had seen her screen test for *Intolerance*,
in which Griffith reportedly asked her to fake an orgasm, would expect.
Von would have known that she had posed nude for photographer Alexander "Zan" Stark in the early 1920s. Madge Hunt, another face from
Von's past, who had made her debut in *Old Heidelberg* in 1915, would
be the Mother Superior. In the African scenes, veteran actress Florence
Gibson, seen as a saloon drunkard in *Greed*, would play Patricia's aunt.
The role of her employee, Coughdrops, a tubercular, tattooed harlot,
went to a Canadian, Rae Daggett, who worked in Poverty Row and
was apparently an extra in *Greed*. She made a handful more films in the
1930s. Estimable Griffith alumna Madame Sul-Te-Wan, one of silent
Hollywood's better known Black actresses, played the mysterious Kali
Sana, another brothel employee.

And Gloria? She had already taken an advance on her salary and was
rehearsing her role in the most Hollywood way. At a party hosted by
Mary Pickford, Gloria was seated next to the guest of honour, Prince
George, the Duke of Kent. The queen of the movies hit it off with the
British royal, absconding from the party, which was far from as lively as
the prince had hoped, with a group of handpicked revellers.

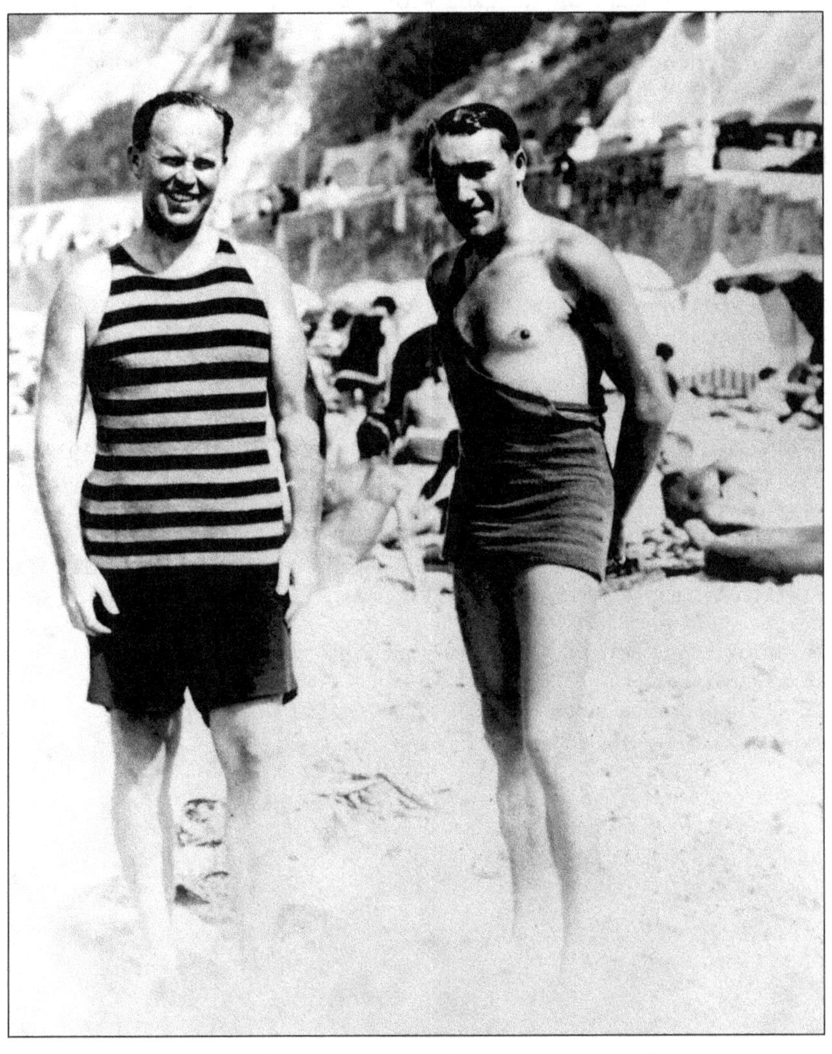

All smiles before production began on *Queen Kelly*:
Joseph Kennedy and Henri de La Falaise on the beach in Biarritz.
Everett Collection.

Gloria loaded her car with champagne and drove everyone to a night-club, Roscoe Arbuckle's Plantation Café, to dance. From there, back to Gloria's house, where the party continued until dawn, with a full band, and Chaplin entertaining the gang with a selection of skits. When the sun came up, Gloria made everyone breakfast and drove the Prince first to his hotel and then to the airport. Joe missed out on all the fun as he was in Europe with Rose and Henri, marking his 40th birthday with a holiday. Who could resist calling this a case of life imitating art before the fact? In just a couple of months' time, Patricia was about to spend her wild night with Wolfram.

1.   Telegram from Sullivan to Derr, 16 August 1928, JPK Papers.
2.   *Hostage to Fortune*, 77.
3.   Letter from JPK to HDF, 13 March 1929, JPK Papers.
4.   Telegram from Sullivan to Derr, 13 August 1928, JPK Papers.
5.   *SoS*, 359.
6.   "'Talkies' just a fad, says Joseph Schenck", *New York Times*, 22 August 1928, 30.
7.   "Gloria Swanson Contracts for Photophone Synchronization", *Motion Picture News*, 1 September 1928, 725.
8.   "News Gazette", *Close-Up*, November 1928, 50-51.
9.   Cari Beauchamp, "The Mogul in Mr Kennedy", *Vanity Fair*, June 2025, 111.
10. Peter Vische, "J.P. Kennedy—and Progress", *Exhibitors Herald and Motion Picture World*, 7 July 1928, 20.
11. "Movie Chief's Rapid Rise", *New York Times*, 3 June 1928, 10.
12   Quoted, Beauchamp, 207.
13. Quoted, Beauchamp, 213.
14. *SoS*, 368.

11
The Whip

The *Queen Kelly* shoot began with a bad omen on 1 November 1928. Gloria's first scenes were shot in a future Hollywood graveyard. The sequence in which Patricia first meets Wolfram was filmed at Gopher Flats on the Lasky Ranch. This pleasant green space in the San Fernando Valley had been a popular film location since the 1910s, but in the 1940s it would be bought up by Forest Lawn Memorial Parks to bury the dead. That wasn't the dark cloud on the horizon, though. Gloria was beset with gloomy thoughts. On the first day of filming, while in make up, she said: "I can't see this picture finished." Gloria would always refer to this as an "extrasensory" experience, a moment of precognition that bolstered her belief in parapsychology and her own clairvoyant tendency. She also had solid grounds for doubting the success of this joint venture.

Gloria was under considerable stress even before shooting began. The delayed start had already caused speculation that she and Von were ready to call the whole thing off, rumours swiftly denied in the trade press. Plus, all was not well between her and the Marquis. The night before filming began, Joe radiogrammed Henri saying, "SHE SEEMS CONSIDERABLY UPSET OVER CABLE FROM YOU." Gloria was tiring of the marriage, which no longer felt new and romantic. It's possible she suspected more infidelity or simply resented Henri developing his own new identity as a movie man in Paris. Henri had good cause to be alarmed by the fact that Gloria had nipped over to New York to visit Joe, and at his urging her children had been to the Kennedy home to visit Rose and the kids for Halloween. Gloria stayed in Manhattan, where she made sure that whenever she went out with Joe, a third party was present—a precaution Joe felt unnecessary. Gloria had returned to Hollywood while Joe stayed on the east coast a few days more to attend the opening of the Keith Memorial Theater, along with three of the people outside Hollywood that he most wanted to keep on side: Rose, Cardinal O'Connell and the president of Harvard. Whatever was disturbing the marital harmony, Joe was determined that it would not disrupt the shoot. "EVERYTHING HERE PERFECTLY

OKEY [sic] FAR AS YOU CONCERNED," he told Henri. "HAVE NO ANXIETY AND DONT UPSET HER BECAUSE WE NOW ALMOST THREE MONTHS LATE."[1]

They certainly weren't on schedule and never would be. The screenplay for *Queen Kelly* represented around 30 reels, more than five hours. Before they even began filming, Von was told to start cutting scenes. "The first day on the set I was informed that I was $100,000 over budget," he later told a magazine. "When I asked how this could be, they told me it was the accumulation of Gloria Swanson's salary and her personal publicity. So I was told to take $100,000 worth of scenes that were in my script and throw them out."[2] In fact, Von's profligacy, not Gloria's, was to blame in this case.

Gloria retained almost all the paperwork relating to the production so it's possible to see pretty much exactly what was shot and who was on set on a certain date. Also, how many scenes were added to the screenplay and precisely when shooting began and ended. The stats are hairraising. On day one, the cast and crew were called with a bugle blast at 7am, started shooting at 10am, and were done by 5pm. Chaos set in as early as the second day: called once again at 7am, the team were not sent home until 6.15 the following morning. Almost every day, new scenes were added. Von fully intended to work painstakingly, sometimes all day and all night, and to take only one day off for Christmas. "Assistant directors became haggard-eyed," wrote one magazine. "Property men barely ambled instead of ran. Actors slept standing up."[3] Von, however, seemed to thrive. Cinematographer Paul Ivano remembered the director shooting daylight scenes all night with strong lighting and then, as dawn broke, ordering the set to be draped in black canvas to set up for a night scene. When cast and crew retired gratefully to their beds, Von was said to repair to one of Madam Francis's brothels. Arriving on set a few weeks into the shoot, Joe was horrified to see the cast and crew stumbling around as if drunk, due to extreme sleep deprivation. He ordered a clampdown on overtime, promising the company a day off every time they were kept working through the night.

The first scenes taken in the outdoors were reshot anyway. Von had hired Gordon Pollock as cinematographer, due to his skill with glass matte photography and process shots. Ivano, a French cinematographer of greater aptitude was hired to assist. The inevitable happened when Gloria and Joe saw the superiority of Ivano's work and the roles were reversed. Or as Ivano put it, "Ask anybody, I photographed *Queen Kelly*. Gordon got the $ and I got the pleasure." A doubtful pleasure. Von and Ivano created beautiful images together, with Ivano adapting to the director's style and perfectionism with relative ease, but they were both such strong personalities that they clashed day and night.

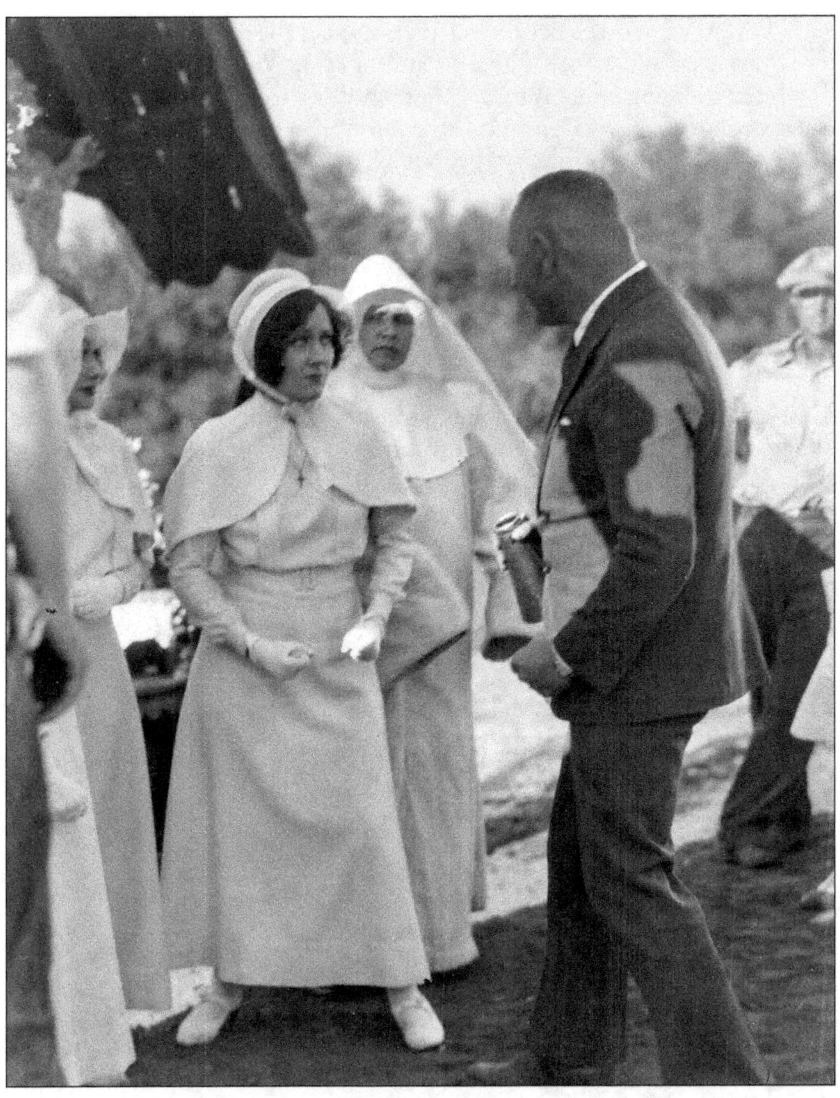

Gloria Swanson and Erich von Stroheim rehearse the meet-cute.
Milestone Film & Video.

In fits of rage Von would fire Ivano several times a week, sometimes during the same day. One time, camera assistant William Margulies remembered that the star-producer was forced to intervene.

> [Von] says, 'You're fired.' So Paul walks off the set. Gloria comes on the set and says, 'Where's Paul?' I said, 'Von Stroheim fired him.' 'So, you sonofabitch, I wait ten years to find a cameraman to photograph me and you fire him.' She says, '*You're* fired!' And he walked off the set. About a half hour later they all come back with love and kisses.

Gloria had not had to play such a heavy-handed role as producer before and it didn't suit her temperament. She had always wanted Joe to be the producer so she could concentrate on her performance. Joe had delegated the job to LeBaron, who was concerned with his new role at RKO and in turn passed the job on to his assistant, Louis Sarecky. Gloria kept Joe in the loop but he didn't believe things could be as bad as she said. When Derr complained to Von about rising costs, the director blamed everyone but himself.

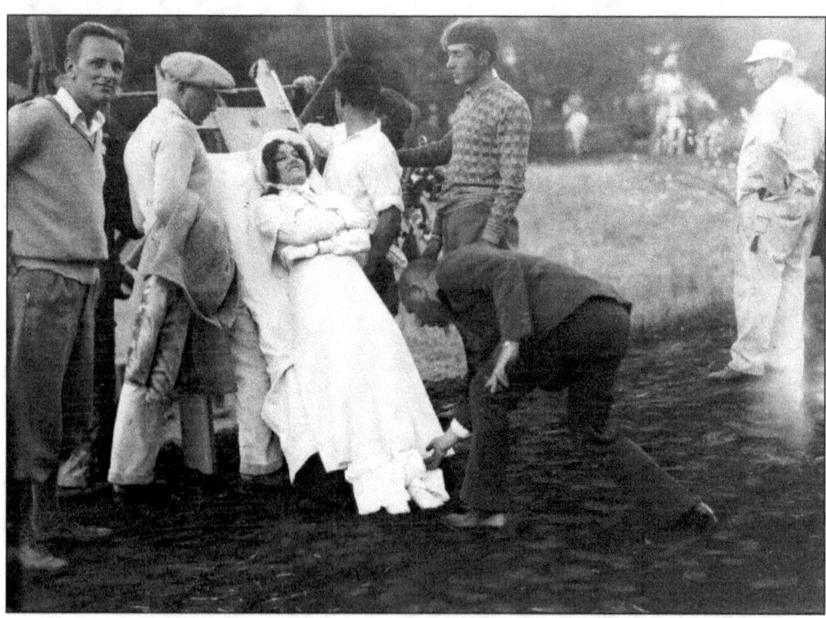

Erich von Stroheim adjusts Gloria Swanson's bloomers…
for an abandoned trick shot?
Harry Ransom Center/Milestone Film & Video.

Still, copious behind-the-scenes photographs capture what looks like a jolly and productive working environment. Several images were printed of the team shooting the meet-cute between Patricia and Wolfram on the Gopher Flats. This is Gloria's first appearance, which would prove to be one of the film's most controversial moments. Patricia and her fellow convent girls are out for a walk, crocodile-fashion, when they meet Wolfram and his cavalry squadron travelling in the opposite direction. Wolfram halts the squadron as he and Patricia lock eyes; they share a mutual and instant attraction. Patricia curtseys — and her knickers fall to the floor. This audacious bit of comic flirtation may well have been borrowed by Von from a German play of 1910, *Die Hose*, by Carl Sternheim, in which a peasant girl loses her underwear when she watches a military parade pass by. Perhaps Von had considered it for *The Wedding March*. It is guaranteed to make even a 21st-century audience gasp. Cast and crew clearly found it deeply funny. A bizarre behind-the-scenes photograph captures Gloria on set and in costume, strapped to a board, smiling and smoking a cigarette, with her bloomers around her ankles. A spoof on the scene or an attempt to film the panties in motion? In the end, the fall from grace was accomplished by a simple cut to a shot of her lingerie-draped feet. Wolfram laughs and Patricia, first flustered then enraged (owing to her "Irish temper"), picks up the knickers and throws them at Wolfram, who stashes them away in his saddle-bag.

Gloria was initially delighted by the beauty of Von's work. "My own scenes passed before me each day in the rushes like paintings created by a master of a girl I didn't quite know. Erich von Stroheim had stripped a dozen years off me. I looked sixteen." Gloria does indeed look radiant, although her heavy makeup, in particular her false eyelashes, doesn't quite convey the idea of a teenage convent girl. Von was more critical, continually pointing out what could be improved or what would have to be retaken. "We shot the sequence of the convent girls and the man on horseback so many times that I lost count." [4] Von blew up when he saw the soldiers' helmets were gold and not silver gilt as he requested — a difference barely perceptible in black-and-white. Gloria lost track of time, "hypnotized by the man's relentless perfectionism". Still, she had made enough films to know that they were falling terribly behind, and began to tally the takes. The production reports record that they filmed the meeting scene on seven separate days.

On one of these days, Ann Morgan, usually employed as Elinor Glyn's dressmaker but playing one of the supporting roles as a nun on *Queen Kelly*, relayed to Gloria something alarming that happened after the star had left the scene of the lovers' first encounter. Von filmed Byron holding the underwear to his nose and breathing deeply. Gloria recalled being immediately horrified. "The very idea of putting such an

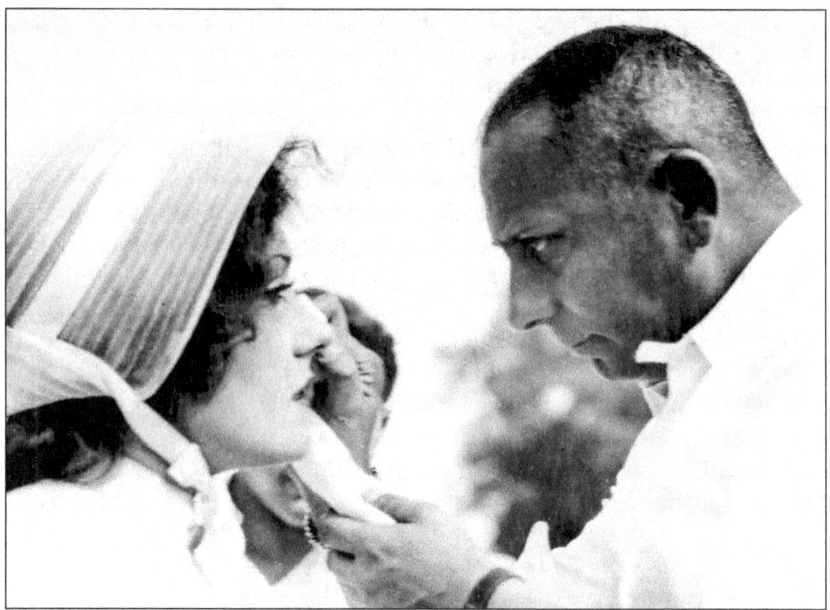

'Like paintings created by a master': Erich von Stroheim's perfectionism impressed Gloria Swanson at the start of filming.
Harry Ransom Center/Milestone Film & Video.

act into a film was so unthinkable in 1928 as to be unmentionable, even in the Formula. That, in fact, I thought, might be the very reason von Stroheim thought he could get away with it. And from then on, I began to watch him more closely." Perhaps she did, but she didn't take action. She writes in her memoir that the gesture, viewed in the rushes, was subtle but unmistakable and given that "everything else was so beautiful, I decided not to exercise my veto on the matter until the proper time came".[5] It's possible that Gloria, too, thought they could get away with it—or even that she wished they would.

Ivano recalled watching the rushes of the knickers scene with Joe, seated between Gloria and Von. Joe asked Ivano for his thoughts, but his response, that "photographically it's fine, but I'm not sure if you'll get away with it",[6] earned him two kicks on his ankles—one each from Gloria and Von. This undermines Gloria's claim to have been ignorant of the gesture. There is no doubt that Von intended it to go in the finished picture. It cues up a whole series of similar images, related to Wolfram's love for Patricia: principally those of him sniffing a handkerchief filled with hay, and then orchids, but also him clutching her black robes, her toying with her napkin, and even the scene where they both have handkerchiefs stuffed in their mouths as they escape a smoke-filled convent.

Ivano was right, however. This was exactly the sort of thing the Hays Office—the same body that demanded the monkey in *Sadie Thompson* had to wear trousers—frowned upon. Anita Loos, who found the scene wickedly amusing, nevertheless described it as "merely an expensive self-indulgence, for even in those days before censorship the studio itself would never have outraged public opinion by including it in the picture".[7] Joe shouldn't even have had to ask whether it was appropriate and LeBaron should have shut down such shenanigans, which were ultimately wasteful. The fact that he didn't proved that Von was essentially working unsupervised, possibly in cahoots with his star, and apparently taking full advantage.

Not for nothing did Gloria later call this film a "naughty little number". There is barely a frame in which Von is not making some kind of mischief. *Queen Kelly* opens in the palace in Kronberg, where we meet the royal characters, Queen Regina and "Wild Wolfram". These scenes are the perfect illustration of Von's famous line about the difference between him and Ernst Lubitsch. "Lubitsch shows you the king on his throne, then follows this with the king in his bedroom. I show you the king in his bedroom, first, so you'll know what he is when you see him on his throne."[8] The king is here a queen (Seena Owen), whom we first meet as she rouses herself from a drunken slumber, naked in her palace boudoir, which is adorned with cavorting cupids, an altar to amorousness. Von initially intended for Owen to play the scene nude, but after she protested he conceded first a pair of flesh-coloured tights and then a cat to cover her modesty. There are other cats lounging in the bed, and Von wanted one of them to arch its back and bristle, playing the role of a feisty little familiar for the Queen. Nothing the crew did could make the cat throw a hissy fit, not even dragging Ranger the Wonder Dog in from elsewhere on the lot to enrage it. The cat remained calm and was allowed to sleep. This was taken as a sign that Von had chilled out himself or that he was picking his battles. "Two years ago," said English film journalist Cedric Belfrage, "he would have got every dog in Hollywood into the studio."[9] A quote fed to the papers had Von claim to have "changed my attitude. One naturally does as one grows older. I am more philosophical about the making of pictures. I am so to speak, aged in wood, mellower."[10]

Regina reaches for the champagne to soothe her hangover as we learn this woman had inherited the "blood mania" of her forebears and "knows no law but her own desires". Next to her bed is a portrait of her betrothed Prince Wolfram, for whom she harbours a "morbid, jealous passion" (we will later learn that Patricia keeps two postcards of his face under her pillow). Next to that, a still-life of regal debauchery: a copy of the Decameron alongside her Bible and rosary, an ashtray overflowing with

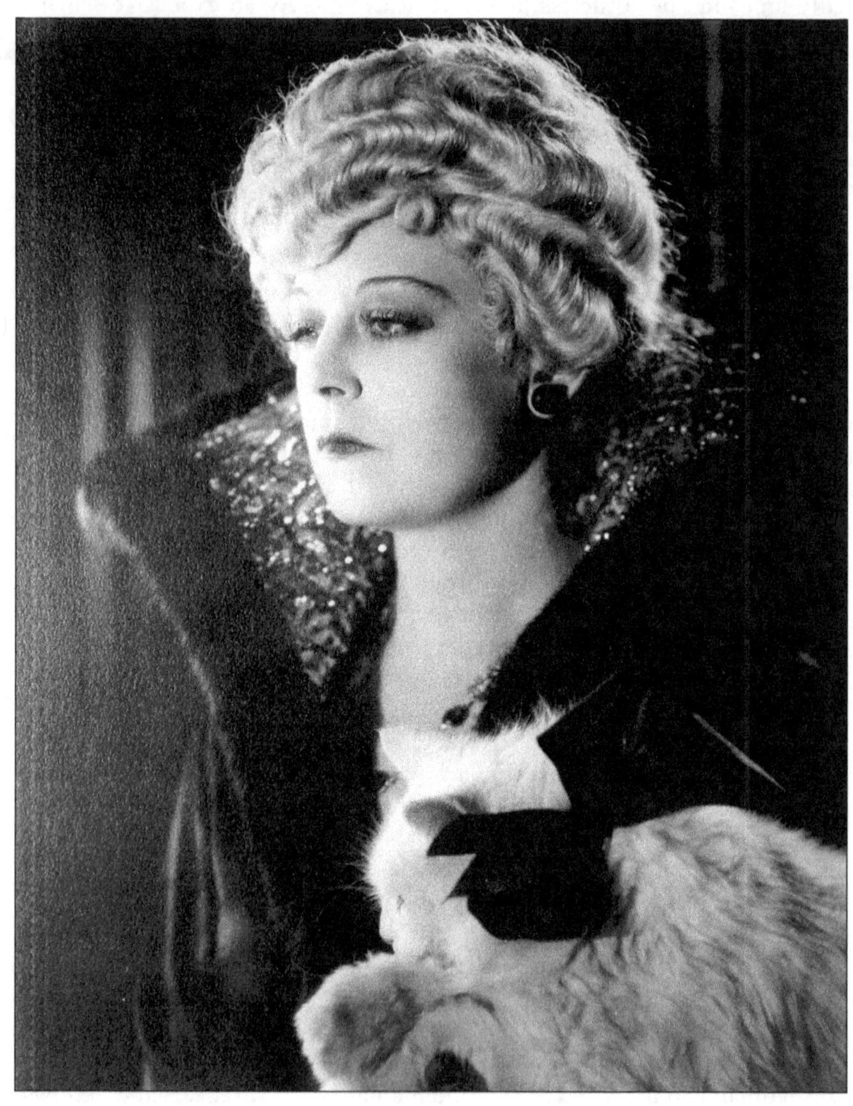

Seena Owen as Queen Regina. The crew called her 'Poor Seena'.
Milestone Film & Video.

the butts of cigars and cigarettes—evidence that she had male company last night, and plenty of it—and a packet of the barbiturate Veronal, which may explain her grogginess.

On set, Owen was referred to as "Poor Seena" because her role involved so much nudity and because Von required so many takes that the cat began to scratch her. Mittens had to be made for the cat. Von's own claws were sharper. Unable to deploy harsher methods on Gloria, who was in charge, he directed them instead at Owen, who discovered, as Mae Murray had before her, that he could be a tyrant. He blamed his military training. "I must undermine this surface of acquired false technique and bring out the real feeling that is like a kernel beneath a girl's superficial charm," he told a journalist when he was making *The Wedding March*. "I glower at them. Never in their lives have they been spoken to as roughly as by me. I crush them, beat them down with satire, with harsh words, with scorn. They are ready to quit. Then I get at the real soul and guide its natural unfoldment."[11] On the one hand, Fay Wray always spoke fondly of her time with Von and his method, but Murray certainly did not. We can assume that being directed by him was often, if not always, brutal.

A dissolve, one of many, almost all achieved in-camera, shifts the scene to the palace grounds and the return of Wolfram from his own night of debauchery. He has enjoyed his time away from the queen, whom he does not love, and is racing home on horseback, waving a pair of stockings aloft, driving a carriage laden with intoxicated young women wearing negligées, referred to in the cutting script as "pifflicated janes". Ivano claimed these extras were all supplied by Madam Francis—which if true would be another example of Von's dedication to authenticity. During the shoot, one of the girls fell out of the carriage, sustaining cuts and bruises; the production records name her as actress and dancer Jean Doree, who appeared in comedies for Universal. She was not, as far as can be ascertained, an employee of Madam Francis. We can be sure that the Prince is prolifically promiscuous, and later scenes in his dressing room show that his folding screen is découpaged with portraits of women—all conquests, no doubt. A military band heralds Wolfram's arrival and the Queen comes to the window to welcome her returning lover, still naked, now furious. Von undermines the pomp of the regal household not just by exposing the vices of the upper-classes—Wolfram is so plastered that he falls off his horse—but by showing us staff at work around them with carpet sweepers, dusters and mops. The Prince's female companions taunt him with his royal titles before they depart. This is "Majesty, me foot" writ large.

Partly as punishment and partly to sober him up for a surprise announcement, the Queen orders the hungover Wolfram to do drills with his squadron in the heat of the day—which is where he meets Patricia. This too is an extravagant scene requiring a vast number of soldiers on horseback in full dress uniforms, complete with *pickelhaube* helmets topped with enormous eagles, and long shots taken at a great distance to obscure 1928 Los Angeles in the background. Gloria is terrific, by turns vivacious and furious. Byron, who mostly took character parts after this failed attempt to launch him as a Hollywood leading man, plays Wolfram as a self-assured lush, with outbreaks of winning charm. Gloria often chose quite muted leading men, but Von had a way of boosting the energy of his male stars—as with John Gilbert in The Merry Widow. Although the shoot took place in winter, the setting is springtime and Von's beloved blossom abounds, bringing with it an air of old-world romance as the lovers make a wish on the new-mown hay—a surprisingly sensual moment, largely thanks to Gloria's performance of the gesture.

When Patricia plaintively mimes to Wolfram her request for the return of her underwear, you see the truth of Gloria's claim that she played comedy "like Duse". It's funny because she plays it so straight, but it's also rather sweet. Likewise, back at the convent she defends herself in front of the Mother Superior by saying that she lost her temper—but gestures to her ankles, where something else was lost. Patricia is punished, but not before provoking a ripple of giggles among the nuns, both young and old. This film proceeds on two tracks at once, having its cake and eating it. In one of the most beautiful shots, Gloria is shown in close-up, her eyes damp with tears, and candles flickering and dripping wax in the foreground, as Patricia kneels before a statue of the Holy Mother. She prays, not as instructed, to be purified of sinful thoughts, but to see Prince Wolfram again—the same wish she made on the hay. She is carrying a letter in these scenes, unopened on screen, but the screenplay reveals it to be the message from her aunt enticing her to come visit her and marry Jan.

The Queen's surprise for Wolfram is that their wedding has been brought forward to the following day. This news is announced at an extravagantly shot dinner scene, referred to as the wedding banquet: a long table sagging with candelabras, glassware and dishes, 166 diplomatic guests, the prime minister, a papal nuncio and serving staff, plus the royal orchestra playing on the balcony. Back in the Prince's chambers, his smirking adjutant taunts him with the demise of his bachelor days and the fact that he will never see Patricia again, wafting the handkerchief full of hay under his nose. The Prince takes it and inhales deeply, mixing the memory of this scent with another.

Although it is already the small hours of the morning, soon Wolfram and his increasingly fretful companion break into the convent, climbing a ladder to enter an open bathroom window. As they creep down the corridor, the camera swings left to right from the Prince's perspective to confirm we are in the vicinity of the *Schlafsaals,* or dormitories. A plan forms when Wolfram sees the fire alarm. They run through the halls waving torches made of tar paper, to create enough smoke to suggest a fire, then set off the alarm to empty those dormitories. Panicked nuns awaken in rooms thick with smoke and run to the dormitories to round up the girls. Von seemed to forget his newfound serenity when shooting this sequence. After the first take, recalled Ivano, he threw down his megaphone and yelled, "Cut! Not good! Since when do you girls go to bed with all your clothes on? I want to see a little bit more of your bodies."[12] You might expect LeBaron or Gloria to protest, but the actresses dutifully removed some of their underwear and repeated the action. In all the rush, one actress had to be taken to hospital after falling on her face. To augment this scene, Joe put in a request for stock footage of a fire in a German convent and for images of a German fire department, which couldn't be found—but Von's smoke-choked chapel is very effective on its own. Wolfram spots Patricia spinning in confusion and carries her, as she falls unconscious, to the window and down the ladder, then through the moonlit convent gardens to his waiting car.

Their return to the palace is far from private, witnessed by multiple guards, lackeys and footmen who watch Wolfram carry the girl to his private rooms and eject his adjutant—who reminds him that this is "the Queen's palace". What follows is the central sequence of double-think in *Queen Kelly.* Wolfram and Patricia will share a lavish private supper, which she hungrily devours. She tastes champagne for the first time (it makes her sneeze) and learns how to eat oysters. When Wolfram removes the army coat that he has wrapped around her, Patricia remembers with a shock that she is not dressed: "Holy Mother of Patrick! I'm in my night-shirt!" They share mutual declarations of love and he carries her to his bedroom and lays her on the bed, while romantic intertitles quote Heinrich Heine ("Sing me dead and kiss me dead; Heart and soul and body—take me!"[13]). All this is intercut with a scene of the Queen taking a bath that might impress even DeMille—she is naked in the tub, with her cat, drinking champagne.

There is little doubt, despite the script's later insistence that Queen Kelly is a virgin, that this is a seduction scene—from Wolfram's abduction of Patricia and her fear when she wakes up on his sofa to their repartee over a candlelit supper and the retreat to the bedroom. Wolfram is very insistent, placing his arm around her and saying, "You're not going to run away—after I've burned down a convent to see you again!" Pointedly, he makes her complicit in her own deflowering: his beauty made her do it, and she was "naughty" to faint in his arms. He

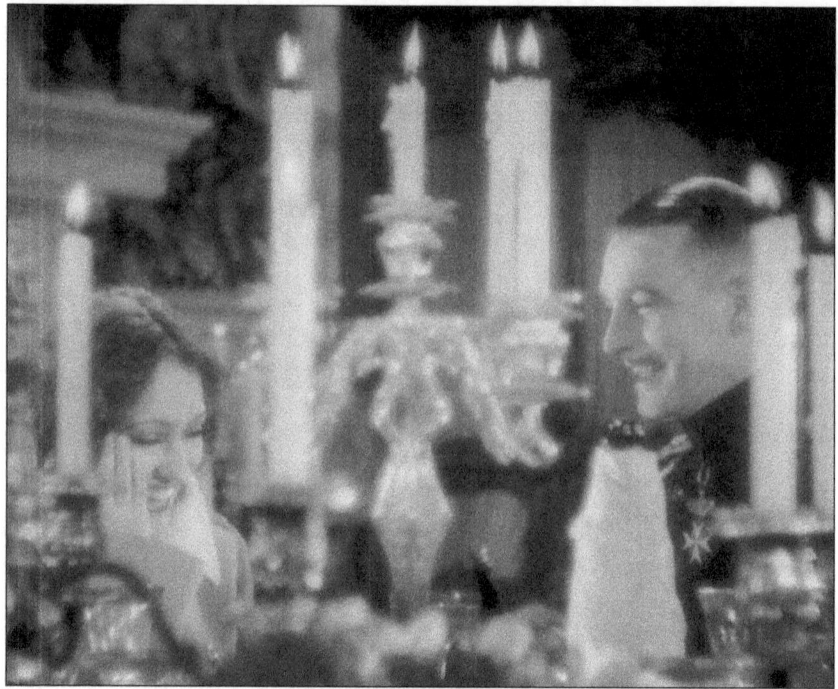

Seduction by candlelight in *Queen Kelly*. Milestone Film & Video.

encourages her to act out the fire-setting herself. Perhaps, like the convent conflagration itself, this is smoke without fire, but it seems unlikely that the Hays Office would see it that way. This is also one of the most extravagant scenes in the film: the heaps of caviar, dishes of foie gras and lobster on the table, the bottles of champagne. All the food was real, as was the champagne—a choice that was not just expensive but illegal, during Prohibition. After the gentle clowning of the supper scene, the tone shifts when Wolfram gives Patricia orchids. They embrace in front of a large mirror, and Patricia runs to the balcony, weeping because she will never see him again. She lies in Wolfram's arms as they profess their love for each other. He kisses her passionately and then carries her to the bedroom.

What is going on in the bedroom? Ask the Queen, who emerges from her bathroom, dressed in an ostrich-trimmed peignoir and still clutching that implacable cat. She visits the prince's chambers and listens at the bedroom door, then finds a window to peek in… The fact that the lovers on the bed are still dressed and Wolfram's feet are on the floor may not have satisfied Will Hays, and it certainly does not satisfy Queen Regina, who looks genuinely distraught. What follows is possibly the most famous sequence in the whole film. Frothing at the mouth, Regina lashes out at the couple with a whip. Patricia weeps when she learns that Wolfram is engaged, and he begs her forgiveness, to no avail. Outside the chamber Regina rips Wolfram's coat from Patricia's back and attacks with her whip, chasing her all the way down that giant staircase, screaming that the prince belongs to her—all while the footmen openly laugh. This whipping set piece is remarkable for both its perverse violence and the grandeur of its setting. It features in several of the film's most frequently reprinted stills, showing the queen in her negligée wielding the whip, and Patricia in her nightgown, her long plaits unbraided—a graphic suggestion of the film's sex and violence, as well as its beauty. In the film's unrealised African scenes, Jan froths at the mouth in the throes of his disease and he brandishes his own whip. There is a direct parallel between the two characters of Jan and the Queen. Punishment by whipping was a popular trope in silent cinema.

A distressed Patricia walks to a bridge, driven by a suicidal impulse. Back at the palace, Wolfram tells the Queen that he wants to marry Patricia and she orders him thrown in solitary confinement. Byron arches one eyebrow in response. Patricia contemplates the icy water, suffering super-

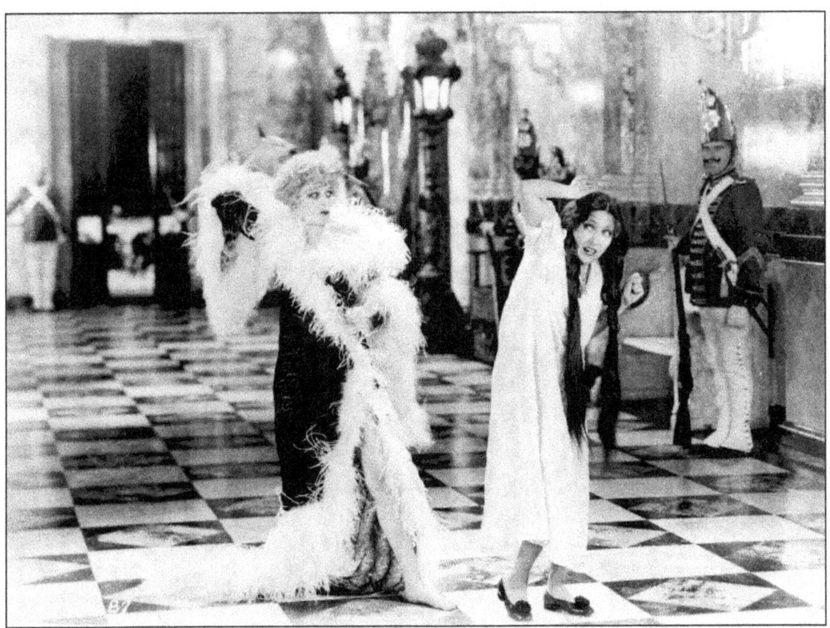

Excess both of emotion and décor in the whipping scene from *Queen Kelly*.
Milestone Film & Video.

imposed visions of Wolfram and Regina, her face striped with blood from the lash. Abruptly, she jumps and is rescued by a passing policeman, who brings her back to the convent. There, a cable from Jan tells her to come to her aunt's deathbed in Dar Es Salaam. The next morning, the prince is seen in his cell telling his adjutant that he cannot live without Patricia, and, in a moment of solitude, he plays the violin, serenading her convent robes, which he has kept as a memento.

Apart from the wedding banquet scene, not filmed until the following year, the cutting scripts and production records tell us that the company had captured this much of the story by 21 December, despite delays, retakes and night shooting. The scene of Patricia's return to the convent

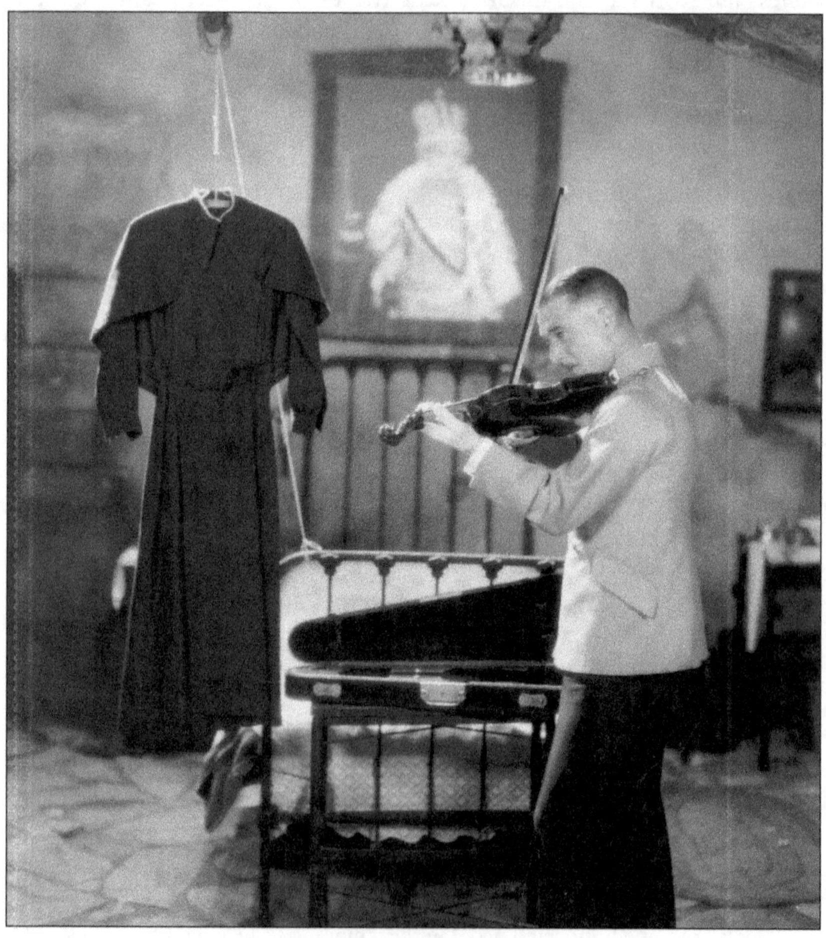

Walter Byron as Wolfram serenading Patricia's convent gown,
under Regina's watchful eye.
George Eastman Museum/Milestone Film & Video.

and some other shots have not survived as they were cut from the film's eventual, truncated release, but this is well over an hour of screen time, and depending on who, and when, you asked, it represents about a half, a third or even a quarter of the complete film. This, after seven weeks of a ten-week schedule.

Three weeks in, it became obvious that the budget was climbing up to $450,000, with Von working at a pace of 4.8 scenes a day, meaning the shoot would take 103 days. After four or five weeks, Joe really began to start worrying. As his train sped towards New York, Eddie Moore was messaging him about Byron's contract. Did it include talking? And could it be extended, because the shoot was clearly going to drag on? Von's contract from Powers also needed an extension, due to the delay in starting the shoot.

Joe's men had arranged for the purchase of footage of East Africa from explorer-filmmakers Martin and Osa Johnson for establishing shots of the Dar Es Salaam locations, but by early December it was still impossible to see any of this film. The Prince of Wales was on a tour of Britain's East African territories, and Derr had the bright, if bizarre, idea of Pathé using some of the Johnson footage to fabricate newsreel images of the Prince's tour, as the real thing would not arrive for weeks. He was also keen to splice the eventual footage of his visit into Johnson's footage to cover Wolfram's arrival. Not too difficult to imagine the Royal displeasure that would have ensued, had a Hollywood studio tried to use the heir to the British throne, the future King Edward VIII, as a double for a dissipated Ruritanian playboy in a risqué melodrama. At least Von would have been amused.

By early December, all the FBO films in production when RKO took over were finished, so *Queen Kelly* claimed more of Joe's attention. It seemed that everything was going wrong at once. Von was taking days to shoot the love scene, constantly adding more setups. Derr, clearly out of his depth, was struggling to understand how films were made and whether Von was demanding an unusually high number of setups and takes. He tried, unsuccessfully, to get hold of a copy of *The Merry Widow* and have someone count how many shots it contained. Derr's primary plan of action was to get Von to speed up and reduce the scope of the film. "UNQUESTIONABLY STORY IS A PICTURE AND A HALF AND HE KNOWS IT," read Derr's panicked telegram to Joe.

Von made a big concession, agreeing to shoot the African scenes in a studio rather than on location in Catalina, where Gloria had shot *Sadie Thompson*, due to the time and cost and the risk of rain stopping the shoot. He also dropped the idea of showing Queen Regina lying in state after her death. However, he was reluctant to make any more of the cuts Derr thought were needed to trim the film down from 14 or

15 to ten reels. "EVERYTHING SUGGESTED HE CALLS MILE-STONES I WISH HE HAD ONE AROUND HIS NECK," wrote a clearly desperate Derr. Von was fighting to save his beloved royal set pieces: the elaborate wedding banquet, and the climactic coronation, Glazer believed the banquet was necessary but need not become a spectacle: "Any elaboration or elongation of it, no matter how tricked up with pomp and ceremony, can only retard the action of the story at this point."[14] Derr and Glazer both argued for the removal of Patricia's jump into the river (just about to be shot), and Derr also wanted to delete Patricia's second suicide attempt. Glazer and Derr were trying to encourage Von to find a new ending altogether, which was "NOT ALL WRITTEN BUT SLOWLY WORKING OUT IN VONS MIND." A division between two camps was hardening, with Von working on the story alone, while Derr and Glazer collaborated on a list of potential cuts.

Joe had already sought a second and even a third opinion, calling in some big names from Hollywood. It was at this point, not the following year, as Gloria later claimed, that screenwriter and director Edmund Goulding was brought in, first to write a new ending—the one Von thought he was writing alone. Joe had also been seeking advice from Paul

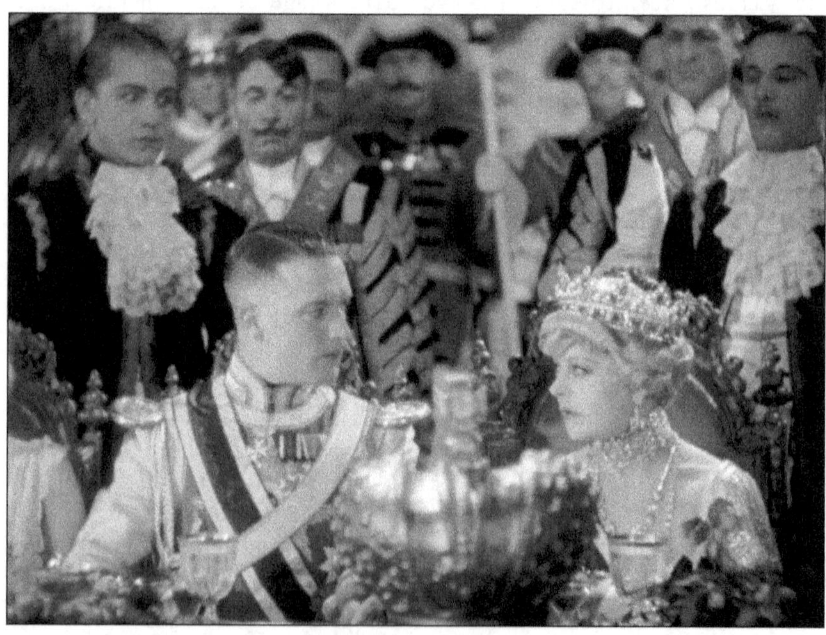

One of Von's many milestones: The 'Wedding Banquet'.
Milestone Film & Video.

Bern, Pathé's head of production, who responded to this crisis with a list of suggestions in a memo sent to Joe and Goulding. He agreed with Derr and Glazer: drop the banquet, the suicide attempt, the scene-setting and a parade on the streets of Dar Es Salaam, and "the marriage of Kelly by the colored priest." He went further, suggesting the story would have "infinitely more pathos" if we never see Patricia as "the resplendent, gorgeous Madame" at all, but catch up with her much later, worn down by life, still a virgin but already "a drunken sot". The Prince should arrive in a similarly diminished state—"a very simple, distraught figure, accompanied only by an adjutant in plain, ordinary uniform. Then I will believe that he has made some sort of sacrifice for her."[15] This was the kind of delicacy and narrative economy that both Joe and the Hays Office would welcome. But it would delete the enthralling figure of Queen Kelly and reduce the Swamp scenes to a bare minimum. Von could never agree to that.

A week later, after Joe had pledged more money to the budget and with the love scenes finally completed, Gloria and Von dutifully sent cheery dispatches to the United Artists sales convention in Chicago, where Derr presented a trailer of highlights. To hear them tell it, all was going swimmingly on *Queen Kelly*, which would be ready for distribution early in the new year. Gloria praised Von: "HE TRULY IS THE GREAT VON STROHEIM." And Von hymned Gloria, though a little less effusively: "WITH THE EXCEPTION OF JACK GILBERT IT HAS NEVER BEEN MY PRIVILEGE TO WORK WITH A REAL ARTIST IN A ROLE OF SUCH IMPORTANCE."[16] At the convention, Al Lichtman reiterated the studio's commitment to talking pictures, including the "part-talkie"[17] *Queen Kelly*. Bookings were slow, though, which likely reflected exhibitors' lack of confidence in one of Von's films being ready for the projected date. After all, *The Wedding March* had only just appeared, more than two years after shooting began.

By Christmas, however, Von must have known that he was on borrowed time—he spent a lavish $75 on a Christmas bouquet for Rose in order to butter up the boss's boss. The holiday was anything but a respite for the *Queen Kelly* crew, as the RKO takeover of FBO meant that the entire production, sets and all, had to be shipped to the Pathé premises in Culver City in thousands of crates. It cost a great deal to rebuild the palace in its new location. And while Gloria Productions had been charged $5,000 a week for shooting on the FBO lot, Joe would set the bill at Pathé for twice that figure. By the end of 1928, total expenditure on *Queen Kelly* was already $700,000.

Most of the *Queen Kelly* team barely took Christmas off at all. There were retakes on Christmas Eve and an epic story conference from 8pm to 2.30am on Boxing Day, but they were pleased to view a rough cut of the European scenes that convinced everyone they were on the right track. On Christmas Day itself, Fred Thomson, the Western star that Joe had muscled out of FBO, had died in hospital—Frances Marion told everyone he had lost the will to live after the way Joe treated him. While his fans mourned, Joe collected the life insurance money and ordered that all FBO's prints of his films be sold for scrap. Away from the set, Gloria spent the holiday with her husband and children, as Henri had returned to Los Angeles. She had another reason to be happy. Amid the chaos of the move to Culver City, Joe had given her a Christmas gift: an ultra-luxurious new bungalow on the Pathé lot, even more lavish, she thought, than the one William Randolph Hearst had bought for his mistress, Marion Davies. It had a grand piano in the living room, a kitchen, a wardrobe and fitting room, even a private garage. "I could only surmise that Joe Kennedy was starting to do very well for himself in the movie business," she wrote. "And that he loved me."[18] She was going to foot the bill in the end, for the bungalow, and everything else.

1. *Hostage to Fortune*, 78.
2. Cedric Belfrage, "Classic Holds Open Court", *Motion Picture Classic*, June 1930, 82.
3. Ibid, 105.
4. *SoS*, 369.
5. *SoS*, 370.
6. Quoted, Koszarski, 249.
7. *A Girl Like* I, 126.
8. Herman G Weinberg, *The Lubitsch Touch: A Critical Study* (E.P. Dutton & Co, 1968), 102.
9. Cedric Belfrage, *Film Weekly*, 31 December 1928, quoted, Peter Noble, *Hollywood Scapegoat: The Biography of Erich von Stroheim* (Fortune Press, 1950), 76.
10. "Miss Swanson's new role", *New York Times*, 27 January 1929, 154.
11. Myrtle Gebhart, "Apple Blossoms and *The Wedding March*", *Picture-Play*, December 1926, 11.
12. Ivano, quoted in Koszarski, 250.
13. From the Heinrich Heine poem known as "Auf den Wolken ruht der Mond" or "The moon rests on the clouds", published in *Buch der Lieder* (1827).
14. Memo from Benjamin Glazer to Derr, 10 December 1928, JPK Papers.
15. Memo from Paul Bern to Derr, 7 December 1928, JPK Papers.
16. *SoS*, 371.
17. "United Artists Sales Leaders in Chicago for First Convention", *Exhibitors Herald and Moving Picture World*, 15 December 1928, 25.
18. *SoS*, 372.

12

The Manure Pile

The new year of 1929 brought the Queen Kelly shoot to the Pathé lot. In the projected final three weeks, Von had to film his African scenes, his beautiful wedding banquet, and the coronation finale. He was at least a month behind schedule. As Gloria calculated it: "We had another four months of shooting to go and twenty more hours of film, most of which would end up on the cutting-room floor, unless a great change occurred soon".[1] And yet, on the first day of work, 2 January, none of the principals stepped in front of the camera. Instead, Von directed background players, including sailors and what the script called "girls", in suggestive background shenanigans in a hallway — a sequence that could never have made it to the screen in 1929.

This is the scene that Patricia first encounters when she sets foot in her aunt's establishment. The production reports coyly refer to "Upper hallway café", but it is certainly not a café. A Chinese sailor and a "negro girl" go into one door together, while a sailor kisses a Spanish girl goodbye as he emerges from another door, and a "beachcomber"[2] kisses a French girl in another doorway. A blonde girl runs out of a fourth door screaming, only to be chased by two sailors and a girl in black and carried back into the room. The French and Spanish girls laugh in Patricia's face when they see her gawping. With girls coming and going in and out of doors along a corridor, Von clearly meant this scene to be a parallel with the novices emerging from their dormitories in the convent fire, complete with a girl carried in a uniformed man's arms. Offensive as many would find that comparison, the Hays Office would not need that detail to object to this scene. It is unmistakably a hallway in a brothel, and the screaming escapee suggests the brutality of forced prostitution. This scene only survives in the evocative description in the cutting script and a rarely reprinted production still, which clearly shows the sailors and girls in the corridor, the screaming girl carried aloft by sailors, as well as a Black maid in native dress in the foreground. Von had effectively wasted a day's work. Did Gloria, LeBaron or Sarecky have the nerve, or sense, to tell him?

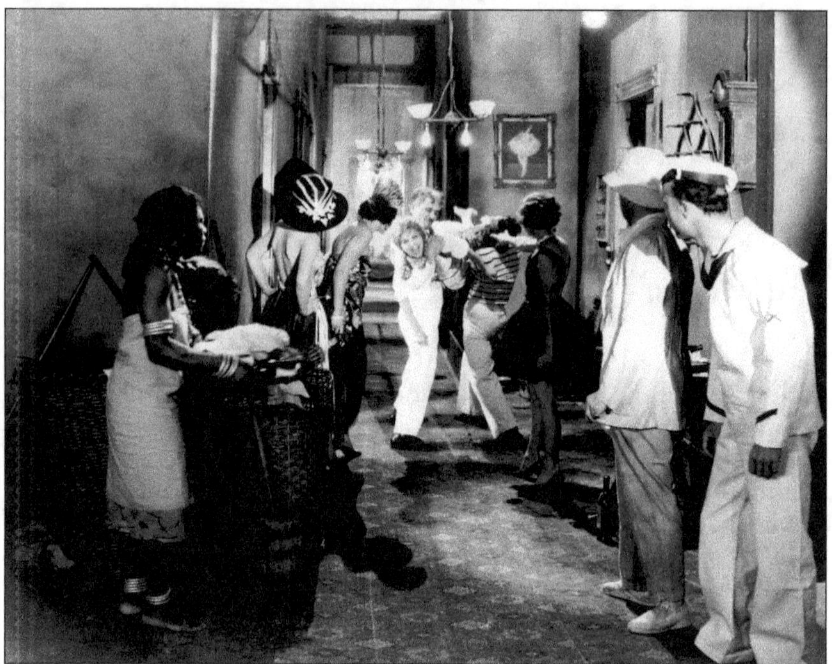

The goings-on in this hallway make The Swamp's real business unambiguous.
Milestone Film & Video.

Over the next three days, Von shot Patricia's arrival at the brothel, her welcome from Kali Sana and Coughdrops, her aunt's deathbed wish, and her first encounter with Jan. This is a remarkable sequence, marked both by Von's insistence on bitter realism—as Jan glowers in the doorway, we glimpse a couple in the corridor behind him—and his tenderness, as Patricia embraces her dying aunt. Gloria posed for photographs grinning in her costume, standing between Von and Henri with her hands on their shoulders as they looked studiously at the script, as well as for stills with Daggett and Sul-Te-Wan. On the Sunday, Derr called a meeting with Gloria and Von, demanding that they start trimming the screenplay. The coronation and "other excessive scenes," likely a reference to much of the colour in the bar, such as Kelly tasting various kinds of champagne, had to go. Von's favourite scene, the tree in the swamp, with the lovers in peril, was for the chop. *Motion Picture Magazine* later reported:

The high-light of the yarn was to be when Gloria Swanson, clinging desperately to a tree, is rescued just as the huge stick sinks eighty feet into a swamp. This was the scene Von counted on. It was to furnish more excitement, heart interest, et al. than the other fourteen or so reels combined. It was his brainchild. It was, so to speak, his baby. But, phooey! Along came a supervisor with his big stick, or knife, and hacked the whole thing out. Too expensive. Out with it.[3]

It was a carrot, not a stick, that persuaded Von. Extremely reluctant to kill this particular darling, Von called Joe in Florida and extracted from him a promise that he would retain the rights to "the swamp idea". As he put it to Joe: "Some day that will make a great picture." Joe was having dinner with a priest, and you might think not inclined to discuss any of this in such company. Seeing how sincere Von was, Joe agreed, but only "AFTER the picture was satisfactorily shot"[4], meaning on time and on budget.

Von agreed to finish *Queen Kelly* so that he could go on to make his "great" swamp film later. In the revised plan, everything would be shot silent "except for synthetic sound"—dialogue and effects, dubbed on

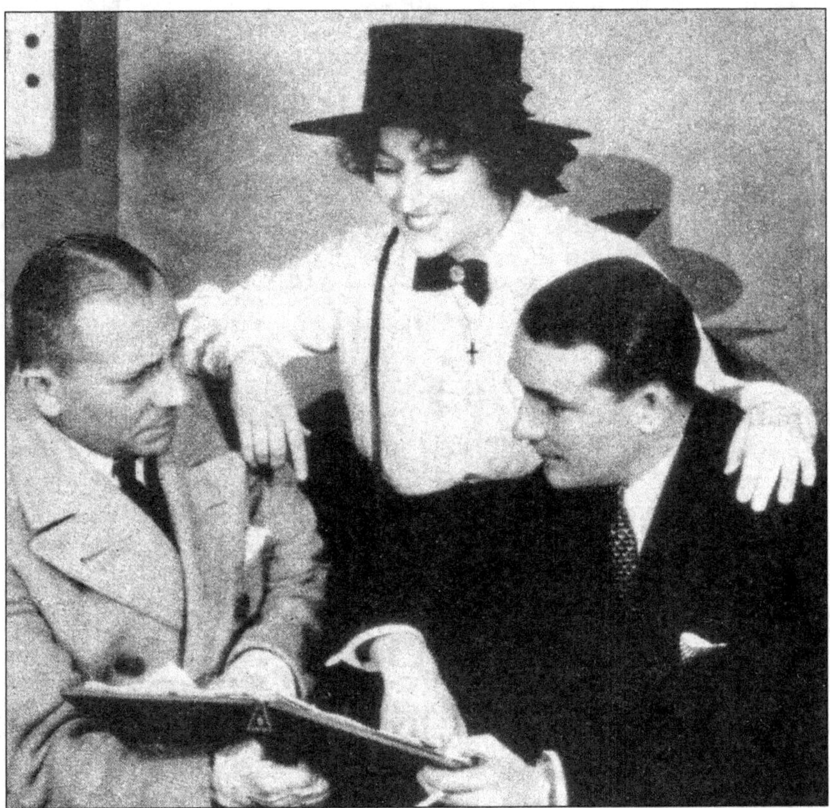

Erich von Stroheim, Gloria Swanson and Henri de La Falaise on the set of *Queen Kelly*. Harry Ransom Center/Milestone Film & Video.

afterwards. Patricia would marry Jan, then a title card would carry the film forward eight months, to find Patricia as Queen Kelly, the hard-drinking, black-clad madam with a whip and a police dog. She is working in the bar, folding towels and counting cash, when she reads in the newspaper that Prince Wolfram is arriving on a tour of duty, and hits the booze. When he arrives she is kissing a sailor. Horrified, he exclaims, "So this is where you live… this… what you are." She ejects him from the bar and Jan attacks her. Weakened and distraught because she believes she has lost Wolfram forever, Kelly appears to give in, saying to Jan, "I'll go with you. I'll go with anybody! Everybody!" Jan drags her upstairs and at this point the screenplay has an attempted rape by a Chinese sailor, but that was removed later. Kelly locks herself in a room with a bottle of poison. Wolfram returns and breaks into the room to find Kelly has already taken the fatal dose. He sends for a doctor, and the dying woman and her prince talk regret, love, forgiveness… Kelly even prays in Latin. After the doctor arrives to take care of Kelly, Wolfram prays to the Madonna in a chapel. Kelly is seen recovering in hospital: "Don't forget my name is Kelly—When we Oirish get a fighting chance—We fight like hell!" The governor arrives with news of Queen Regina's death and so Wolfram proposes to Kelly, allowing for a happy ending, with the "'Majesty', me foot. Just 'Queen' Kelly!" sign-off.

A fan magazine feature reported that Von was a changed man, no longer the long-winded perfectionist of old but a newly efficient, obedient producer who stuck to his shooting schedule and followed his supervisor's orders. "He was, so to speak, presented with a first reader (in plain wrapper), entitled: How To Be Thrifty Though Arty."[5] It wasn't true; Von didn't work any faster. By the time his ten weeks (allowing for the Christmas break) were up, he had only got as far as completing Kelly's wedding to Jan. On 17 January, the day that scene was finally wrapped, Gloria and Derr brought in Edmund Goulding, a talented writer-director who knew the Movietone process well, for an emergency meeting. Both Glazer and Goulding had prepared dialogue scripts for scenes that took place after the eight-month ellipsis, and Josiah Zuro, a classically trained film composer on the Pathé books, was being consulted on a choice of song for Gloria to sing on the soundtrack—which had possibly been written by Goulding. Gloria, meanwhile, who was performing Patricia's arrival at the brothel and her grisly wedding every day, was becoming frantic with worry and feeling isolated. Henri was in Palm Beach, for a short break before he returned to France, with Joe and Eddie Moore, who were playing Bunco on their traditional vacation. On set, she felt that Glazer and LeBaron were merely going along with Von's impossible shooting pace and his "apocalyptic vision of hell on earth… full of material that would never pass the censors".[6]

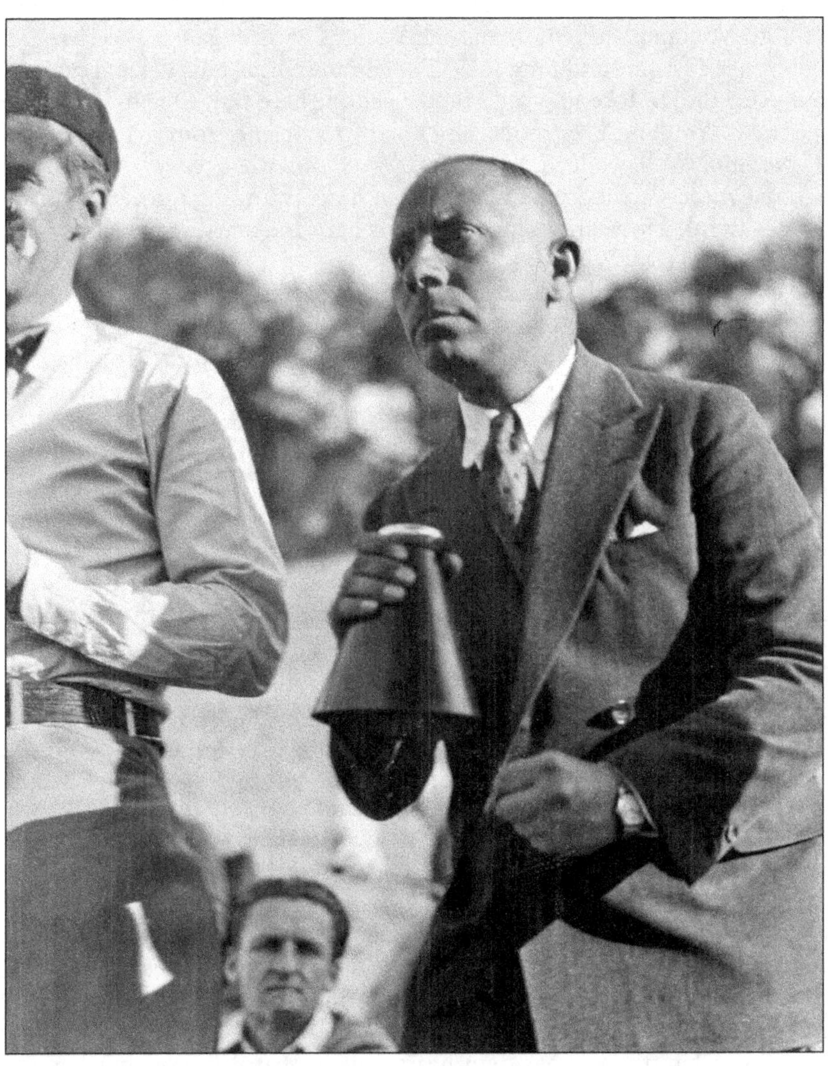

Killing his darlings: Erich von Stroheim directing *Queen Kelly*.
Harry Ransom Center/Milestone Film & Video.

Gloria recalled reaching breaking point during the filming of the wedding scene when Von instructed Tully Marshall, in detail, how to drool tobacco juice on to Gloria's hand as he placed the ring there. "I had just eaten breakfast, and my stomach turned. I felt nauseated and furious at the same time." She said "Excuse me, I must make a phone call" to Von and walked off the set. Back at her bungalow she changed out of her costume and rang Joe. "The minute I heard his voice, I poured out everything. 'Joseph, you'd better get out here fast. Our director is a madman. You and everybody else tried to stop me from making *Sadie Thompson*. Well, believe me, *Sadie Thompson* was *Rebecca of Sunnybrook Farm* compared with what *Queen Kelly* is turning into. It's ruined! And—awful! Now, are you coming out here and starting to make decisions or aren't you?'"[7]

It almost certainly wasn't the brothel wedding scene itself that broke Gloria. On 18 January, Von spent a day on one of his beloved milestones, the wedding banquet (which didn't require Gloria), shooting from 9am to 11pm. A script dated 19 January sets up what exactly is due to be filmed in the rest of the shoot, following the cuts agreed on 6 January. On 19 and 21 January, the crew shot scenes 261, 262, 277 and 278, in the "Upper hallway café" and "Kelly's bedroom", which called for 30 or 31 "types" in the extras list. These are scenes immediately following the wedding, which are especially controversial, and the relevant pages are missing from most of the copies of the screenplay that Gloria saved. According to the 19 January script note they consisted of "the business of Kelly driving the 30 people out of her room and down the hall".

In the preceding scene, Jan has led "about fifteen tarts and about fifteen sailors, soldiers and planters" upstairs to the bedroom where Kali and Coughdrops have taken Patricia to prepare for her wedding night. Jan arranges them in a semi-circle in pairs, as if about to see a show. They are "hugging and kissing, drinking and are generally excited at the anticipation of the expected hors d'oeuvre to their own dinner". There is a curtain between them and the bed where Patricia is sleeping. Jan opens the curtain and Patricia wakes, swiftly realises that he has come to consummate the marriage and crawls away across the bed, then picks up the scissors that Coughdrops used to make her veil. In scenes 263-276 (not filmed) Patricia backs into the next room, where her aunt lies dead, moving further back until she is against the bed. At first she points the scissors at Jan, then at her own heart, saying that if he touches her she will kill herself. Jan advances, but Patricia says she will do "anything— but that!"[8] In scenes 277 and 278, Jan announces, in front of the jeering crowd, that Patricia will be the "new madame". Patricia reluctantly agrees, but immediately marks her territory by taking a swing at the crowd with Jan's crutch, as she drives the mob from the room. "One tart walks defiantly into her path, whereupon Kelly grabs her by the hair, yanks her about."[9] In the following scene, Patricia sits down wearily on the bed and Kali and Coughdrops give her cigarettes and whiskey to anaesthetise her distress, as an iris ushers in the film's ten-minute intermission. After that, the story will return to The Swamp, eight months later, with Queen Kelly established in her post.

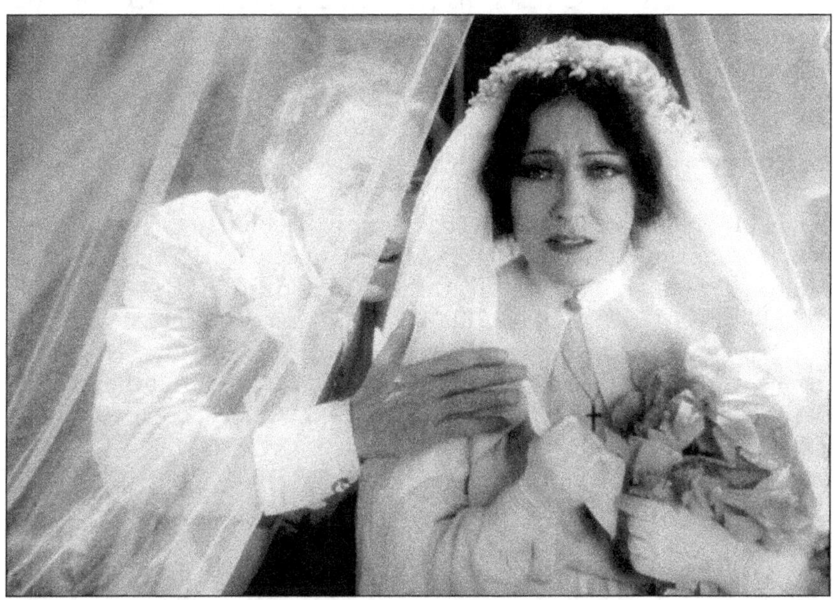

Tully Marshall as Poto-Poto Jan and Gloria Swanson as Patricia, the terrified bride. Milestone Film & Video.

These scenes contain material that violates one Don't and several Be Carefuls in what was known as the Hays Office's Magna Charta and appear more perverse than anything in *Sadie Thompson*. Wedding nights were to be treated with delicacy, not represented as a live sex show in a brothel, involving a corpse and a violent standoff. The blocking of this scene, with Patricia backing out of one space and into another, Jan following her, creates another of Von's parallels—it is a distorted reflection of her night of love with Wolfram. Also, as Patricia agrees to every task required of her as proprietor of The Swamp, this scene is the most explicit in terms of the brothel's day-to-day business. Patricia agrees to "deal out the booze", "count the towels", "take in the dough", "an' everythin'!"[10]

According to Ivano, it was during this violent scene that Von instructed Marshall to spit on Gloria's hand—a gross addition to a sordid sequence. For Gloria, already sick with worry, and having endured such a brutal wedding night with her first husband, this sequence could have been distressing to film, with or without the tobacco juice. There is the possibility that someone got hurt in the mêlée, or alternatively that Gloria, who wasn't very strong, was unable to summon up the violence required. It could even be the case that Von started shooting an orgy scene, as was his habit.

Did Joe answer Gloria's distress call and jump into action? Yes and no. It seems that he stayed put in Palm Beach a while longer to handle the situation remotely, while waving Henri off to Paris. Rose had just arrived in Florida, along with Eddie Moore's wife, Mary. At some point, Joe had called in yet another outside opinion, tasking Pathé screenwriter Eugene Walter with viewing the *Queen Kelly* footage and reading the screenplay. Walter's report on *Queen Kelly*, sent by Derr to Eddie Moore in Palm Beach on 25 January, is absolutely excoriating. He makes some good points about how as it stood Gloria's character was rather passive ("EITHER THE MOST EXASPERATING SAP OR A POTENTIAL PROSTITUTE"), underdressed and not a star role, but exaggerates this and seems to see no value added by her performance. "CLIENT… AT NO TIME DOES ONE SINGLE SOLITARY THING WHICH WOULD SHOW ANY EVIDENCE OF STRENGTH OR OF INDIVIDUALITY OR OF CHARM OR OF ANY OF HER ATTRIBUTES STOP HER CHARACTERISATION AS WRITTEN COULD BE PLAYED BY ANY THIRD CLASS LEADING WOMAN." He rightly points out that audiences were unlikely to consider Kelly an innocent or even a virgin if for several months she has been living off immoral earnings. Gloria was in agreement, as far as the costumes went, at least. So far all she had worn on screen was a cotton nightie, a man's overcoat, and "convent togs"—a far cry from her "clotheshorse" days.

Mostly though, Walter is "SO SHOCKED AND SO REVOLTED", in particular by the African scenes. Like so many others, he is disgusted by the marriage of Jan and Kelly, "WITHOUT REVERENCE" at the aunt's deathbed and administered by a "COLORED PRIEST WHO ENTERS WITH VESTMENTS TRAILING THROUGH IMPROPER ATMOSPHERE". Walter finds the wedding scene "IN EXECRABLE TASTE" but what follows is worse: "HUSBAND AS REPULSIVE REPUGNANT MAN ENTERING BRIDES CHAMBER WHILE HE BECKONING TO CROWD OF THIRTY OR FORTY PROSTITUTES TO ACT AS AUDIENCE." It is implicit in his report that this is a scene he has seen as part of the rough cut or rushes, not merely read in the screenplay.

Elsewhere, Walter seems to have little sympathy for how Von's story was constructed and how he was building up a series of comparisons and

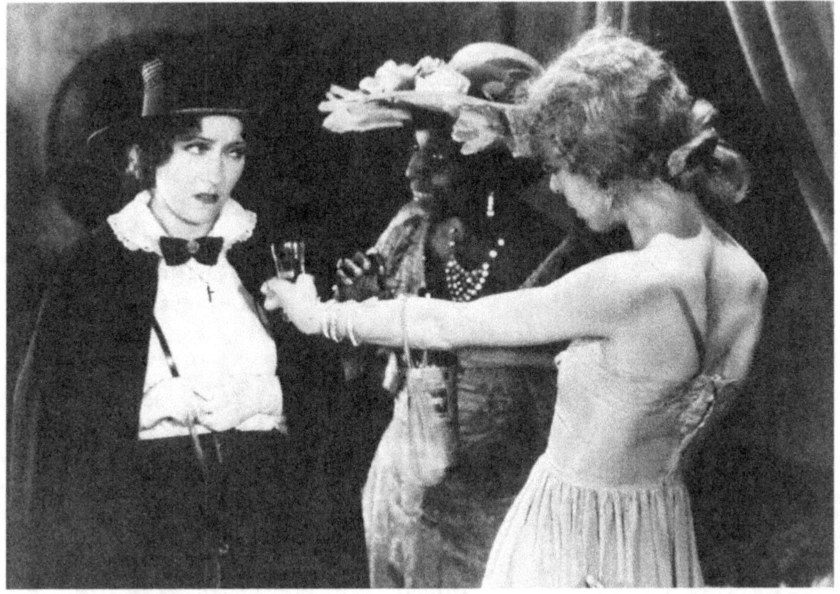

'Magnificent' but 'manure': Patricia (Gloria Swanson) greeted by
Kali Sana (Madame Sul-Te-Wan) and Coughdrops (Rae Daggett) at The Swamp.
Milestone Film & Video.

contrasts: Black and white, European and African. Almost as an aside, he comments: "PRODUCTION IS MAGNIFICENT BUT IN MY HUMBLE OPINION IT IS MOSTLY GUILDING [sic] TO THE MANURE PILE." Walter concentrates on what is best for Gloria as a star, Joe's most valuable asset, and what the Hays Office will pass. He has a suggestion for "REWRITING AND DISINFECTING WHAT HAS BEEN DONE", which Derr suggests adopting: "AT LEAST WE WILL NOT BE CRIMINALLY NEGLIGENT IN KILLING STAR VALUE."

This sounds like the ammunition Joe needed to fire Von, yet he couldn't quite use it that way. Derr writes that he offered Von's manager Harry Edington two options, either a mutually agreed termination of the director's contract or to draft a legal notice saying that Von had violated his contract "IN TIME AND MONEY". Edington requested whichever option was most lucrative to him personally. Derr suggested no further money be sent to Von but that they avoid stating "ANY DISSATISFAC-TION IN STORY AND PICTURE AS YOU HAVE NO LEGAL GROUNDS ALONG THOSE LINES FOR TERMINATION."[11] Joe was going to sack Von on grounds of spending too much money and taking too long, even though his real problem with the work was the content. The implication is that had Joe thought *Queen Kelly* was a good film, he might have indulged a little more of Von's extravagance. But Joe was wrong about *Sadie Thompson* and he was wrong about *Queen Kelly* too. In hindsight, the most efficient way to rescue *Queen Kelly* would have been to let Von finish what he had started, in some fashion. At least it would have been released, in 1929, albeit heavily cut. But with Gloria so upset and the scenes Von was shooting causing such violent reactions, any option seemed more attractive than keeping the director in place. Joe called Von and fired him over the phone.

When Joe eventually made it to the set, it was a heartbreaking scene, whichever account you follow. Gloria was in hospital, according to Joe, suffering from what was "practically a nervous collapse,"[12] having lost a lot of weight and feeling hostile towards the film and anyone associated with it. As Gloria remembers, she greeted him, composed and clear-minded, in her bungalow on the Pathé lot. Joe's first stop on arrival had been the screening room, where he watched the offending footage.

> An hour later he charged into the living room of the bungalow, alone, cursing von Stroheim and LeBaron and Glazer. Stopping abruptly, he slumped into a deep chair. He turned away from me, struggling to control himself. He held his head in his hands, and little, high-pitched sounds escaped from his rigid body, like those of a wounded animal whimpering in a trap. He finally found his voice. It was quiet, controlled. 'I've never had a failure in my life' were his first words.[13]

Joe flew into a rage and embraced Gloria, sobbing. The lady was not sympathetic to the plight of the man who was once her White Knight. She wanted to tell him that to experience one's first failure at the age of 40 is nothing to complain about. Instead, she tried to rally her lover and colleague—the only person she trusted to get her out of this mess.

> 'Don't cry' is what I said. 'We'll try to save it.'
> 'I don't want to see any of them again,' he moaned.
> 'Then we'll do it without them,' I said.[14]

This could have been the fight that ended Gloria and Joe. Gloria had just learned that she had been Oscar-nominated for *Sadie Thompson*, the film Joe urged her to give away, and she taunted him with his lack of judgment. He reminded her that she was in debt to him, for every cent spent on *Queen Kelly*. In desperation, Gloria turned to Jesse Lasky for help, which he could not supply. This act of betrayal, however, caused another massive row with Joe.

Gloria started looking for new collaborators to help her finish the film. She wasn't quite as isolated as she thought—some people were grateful for her decisive action in getting Von sacked; it was as if Patricia had ripped the whip from the Queen's hands and given her a dose of her own medicine. To hear them tell it, Gloria had dethroned a tyrant. A few wags on set wrote her a mock telegram, in honour of the occasion.

AT A MEETING OF THE BOARD OF DIRECTORS OF THE SALVAGE ASSOCIATION CHARTERED IN THE LAWS OF COBURG, NASSAU, TO DO A GENERAL SALVAGE BUSINESS OF EVERY NAME AND NATURE, IT WAS MOVED, SECONDED AND SO VOTED THAT THIS ASSOCIATION IN TOTO AND IP SO FACTO EXTENDED TO THE NEW GENERAL MANAGER OF THE GLO PRODUCT COMPANY, INC. THEIR BEST EFFORTS IN THE SALVAGING OF THE TITBITS OF QUEEN KEL (TO-WIT: THOSE BITS NOT DEPICTING THE INSANITY OF THE DIRECTOR) AND CAN ASSURE YOU OF OUR UNSWERVING LOYALTY IN THIS STUPENDOUS, GIGANTIC, COLOSSAL AND JUMBOAIC ADVENTURE AND IT IS IN OUR BEST JUDGMENT POSSIBLE FOR US TO PLACE IN YOUR HANDS MOIST BUT NOT ALL WET TWO AND ONE FRACTION REELS OF THE FORESAID PRODUCT AND IN THE MEANWHILE MAY THE GOOD LORD HAVE MERCY UPON OUR SOULS.[15]

The note is signed by a collection of Gloria's personal friends and Joe's colleagues—some comically misspelled, e.g. "Josiah P. Kennedy", "C. Bee DeMille" and "Billie Hayes". Barney Glazer was there, but no sign of LeBaron or Sarecky. The first signatory was "Esmond," or rather Edmund, Goulding. Gloria tells a pretty story about him approaching her in Hollywood with an offer of assistance after the film collapsed, but even if that were true he had been plugged in to the drama since before Christmas. Goulding knew all about *Queen Kelly* and had no solution. He told Gloria she should "shelve it". Instead, he promised he could write her a talkie and have it finished before anyone found a way to salvage their "old-fashioned"[16] flop. This would keep Gloria in the public eye and give UA something to distribute in the spring, as promised. But this didn't satisfy Joe, who wanted to find a way to recoup some of the vast amount spent on sets and costumes for *Queen Kelly*—an expense clearly visible in the rushes. As an asset, the film had undeniable value, if only it could be exhibited. To get *Queen Kelly* into cinemas, it needed an ending, a disinfectant, and as the days of 1929 began to tick by, it absolutely needed sound, too.

What did Von say about getting fired from *Queen Kelly*? As little as possible, to the end of his days. To hear him talk about it, you'd think his last day of shooting coincided with the premiere of *The Jazz Singer* in October 1927. He maintained that he and Gloria had always been on good terms and it was the talkies that killed his *Queen Kelly*, with Joe telling him in no uncertain terms that "The worst talking film would take more at the box office than the best silent film."[17] This was another Hollywood battle that he had lost. And he had just one more fight left in him.

1. *SoS*, 372.
2. Slang for a European drifter, bumming around in the tropics.
3. Tod Welch, "Von Schedule!", *Motion Picture Magazine*, May 1929, 104.
4. Letter from E.B. Derr, 5 October 1929, JPK Papers.
5. "Von Schedule!", 42.
6. *SoS*, 372.
7. *SoS*, 373.
8. Erich von Stroheim, *Queen Kelly: the Complete Screenplay*, edited by Bret Wood (Scarecrow Press, 2002), 157.
9. Ibid, 164.
10. Ibid, 162.
11. Telegram from Derr to Edward Moore, 25 January 1929, JPK Papers.
12. Letter from JPK to Henri de La Falaise, 13 March 1929, JPK Papers.
13. *SoS*, 373.
14. *SoS*, 374.
15. Message to GS from Esmond Goulding et al, GSA.
16. *SoS*, 377.
17. *Saint Cinema*, 47.

13
The Misfit

For a little over five weeks, the *Queen Kelly* sets lay idle. Every day until 2 March the production reports offer a variation on "Script work — company not called." A lot of talk and no action. The actors disappear one by one from the call list as their contracts come to an end. Eventually only Byron, whose term had been extended in the autumn, is listed. At $10,000 a week, plus cast and crew salaries, it was an expensive waste of time. In these five weeks, even Von could feasibly have finished the film, had he not been given his marching orders. At least now that Joe was in Culver City he could be more effective at managing the crisis, which largely meant keeping up the pretence that *Queen Kelly* was actually still in production. He renewed the loan and continued to promise United Artists a film for the spring, although Lichtman quite rightly pointed out that tentative release dates were no use. He needed proof that the film would really be available for distribution. Joe also briefed the trades that Von had left the producers no choice but to sack him after he had exhausted their patience and thrown away their time and money.

Soon, however, Joe was called back east because his father was dying, and this is when he finally updated Henri in Paris as to the state of play with Gloria and the film. By this time a plan had finally been formed to complete *Queen Kelly* with dialogue and music at an estimated cost of $225,000. This version opens with Patricia singing "Ave Maria" as part of the convent choir. The story, taking place entirely within the European kingdom, was now a love triangle, with the choirmaster vying with the Prince for Patricia's heart. The convent and palace sets were reconstructed and plans were made to rehire all supporting players who had been fitted for costumes. Paul Stein, another Austrian film director, who was working between Berlin and Hollywood, now under contract at Pathé, was assigned to shoot new scenes for the beginning and ending of the film. According to the trades, these scenes were written by Austrian playwright Leo Birinski, then working in Hollywood at the time. Danish actor Otto Matieson was slated to appear, presumably as the choirmaster. A new release date was announced, in late summer. Joe assured Henri that *Queen Kelly* "is the chief concern now, as there is already over a million dollars invested with nothing to show", exaggerating the figures involved. But he was not optimistic: "Whether it will ever get started, whether it will ever see a finish, whether (when it is finished) it will be any good, I can give you no information whatsoever."[1]

There was good reason for Joe's trepidation. Stein shot tests for three days, and after viewing the footage, Gloria rejected it all. Plus, she hated the ending, which was a fade-out on her sobbing face as Patricia struggled with her choice between two lovers and between the convent and the palace. Joe, who was back on the east coast with his father, called Henri with the bad news: "Picture likely be shelved. Approximate loss between eight hundred and million." He gave Glazer the task of supervising an edit of Von's footage, which would run about an hour, so that he could decide whether to extend it into a full silent feature, add dialogue, or "scrap the misfit".[2]

Meanwhile, Gloria put forward *The Trespasser*, Goulding's quick-fix solution of a fast-turnaround talking picture to get her back on American screens and up to date with the coming of sound. This was a prospect that made Joe cheerful enough to whack his thigh again. "The curse of *Queen Kelly* was removed," recalled Gloria, "and we struck a bargain."[3] Gloria would always be proud of her first talkie, partly because she remembered that it was made so swiftly, in just three months "from day one in my breakfast room, when Eddie [Goulding] and Laura [Hope Crews] and I began on the script, until the picture was edited, scored, and ready for shipment to United Artists".[4] The shoot itself took just 21 days. As per her contract, Gloria's fee was $50,000, the same as for *Queen Kelly*. Writer-director Goulding proved himself a valuable collaborator, even penning the melody for the theme song, "Love, Your Magic Spell is Everywhere", sung by Gloria—who croons prettily throughout the film, reviving her childhood dream of becoming a singer. Yet Goulding had cause to regret his efforts when he realised that all he would receive for his work was his Pathé salary. The song was a hit but he made no money from that either. He and the lyricist Elsie Janis had signed away all the rights—to Joe, of course. Goulding's lawyer, Fanny Holtzmann, threatened to sue Joe, but his response was vicious enough to dissuade them. "You have that Jew girl go after me and I guarantee you'll never be on a screen again. I'll tell a federal jury about some of those wild Goulding weekends and you'll be deported for moral turpitude."[5] Goulding was bisexual and his parties were risqué indeed, but this was clearly blackmail. Not only that, it was rank sexual hypocrisy from a man still intent on selling *Queen Kelly* to the American public.

The Trespasser is a smart pre-Code melodrama, a riff on *Stella Dallas,* with Gloria playing Marion, a Chicago stenographer who elopes with a wealthy young man, only for him to abandon her after their wedding night due to his father's disapproval. Marion is left to raise their son alone, but when their paths cross in years to come, he is married to a woman from his own class who is unable to have children, and Marion knows that she must make a great sacrifice. Unlike *Stella Dallas*, this story has a happy ending. Joe adored the script, writing to Gloria from his train to Los Angeles, "If that isn't the greatest motion picture that anyone ever shot I want to go back to stock manipulation."[6] A few days after Joe arrived in Hollywood to share in the good mood on set, his father died, and it was impossible for him to return home in time for the funeral.

The Trespasser holds up well, especially in comparison to other talkies of the period, with fluid, overlapping dialogue and a fine central performance from Gloria. When it came to showcasing Gloria, it was everything that *Queen Kelly* was not, offering her the chance to play a romantic and noble but also spirited character, a modern and independent woman in a succession of glamorous settings, plus outfits by her favourite designer René Hubert. The film was previewed in the US in July but the world premiere was in London in August, followed by a show in Paris, before opening in New York and Chicago in November.

The trip to the European premieres was fraught. Joe wanted to accompany Gloria, so for respectability's sake Rose had to come too, and they picked up Henri once they arrived in Europe. Gloria brought her friend Virginia Bowker for moral support; Rose travelled with her sister likewise. It gets worse. Opening a cable by accident, Gloria discovered that Henri was having an affair with actress Constance Bennett, newly hired at Pathé. She hit the roof, which meant that soon *her* lover and his wife were in the bizarre position of having to placate her rage and persuade her not to divorce Henri on the spot. As if she needed any extra incentive to be discreet, Gloria's contract with Gloria Productions contained a morality clause of a kind: "The Artist agrees, during the making of said pictures, to conduct herself with due regard to public conventions and morals, and agrees that she will not do or commit any act or thing which will tend to bring her into public scorn, ridicule or dispute."[7] So, ideally no divorce. Still, when they returned from the trip, the press got wind that the marriage was failing, and Henri told friends he planned to divorce Gloria and marry Bennett as soon as possible.

The premieres were a sensation. Each night, Gloria was thronged by admirers who had been waiting a year and a half to see her on screen again. American trade ads boasted of the biggest traffic jam Broadway had seen in years. *The New York Times* raved: *The Trespasser* was "gifted with originality from beginning to end", Gloria's singing voice "was most pleasing" and that she gave "even a better performance than she did in

Sadie Thompson, for here she is more of an actress than ever, speaking lines naturally and without unnecessary pantomimic gestures".[8] The Trespasser broke all United Artists box-office records. Joe, knowing he had a winner on his hands, pushed the picture as hard as he could. For the second time Gloria was nominated for the Best Actress Oscar, though she lost again, this time to Norma Shearer, wife of Irving Thalberg, in *The Divorcee* (Robert Z. Leonard, 1930)—a comparable, but less sentimental film, adapted from Ursula Parrott's hot new novel, *Ex-Wife*.

Joe's name had been at the top of *The Trespasser*, "Joseph P. Kennedy Presents", but he didn't consider it his triumph. *The Trespasser* was Gloria's project, whereas *Queen Kelly* his was, so he still had something to prove. Once the hoop-la of *The Trespasser*'s release had died down, they got back to work. So far $648,611 had been spent on *Queen Kelly* and Joe reasoned that there must be a way to make back some of that money. Goulding, when consulted, reaffirmed his opinion that it was beyond rescue. After he discovered that Joe had stiffed him on his contract, he publicly flounced over to Paramount.

Playwright Laurence Eyre and Laura Hope Crews, the actress-turned screenwriter who had worked on *The Trespasser*, came up with a new dialogue screenplay, the sets were rebuilt as well as possible (for the third time), and principals Owen and Byron were put back on contract. In this version, Patricia is not Irish at all, she is Princess Victoria Maria, rightful heir to the throne of Coburg Nassau. Abandoned at the convent as a baby, she took the name of the Father Kelly who raised her. Still, the last line is "No—just Kelly!" There were no African scenes, but in September Scollard had finally arranged to take delivery of the Johnsons' East African footage—presumably because it had already been paid for and they might be able to sell it on to a third party, possibly even Von, for his swamp film. This version uses as many of Von's existing European scenes as possible and weaves in a story of civil unrest, with Gloria's character joining the mob, led by a poet, intent on enacting a bloody revolt against Queen Regina and her oppressive bread tax: a fine sentiment for American audiences waking up to the aftermath of October's Wall Street Crash. One can only imagine what such committed capitalists as Joe and Gloria thought of such eruptions of bolshiness, however. The romance between Kelly and Wolfram stays largely the same, with the wish on the new hay, and the whipping scene. When the Queen announces her wedding to the Prince, Kelly tears down the proclamations posted around town, and after she and Wolfram declare their love, he is arrested. Deathbed confessions reveal that Kelly is the true Queen, Regina the imposter, and so the people liberate the Prince from prison. In the grand finale, the lovers embrace as the people sing their national anthem.

The director of this version may have been more keen on the story of workers revolting against a royal terror. The third director to tackle *Queen Kelly* had an impressive pedigree. Polish filmmaker Richard Boleslawski, or "Boley" as he signed himself, had studied drama under Konstantin Stanislavski in Moscow before the war, and in 1922 he and Russian actress Maria Ouspenskaya started teaching his system in New York to students including Lee Strasberg and Stella Adler, later to make Method Acting famous in America. *Queen Kelly* would be his first directing assignment in Hollywood. At the start of December, Boleslawski started shooting tests, rehearsing and ordering new actors: village "fogies" and zealots to fill the "den of patriots". Zuro was leading choir practice.

Almost immediately, Joe and his team were distracted by a tragedy in New York: a fire at Pathé's Manhattan studio resulting in ten deaths and multiple injuries. The studio closed for business for the foreseeable future. Back in Hollywood, on 12 December, a year since the first crisis in *Queen Kelly*'s production, shooting slowed to a standstill once again. "The new scenes didn't look like Von Stroheim's work or have the same mood or texture," recalled Gloria. "The actors, too, were responding differently to Boleslawski; they seemed like different people. Even the sets clashed."[9] Von's work was of such a high standard and distinctive style that he was, essentially, irreplaceable.

Boleslawski sincerely wanted to match his predecessor's production values and wasn't keen to compromise; he could sound a lot like Von when he started arguing. When Joe asked for cheaper set dressings, Boleslawski conceded that "the picture is yours and you may do as you like" but argued: "There are certain high spots that you rely on me to make effective and prominent." Overuse of the existing Poto-Poto street set in various scenes would, he said "make everyone sick". He continued: "I would rather give up entirely the mad scene with Swanson in the woods than do it in front of two lousy tree trunks." Furthermore, Boleslawski said that a quality result would require a 28-day, not a 21-day, shooting schedule, "to get good angles, good performance, and smooth running tempo".[10] Joe may have been trying to complete an epic melodrama but he wanted to do it on the cheap. Boleslawaski's arguments fell on deaf ears.

Joe called off the shoot and sent the cast home. He wrote to Henri: "KELLY STARTED AND STOPPED AGAIN AFTER THREE DAYS GYPSY CURSE STILL ON IT."[11] He finally admitted to UA that they would have to cancel the *Queen Kelly* distribution contracts "because of the failure of the producer to deliver". Still, the *Queen Kelly* company still did not give up. Ted O'Leary suggested a little slapstick might jazz up the picture. Boleslawski, who described himself as being in a "fighting spirit", tried to persuade Joe that he could finish the film, presenting a new, streamlined scenario, "a conventional story", which would be the "cheapest solution".[12] What he didn't know was that Joe had now decided that the film should instead be a "musical operetta" with songs by Vincent Youmans, the Broadway composer of such toe-tappers as "Tea for Two".

To shoot this new version, Joe wanted to hire Sam Wood, a notably efficient director of comedies and romantic dramas, from MGM, which meant negotiating with Thalberg. He had been talking to Wood since October. He had written a treatment, with Delmer Daves, that would become the Eyre-Crews screenplay. Joe and Gloria lovebombed Thalberg, pointing out how "enthusiastic" Wood was to work with Gloria again and how imperative it was to finish *Queen Kelly*, and that Wood could be all wrapped and ready to go back to MGM in February. Gloria, who had worked with Wood when he was DeMille's assistant and again when he was directing at Paramount at the start of the decade, believed in his ability to get the job done, but held him in little esteem. "Sam Wood was all right, but he was a real estate dealer at heart," she later wrote. "There was nothing of the temperamental artist about him." "We had been grinding out pictures since *The Great Moment* [1921], and each one was worse than the last. The only thing that changed was the number and the length of dresses I wore and the face of the leading man."[13] In any event, MGM would not loan Wood except at a high price, and even then not until April. Another dead end.

Gloria asked Allan Dwan whether he could help, but he pronounced himself stumped by the project. After hours spent studying the various screenplays, Dwan told Joe: "I can't quite get the story line. It's either the story of a nun who turned whore or a whore who turned nun and I can't figure out which it is. But it's one or the other and in any case, it stinks."[14]

Before the decision to make the film a full musical, Joe's team had been trying to find a composer to write a theme song, "with a martial strain", that might not be sung by Gloria herself, but would appear on the soundtrack and could be sold as a promotional tie-in. At one point Irving Berlin was interested, and Irving Bibo submitted a song called "Patsy Kelly". But once Joe had decided on the operetta style, he had grander aspirations. In a fit of hubris he tried to hire none other than Franz Lehár, Austro-Hungarian composer of popular operettas, including *The Merry Widow*. Joe tasked Henri with commissioning "A GREAT WALTZ" from Lehár, apparently unbothered by the fact that American moviegoers most associated the man's music with Von's biggest box-office hit, made for Thalberg and MGM. Another heist by Joe, trying to retrofit one of Von's movies as a talkie, without his involvement, but with the support of his nemesis Thalberg. In this new version, the Prince embarks on "a wild debauch with the girls from the

Vienna opera troupe"[15]—a scene that could have been written for Von to shoot.

Henri, on the ground in Europe, conducted the Lehár negotiations and a set of very different talks with Gloria. He wrote to Gloria to formally end their marriage, saying chivalrously that "The fire has burnt the beautiful temple that was our love. We thought it was built of marble, and we wake up to find it has crumbled like the dust of clay. Little can be saved out of the burning ashes. But let's try and preserve our sweet friendship, our regard for each other, our decency!"[16] Gloria was gratified that he didn't mention her infidelity, and in her memoir she returns the favour by asserting that his romance with Bennett did not start until after this letter was sent. Still, she was distraught to think that her marriage with Henri was over because of her dalliance with Joe. "I would always love this handsome marquis; indeed, loved him more even then, at that moment, than I could ever love the man on whose account we were separating."[17]

Notwithstanding the sad demise of the de La Falaise marriage, the Lehár deal—the last effort to complete *Queen Kelly* as a film of grand stature and a possible masterpiece—had to be completed. On Boxing Day, Gloria cabled Lehár saying, "I HAVE ALWAYS BEEN A GREAT WORSHIPPER OF YOUR MUSIC AND I DEEM IT A GREAT HONOR TO BE ASSOCIATED WITH YOU IN THIS ENTERPRISE."[18] The following day Lehár signed a contract with Gloria Productions to write the waltz, for 11,000 Marks in two instalments, and wrote back to Gloria requesting "AS YOUR ADMIRER A PHOTO OF YOURSELF".[19] Sadly, Gloria Productions did not continue to treat the maestro with such reverence.

In early January 1930, Henri and United Artists' Berlin press agent Curt Melnitz held a press conference in the Hotel Bristol where they announced that Lehár had been blown away by Gloria's voice in *The Trespasser* and that was what inspired him to write a full score for *Queen Kelly*. In fact, Lehár had not even seen *The Trespasser*, and was only contracted to write one waltz. When Lehár discovered that these ludicrous words had been placed in his mouth, he threatened to pull out of the contract. He also objected to Youmans writing the score, doubtless offended by the mismatch in musical styles, and by the start of March he was still waiting for a synopsis of the film. Henri did his best to talk him out of walking away, but in the ensuing weeks a series of chaotic cables crossed the Atlantic between Henri and Joe's office. By the time Lehár delivered the waltz, in the middle of March, Joe had finally decided that he no longer wanted it.

More than a month later the illustrious composer was still waiting for any kind of acknowledgment from his Hollywood colleagues. Joe's team were too busy debating how they could repurpose this music that they forgot to write back and say thank you. As soon as they received Lehár's nudge, Joe decided the music was unsatisfactory and they wondered if he could be persuaded to improve it? At least they had paid him his 11,000 Marks—another $2,600 or so on the *Queen Kelly* account. As late as September, Joe would be trying to earn that money back by (unsuccessfully) asking Berlin to write lyrics for the waltz so it could be released as a standalone song. By then the film it was commissioned for was stone cold. On 12 March 1930, *Variety* reported that work on *Queen Kelly* "will not be resumed despite the production cost estimated at $800,000 to date".[20] The actual figure, according to Joe's accounts, was $781,005.90 (nearly $15.2 million today).

It's all too easy to see why Gloria doesn't mention the Lehár debacle and the final demise of *Queen Kelly* in her memoir. Her third marriage, her true love match, was over, and she was feeling bereft and stressed. Her children had been sick with strep throat and Brother had been in hospital to have his tonsils out. Goulding had left, and Joe, whom she had relied on for business support and constant adoration, was finally cooling their affair. Between the coming of sound, the collapse of *Queen Kelly* and the devastating studio fire, the film industry looked less and less appealing to Joe. He was making his final moves to exit the business for good. And that meant departing from his affair with a movie star, especially one who was no longer safely married. In the end, his family always came first, which meant his marriage to Rose.

Gloria's only distraction was that she was busy shooting another talkie. *What a Widow!* was a musical comedy co-starring Lew Cody and Owen Moore, with songs by Youmans, and directed reluctantly by Dwan. Joe was keen on this project, but few people shared his enthusiasm, and Gloria suggested that it was the reason for her affair with Joe finally ending. Playwright Sidney Howard, a Pulitzer laureate who would go on to write the screenplay for *Gone with the Wind* (Victor Fleming, 1939), came up with the title and Joe sent him a Cadillac as an extremely lavish way to say thank you. Gloria was shocked to discover that this extravagance, in Joe's name, had been billed to her personal account. When she challenged Joe over dinner at his Rodeo Drive house, he simply clammed up and left the room. Joe wasn't about to explain himself and she never heard from him again. It's a good story, and essentially correct, but the truth is more complex.

It was while filming *What a Widow!*, as Joe was preparing to exit Pathé, that Gloria and Joe began to fall out and her accountant Irving Waykoff started to piece together what had been going on. Rumours went around the set that Gloria Productions was getting a preferential deal from Pathé because of her relationship with the boss. The reverse was true. Gloria belatedly discovered that Pathé had billed Gloria Productions for all kinds of unwarranted charges, including for salaries of people who may or may not have been working on her films, for hugely elevated studio costs, for accommodating Joe's men in Los Angeles whenever they visited, and—ouch—$19,000 for the bungalow Gloria thought was a token of Joe's love. Gloria Productions had been propping up Pathé's finances, while she was paid $50,000 a movie and now she had to pay back the loans Joe had taken out, with interest. Once Joe's team was caught in the act, Pathé backed off and agreed to write off all outstanding contested bills in exchange for keeping the sets already built at Pathé. The studio had already pressed Von's Poto-Poto saloon set into service as the barroom backdrop for the sleazy but accomplished pre-Code drama *Her Man* (Tay Garnett, 1930), set in Havana. Still, Gloria was in a financial bind. All the money made from *The Trespasser* went to pay debts, and still more was owing. Losing Henri had left her heartsick, but the end of her affair with Joe made her furious. Over the course of 1930 Joe walked away from Hollywood, Gloria and several of his closest business associates, for good. When B. P. Schulberg invited him to join the Academy of Motion Picture Arts and Sciences in November, he politely declined. "I am now definitely out of the motion picture business."[21] In January 1931, Pathé was sold to RKO and Joe officially resigned in May. His reunion with Rose was cemented by the arrival of their ninth and final child, Edward, known as Ted, in February 1932.

What a Widow! had been released in the autumn of 1930 with a torrent of publicity, but it was a flop. No one deserved a Cadillac for this one. Although the fan magazines were largely kind, Mordaunt Hall called it "more than slightly tedious".[22] After its release, Gloria sued for divorce and Henri did not contest the suit. In November 1931, shortly after their divorce was finalised, both Henri and Gloria would marry again. Henri wed Bennett and Gloria married her fourth husband, Michael Farmer. For now it looked as if Gloria's talkie era was about to founder after one film, and her love life was stalling along with her career. "I was completely on my own again," wrote Gloria, "without love and without security."[23] Nor did she have her masterpiece. After at least two years of hard work, double-crossings and false starts, the accursed Queen appeared to be dead. Von had been sacked and Joe had abandoned the film. Only Gloria was left behind, to pay for everything, and to do what she could to save *Queen Kelly* from the curse.

1.   Letter from JPK to HDLF, 13 March 1929, JPK Papers.
2.   "'Queen Kelly' Cut Down to 41/2 Reels", *Variety*, 24 April 1929, 4.
3.   *SoS*, 379.
4.   *SoS*, 385.
5.   Quoted, Beauchamp, 285.
6.   Quoted, David Nasaw, *The Patriarch: The Remarkable Life and Turbulent Times of Joseph P. Kennedy* (Penguin, 2015), 143.
7.   JPK Papers.
8.   Mordaunt Hall, "The Screen", *New York Times*, 2 November 1929, 14.
9.   *SoS*, 396.
10. Letter Richard Boleslawski to JPK, 3 December 1929, JPK Papers.
11. Letter JPK to HDLF, 14 December 1929, JPK Papers.
12. Letter Richard Boleslawski to JPK, 19 December 1929, JPK Papers.
13. *SoS*, 172; 192.
14. Quoted, Koszarski, 256.
15. *Queen Kelly* synopsis, JPK Papers.
16. *SoS*, 399.
17. *SoS*, 400.
18. Cable, GS to Franz Lehár, 26 December 1929, JPK Papers.
19. Cable, Franz Lehár to GS, 31 December 1929, JPK Papers.
20. "$800,000 'Queen' scrapped by Kennedy", *Variety*, 12 March 1930, 4.
21. *Hostage to Fortune*, 90.
22. Mordaunt Hall, "The Screen", *New York Times*, 4 October 1930, 15.
23. *SoS*, 404.

14
The Yank

The "*Queen Kelly* yank" is as excruciating as it sounds. In *Final Cut*, producer Steven Bach's blow-by-blow account of the making of *Heaven's Gate* (1980), the epic Western that brought down United Artists, he describes a point in the shoot when director Michael Cimino was ten days behind schedule, having shot just over half a page of the script a day. Bach and his studio colleagues were freaking out. They called a conference to discuss their options. The first option Bach named after *Cleopatra* (Joseph L. Mankiewicz, 1963), the historical epic starring Elizabeth Taylor and Richard Burton: "Let the production run its course and hope for the best." This was unacceptable to everyone. The second was a more recent reference, the *Apocalypse Now* (Francis Ford Coppola, 1979) option: "Try to control and contain it and thus minimize the overages."[1] This was the option Bach and his team chose, because the third, unthinkable option, which was named for *Queen Kelly*, was to pull the plug. This one "was most difficult to discuss because mere mention of it seemed to curse the project".[2] Indeed, Bach and his colleagues could only guess at how much it would cost. But in time, as delays increased and production expenses continued to rise, Bach had cause to regret opting for "containment" over "the painful but definitive *Queen Kelly* yank".[3]

The question remains: what were the reasons for the original "yank"? When is a film deemed to be unsalvageable, and why? Specifically, why in 1929 were Joe and Gloria unable to keep Von on for a few more weeks to make the masterpiece they all wanted? And why in 1930 did it all come to a shuddering halt?

Gloria's official line, that she walked off set when she realised that Von was shooting a story that she hadn't sanctioned, one that would never pass the Hays Office, has a firm foundation. "It was in a dance hall, but when he got to shooting it it was obviously not just a dance hall," she told Kevin Brownlow. "I was responsible for the money; it had cost $600,000 up to date and he had 20,000ft of film and we'd only shot one third of it. I was a little worried. I just walked off the set one day—a set which was obviously getting out of hand."[4] But this story still doesn't entirely hold water. It's true that the set for the African scenes, the establishment at Poto-Poto Gasse #69,[5] was clearly a bordello, and Von was adding obscene scenes and gestures to the screenplay as he went along, including Wolfram sniffing the underwear and Jan drooling tobacco juice on Patricia's hand. Yet from the first inkling that Joe and Gloria had of the scenario, and in every subsequent draft of screenplay, it is obvious that the African setting includes a brothel, that Jan is a degenerate, and Queen Kelly a madam. Furthermore, Kelly is a fierce businesswoman running a house staffed by girls who have sex with sailors for money. She is not a fallen woman, like Janet Gaynor's waif in *Street Angel*, or even a "tart with a heart", like Gloria's own Sadie Thompson. She has been forced into the position, but Von's conception of her exemplified strength and ruthlessness, not tragedy and fear.

All of which means that at some point Gloria and Joe believed that they could sneak this story of a convent girl becoming a madam, and a palace full of dissolute royals, past the Hays Office, and were at least prepared to try — even if it meant sacrificing a few scenes to the scissors. Far from being shocked by the story that Von was shooting, they had been calculating ways to smuggle it onto the screen, just as Gloria had with *Sadie Thompson*. This was a big gamble. *Queen Kelly* featured one of Hollywood's biggest stars and one of its most renowned directors, plus it had a distribution deal with UA. It is very plausible, however, that Gloria felt overwhelmed by the challenge, as well as personally disturbed by shooting some of Von's more violent and grotesque scenes, including the wedding night. As she said to Brownlow: "There had been a couple of days when I had watched with some trepidation and I thought, 'Oh well, maybe we can get around this by trying to cut it,' but this particular morning it was too much for me to take — because I knew it would be on the cutting-room floor."[6] By the time that Gloria walked off the set she likely felt that carrying on with the original story or reworking it entirely were both equally daunting options. Walter suggested that if the film were to be saved it would need to be disinfected, which would mean completely changing story and characters, which the team had been committed to for almost a year.

Other factors that made *Queen Kelly* controversial. Von and Gloria weren't just pushing at Hollywood's sexual boundaries, but its racial limits too. *Queen Kelly* might have been part of a shift in representation in American cinema, had it been released. The August 1929 issue of European film journal *Close-Up* was devoted to what it called "the negro film". Black journalist Geraldyn Dismond contributed the lead article, "The Negro Actor and the American Movie", in which she argued that Black representation in American cinema was improving, with a diminished use of blackface, and several new films that featured strong roles for

Black actors and larger casts of Black supporting players. It is indicative of the state of racial representation in Hollywood that Dismond largely counts the quantity rather than the quality of roles for Black performers. She mentions *West of Zanzibar* as a film that "used lots of Negroes for the jungle scenes" although it is Universal's *Uncle Tom's Cabin* (Harry A. Pollard, 1927) that she crowns "the outstanding accomplishment of the Negro in the movie world".[7] Dismond believes better is soon to come: "With the talkie, the Negro is at his best." She points to various films either recently released or currently in production, such as *Hearts in Dixie* (Paul Sloane, 1929) and the forthcoming all-Black musical *Hallelujah* (King Vidor, 1929). In this roster, Dismond mentions that "Eric Von Stroheim is working on the Negro sequence of *The Swamp*."[8] Never mind that he was no longer doing so and the film hadn't been called that for a year. The point is that Black journalists were very much aware of Von's film and took their own interest in it, and its downfall.

During pre-production, Von registered his requirement for 138 "negro men and women", an unusually high number for a Hollywood studio film. The casting calls for *Queen Kelly* would certainly have attracted attention among Hollywood's Black community. The trades and entertainment press reported the addition of Madame Sul-Te-Wan to the cast as a named character in January 1929, but only Black newspapers mentioned that one Robert Frazier, with just a couple of film credits, was to play what became the film's most contentious role, the character referred to on screen as "the sky pilot" and off-screen as "the colored priest". His race was certainly an issue for many people. When Joe objected to the presence of a Black priest in the film, Von responded: "The setting is Africa, the priest is a Catholic priest ordained to hear confessions. What's wrong with that? I would not hesitate myself to confess to a Negro priest."[9] Good for Von, however sincere his Catholic faith. Still, *Variety* reported in April 1929: "A considerable portion of the story bearing upon the raw and a racial trend determined Kennedy, when last out here, to kill out those sections he did not approve of."[10]

This story persisted and in September 1929 several Black newspapers ran an acerbic news item from Associated Negro Press about *Queen Kelly*.

The much-heralded sensation was banned by Will Hays, czar of the movies, because one of the prominent figures in the story was a colored priest. Hays, according to the well-authenticated rumors flying around the 'lots,' objected strenuously to the black priest saying it is reported that such an appearance on the screen would affront thousands of decent, religious[11] followers and white audiences. Whether Mr Hays who hails from Indiana and is a Presbyterian elder, as well as a former chairman of the Republican National Committee, knows there are many Negro priests was not explained. He probably would be still more shocked to learn that many foreigners believe Christ to have been a black man.[12]

That last line carries a punch, emphasised by a concluding note about Von, "who is said to believe in strict realism". Could Von himself have started this rumour or did it originate with the *Variety* piece? This story hit the pages following the successful release of the musical film *Hallelujah*, taken by many as happy proof that films with all-Black casts could be viable at the box office. In hindsight that seems optimistic, but such sentiments should have put those who objected to *Queen Kelly's* priest to shame. The hero of *Hallelujah*, played by Daniel L. Haynes, is a sharecropper who becomes preacher and has a relationship with a dancer, played by Nina Mae McKinney—there are tentative parallels between the films. With *Queen Kelly*, it seems to have been the image of a Black

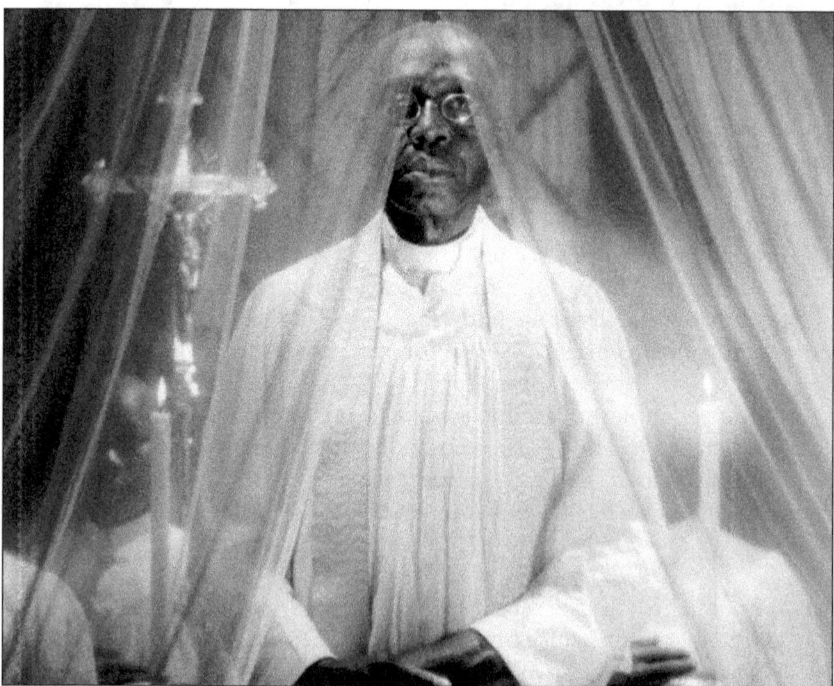

Robert Frazier as the Priest: would his appearance on screen have horrified white audiences? Photograph: Screengrab/Milestone Film & Video.

man marrying a white couple that offended so many eyes, although there were certainly more objectionable aspects to the marriage of a frightened convent girl to a lecherous older man at her aunt's deathbed in a brothel. Hays's alleged objection to the priest's skin colour would have been related to Don'ts 10 and 11: "ridicule of the clergy" and "Willful offense to any nation, race or creed." No matter that any "religious" objection to the portrayal of a Black priest was nothing more than racism.

The Catholic church was deeply important to Joe, whose faith was dear to him, not just for spiritual reasons, but also a marker of his status and, increasingly, for political clout. He was a Democrat, although he had wavered and was about to become more active in the party. In 1928, Joe had supported unsuccessful Catholic presidential candidate Al Smith, after being contacted for advice by Franklin D. Roosevelt, whom he had known since he was at the shipyard and FDR was Assistant Secretary of the Navy. By the time of the 1932 presidential campaign, Joe threw his support behind Roosevelt, despite a few private reservations, with the intention of using such a strategic alliance to move from finance into public office. In this role, his status as a prominent Catholic layman was as important as his track record of success in business. In 1934 Roosevelt made him chairman of the Securities and Exchange Commission, the body that would outlaw stock-market manipulation, and the high-point of his political career came in 1938 when he was appointed the US's Ambassador to the Court of St James's, representing his country in the United Kingdom. In 1961, his dearest ambition for his children was realised when his son John Fitzgerald Kennedy was inaugurated as the 35th President of the United States—the first Catholic to hold that office. As the 1930s began, Joe was working to strengthen his position as a senior Catholic, a man whose endorsement was worth having, even if he didn't always conduct his private life in accordance with this aspiration.

Rose was far more devout than Joe, in thought and deed, and while she had long silently tolerated his philandering, it was in 1929, after the awkward shared vacation in Europe, that she or someone close to her felt the need to take action. Gloria writes in her memoir that in November that year she was brought to a meeting in New York with Cardinal O'Connell, the hardline cleric who had married Rose and Joe in 1914. He wanted to talk to Gloria about "the gravity of Mr Kennedy's predicament as regards his faith". He explained: "I am here to ask you to stop seeing Joseph Kennedy. Each time you see him, you become an occasion of sin for him."[13] O'Connell told Gloria that Joe, knowing that he could not dissolve his marriage, had applied to senior Catholic clergy for permission to live apart from his wife and children, with Gloria. The church firmly opposed this and considered that Joe was bringing scandal on himself by his continuing association with Gloria. Who sent

O'Connell to talk to Gloria? Not Joe, of course, and although Gloria never got an answer to that question, Rose was the first name on her list of suspects. She had remained close to O'Connell and she and the children had the most to lose from Joe's relationship with Gloria. Others, including Hedda Hopper, maintained that it was likely the work of Rose's father, Honey Fitz. "[He] ordered Joe to wind up his film affairs and get out of Hollywood by a given date or certain secrets—still secret except to a few—would burst out into the open,"[14] wrote the well-connected Hopper in her own memoir. There was another incident that threatened to bring Joe and Gloria's affair to light in a way that would have been almost impossible for Rose to ignore.

On Nantucket Sound in August 1929, before the trip to Europe, 12-year-old John stowed away on a boat where Gloria and Joe were having a secret assignation and burst in upon them while they were making love. The poor boy jumped overboard in shock and confusion, but once Joe had rescued his sickly son, a poor swimmer, and settled him down, he and Gloria coached him on exactly what and what not to say to the other adults when they returned to shore. You could say it was JFK's first lesson in adultery—and gossip. We know this anecdote because the neighbours' children talked and the story spread and spread until the White House staff were repeating it to each other even as they facilitated JFK's own dalliances. It certainly could have reached Joe's in-laws that summer. Rose's niece, Geraldine Hammon, claimed that Honey Fitz had rounded on Joe at a family party, threatening to tell his daughter about the affair unless he stopped it. Joe called his bluff, announcing that in that case he would divorce Rose and marry Gloria.

Rose recounts no such confrontations in her own memoir, condescending to "poor Gloria" and describing her as a glamorous family friend, but she does have something quite pertinent to say about *Queen Kelly*, which she described as having achieved "enduring fame in Hollywood as one of the great disasters of all time."[15] "From Von Stroheim's fertile mind came a graphic scene of a convent girl being seduced," she wrote. "And another, of a young[16] priest giving the Blessed Sacrament and Last Rites to the madam of a house of ill repute who was dying."[17] It is telling that she specifically mentions aspects of the story that involved her church—and Joe's. "The personal vision of the story by the great director wouldn't pass the Hays Office and, even if it did, could not be presented under [Joe's] own aegis as a 'Joseph P. Kennedy Production.'"[18] Joe could not be involved with anything that disrespected the Catholic church, and Rose, who was the domestic head of the household, and in charge of the family's relationship with their faith, would make sure of it. Could Rose have put her foot down, or at least persuaded him while they were both in Florida that *Queen Kelly* was a step too far down the wrong road?

In 1966, journalist Florabel Muir, who had been close to the Pathé studio and Joe during the attempts to finish *Queen Kelly*, and claimed to have seen a cut of the film at that time, endorsed this theory. Writing in her *Daily News* column about a forthcoming screening of *Queen Kelly* at George Eastman House, Muir commented that "it's going to be a bombshell!" and filled her readers in on the relevant history. "Realizing the irreparable harm it could do to him as a leading Catholic layman, he [Joe] ordered the entire 800,000 feet of film hidden away in a vault. Truthfully, I thought it had been destroyed." According to Muir, the release of *Queen Kelly* might have changed the course of history—Joe would not have become Ambassador and JFK would not have become president. "And what puzzles me most is—how the heck could George Eastman exhume that old shocker anyway?"[19]

In fact, in 1929 Joe's Catholicism also became an asset to his career in the film industry. The fight for film censorship was passing out of the control of Presbyterian elder Will Hays and into the hands of a group of prominent Catholics, chiefly Joe's friend Martin J. Quigley, the magazine editor, and Chicagoan priest Father Daniel A. Lord, who had been working in Hollywood for some time, partly as an adviser to Cecil B. DeMille on his Bible films. Between them, Lord and Quigley devised what became known as the Production Code, Hollywood's official manual of self-censorship, adopted by the Hays Office in 1930. Joe would have been clued in early enough in 1929 to see the trajectory—censorship was getting stricter, and this was due to the influence of his Catholic peers. Understanding that his position in the industry was allied with these voices of reform and uplift, Joe would have been keen not to be associated any contraventions of the new rules, even though, for a time, studios continued to try to cheat the Production Code, or at least skirt around it. The Lord-Quigley Production Code would be rigorously enforced from the middle of 1934 onwards, following Hays's appointment of Joseph Breen, well known as a "tough Irish Catholic", as the head of the Production Code Administration, partly as a rejoinder to pressure from the National Legion of Decency, a Catholic lobbying group.

By that point Joe was out of the film industry altogether and firmly entrenched in politics instead. He had also made his fortune. In 1935, Joe was worth $180 million, more than $4 billion in today's money, and he had million-dollar trust funds for each of his nine children. Financially he had achieved all his goals, in no small part due to some key decisions he took in 1929. An adept watcher of the markets, Joe was one of the few who saw the Wall Street Crash of October 1929 coming, judging that too much amateur speculation made a fall inevitable. He started selling off his holdings early, then when the crash hit began short-selling—making even more money by betting against the market. While the world despaired, Joe was "whacking his thigh with glee".[20] During the depression that followed, he invested his money into property, blue-chip stocks, and those family trust funds. Did Joe see *Queen Kelly* as another bad investment to be jettisoned, an asset whose value was about to plummet?

For many months, Joe believed *Queen Kelly* had the potential to be a valuable asset, due to the box-office power of Gloria, and to a lesser extent Von, as well as the undeniable quality of his sets and costumes. It looked amazing. But if Von was allowed to continue making it so difficult and offensive to watch, and the Hays Office had to cut it to ribbons, twisting the story out of all sense, then that value would fall—as had happened to *Foolish Wives* and *Greed*—and the film would make a loss. Joe would have known that Von's biggest hit, *The Merry Widow*, had been taken out of his hands. Perhaps he always intended to find a reason to sack him and take control of the edit, as so many producers had done before?

Furthermore, as 1929 progressed, the market value of any silent film was sliding, so while Joe had saved *Queen Kelly* from one commercial disaster by sacking Von, every delay to its release was risking another. Joe fully intended to recoup the costs of *Queen Kelly* from Gloria, but that was not enough. He wanted to be seen as a success in Hollywood, and the success he wanted from *Queen Kelly* was not the satisfaction of a favourable balance sheet but the acclaim due to a man who had made a masterpiece: industry seniority, artistic validation, an Academy Award… Joe was not a man to write off the losses incurred by a mistake to experience, and time and again he had proved his insistence on maximising every scrap of profit from a given situation. It was difficult for him to let go of that dream for *Queen Kelly*, but when he saw that it couldn't be salvaged as a sound film, he had no desire to save it for posterity, to preserve Von's vision or Gloria's performance. When it was no longer capable of turning a profit, *Queen Kelly* was dead to him.

Even Joe, of course, had to face the reality of his first failure. Sales for *Queen Kelly* had been slow, well before the shoot collapsed. Exhibitors never had any reason to believe that it would be ready on time. In fact, the collaboration of Joe and Von was possibly an even worse idea than it looked. Joe needed the kind of swift commercial success that Von was incapable of delivering. And Von, in order to make the film that *Queen Kelly* could be, needed a producer who had the faith and patience to see the project through. Joe was not that man. Gloria seemed to have the necessary faith, but she didn't have the strength or the resources to fight for Von alone, especially not as she realised the scale of the challenge when she was also working at a relentless pace, unsupported by husband, lover or production team—and at her lowest ebb, when she was covered in cold tobacco spit.

There is no way that Joe would have fought for Von's vision and no sensible reason that Gloria should have—not only because of his box-office prospects but because the director was rapidly becoming persona non grata in Hollywood. The coming of sound, with the costs it involved, as well as the intimations of the new Production Code, made Hollywood a more conservative place, financially and morally. In January 1930, Hays wrote to Joe, saying: "There has never been a time when greater care was necessary." Hays was counting on Joe as an ally in what he called "the upward trend of pictures". The reign of extravagant, provocative directors had to be curbed by executives with an eye on the bottom line. DeMille, and especially Von, were in the firing line. They were gossiped about as throwbacks to be put in their place. DeMille was savvy and still making hits, but Von was considered much more difficult to deal with. When Joe briefed the trades against Von after sacking him he further damaged his reputation, and in so doing diminished the value of *Queen Kelly*.

By the time that Joe and Gloria gave up on *Queen Kelly*, it was because they had made the decision that the film no longer had any marketable or artistic value. In truth, that was the case from the moment they fired Von—the one person who could have completed *Queen Kelly* and saved it for posterity, if not for the audiences of 1929.

1. Steven Bach, *Final Cut: Dreams and Disaster in the Making of Heaven's Gate* (Jonathan Cape, 1985), 239.
2. *Final Cut*, 241.
3. *Final Cut*, 252.
4. Transcript of Swanson's interview with Kevin Brownlow for *The Parade's Gone By*, GSA.
5. All of Von's brothels have 69 in their address. If you don't know why, you are probably too innocent to be reading this book.
6. Transcript of Swanson's interview with Kevin Brownlow for *The Parade's Gone By*, GSA.
7 Geraldyn Dismond, "The Negro Actor and the American Movie", *Close-Up*, August 1929, 93.
8 Ibid., 95.
9. Herman G. Weinberg, "Coffee, brandy and cigars (XX)", *Film Culture*, Winter 1955, 27.
10. "'Queen Kelly' Cut Down to 41/2 Reels", *Variety*, 24 April 1929, 4.
11. *The New York Age* sardonically added a [sic] after the word "religious".

12. "Will Hays Bars Movie With Colored Priest", *The St Louis Argus*, 13 September 1929, 5, and various others.
13. *SoS*, 394.
14. Hedda Hopper, *From Under My Hat* (Doubleday, 1952), 169.
15. *Times to Remember*, 175-6.
16. Hardly young. One assumes Rose had not watched the film too carefully.
17. Ibid, 176.
18. Ibid, 177.
19. Florabel Muir, "Gloria Glorified", *Daily News*, 29 April 1966, 68.
20. *SoS*, 391.

15

The Outsider

Queen Kelly was a film made by a band of mavericks and outsiders who took on Hollywood. Out of everyone in that band, Madame Sul-Te-Wan was the biggest outsider, and she likely had the longest memory.

Sul-Te-Wan appears in the final scene that exists of *Queen Kelly*. She plays the brothel worker billed as Kali Sana who attends Patricia's marriage to Jan. In early versions she is Jan's wife. The intertitles introduce her as a "cook" and a newspaper report of her casting had her down as a "colored attendant and bottle washer at the dance hall".[1] Her outfit, however—a long white lace gown, with a parasol, purse and a wide-brimmed flower-trimmed sunhat, plus lots of glittering jewels—is far from suitable for kitchen work. Not to mention her arms-akimbo stance and the way she sways her hips as she strolls around the brothel. Even in the bowdlerised 1928 publication of the *Queen Kelly* script she is suggestively described as "a flashily dressed colored woman" who surprises Patricia by embracing her. In Swahili, Kali Sana means very strong or severe, so if you're really looking for trouble you could convince yourself that Von scripted her character as a dominatrix. In *Queen Kelly*, Sul-Te-Wan isn't filmed like the maids or mammies she played in other films. She has close-ups and two-shots with Gloria, and Rae Daggett, who plays Coughdrops—a tubercular, chain-smoking, tattooed character whose position in the brothel is unambiguous, stripped to her underwear, and jewels. Sana and Coughdrops embrace the villainous Jan and share a toast "to crime! And many of 'em!" Their contribution to the wedding involves improvising a bridal veil from a mosquito net, not baking a cake.

Sul-Te-Wan was born Nellie Wan in Louisville, Kentucky, in 1873, to a former slave and a Hindu minister, who perhaps had mixed Indian and Hawaiian heritage. She began her career in the theatre as a girl, doing laundry for white actresses; she imitated their style and eventually won a talent contest. When she went on stage as an adult, she called herself Creole Nell. Throughout her career she would trade on her own ethnic ambiguity to play a wider variety of roles—at a time when white actors used greasepaint and tape to appropriate any ethnicity that was expedient—

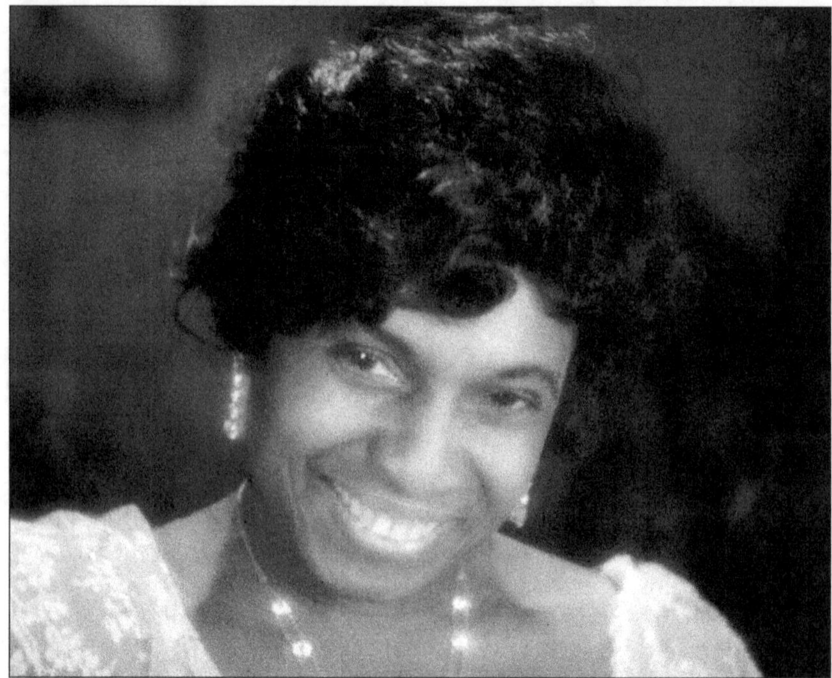

Madame Sul-Te-Wan as Kali Sana in *Queen Kelly*.
Milestone Film & Video.

although Hollywood generally saw her in the narrowest of terms. Her stage career was a success; she even formed her own company, the Black Four Hundred.

She was 42, now Nellie Conley, single mother of three sons, when she became the first Black actress to sign a Hollywood studio contract, beginning a unique career in film. And—of all the films—she started out in 1915 alongside Von on *The Birth of a Nation*. There are conflicting stories about how Sul-Te-Wan caught the eye of D. W. Griffith, but it may have been similar to Gloria's strategy at Essanay Studios. Sul-Te-Wan dressed to be noticed, in a red satin turban, gold earrings and long braids. In one account she introduced herself to the director as "an African queen, East Indian Princess, or [member] of a circus sideshow".[2] However it began, Griffith and Sul-Te-Wan embarked on a long and complicated working relationship. He hired her first as a maid for his white actresses, then gave her a seven-year acting contract. Her role in *The Birth of a Nation* was a wealthy Black landowner who spits at a white character, Mrs Cameron. Reports from the set say Sul-Te-Wan struggled to muster up the saliva, or the nerve, to spit at another actress, and was forced to use soap to make her mouth foam. In any event, this lurid scene was cut as it offended the white censors, but Sul-Te-Wan can still be seen in *The Birth of a Nation* in a variety of smaller parts. This is when she adopted her stage name, Madame Sul-Te-Wan. The name seems to highlight the fact that she frequently played characters with voodoo or witchcraft powers, which may or may not be relevant to her mysterious character in the Tanzanian section of *Queen Kelly*. No one really knows the origin of the name. As her more famous colleague Lillian Gish wrote: "No one was bold enough to ask."

Despite a genuine friendship between the director and the actress (her sons called him "Papa"), Griffith blamed Sul-Te-Wan for stirring up trouble when the film was inevitably attacked by African Americans over its obscene racism, and fired her. She was subsequently accused of stealing from a white cast member to justify the dismissal. A legal letter with the threat of a suit forced the studio to drop all the allegations, and Sul-Te-Wan was rehired as an actress only, with no maid duties. Their friendship weathered this storm and Sul-Te-Wan was at Griffith's bedside when he died in 1948. Her appearance in *Queen Kelly* suggests, but does not confirm, that she kept in touch with Von too.

It isn't always easy to track credits for Black performers in early Hollywood, but Sul-Te-Wan reappeared in *Intolerance* for Griffith in 1916 and kept working. By 1918 she was working for DeMille. In 1920, she appeared in *Why Change Your Wife?*, playing the maid of Gloria's love rival (Bebe Daniels). She also filmed an uncredited role as a member of the congregation in *Hallelujah*. When she was cast in *Queen Kelly*, Grace Kingsley described her as "the noted negro actress",[3] and another paper called her "a clever and well known colored actress".[4] She had a fairly prominent role, well-reviewed too, as Tituba, a slave, in the witchcraft drama *Maid of Salem* (Frank Lloyd, 1937) starring Claudette Colbert. She's excellent, although her character becomes the scapegoat for the village's satanic panic. Even when she took the most minor roles she was part of some iconic films, including *King Kong*, the original *Imitation of Life* (John M. Stahl, 1934), *Sullivan's Travels* (Preston Sturges, 1941) and *Carmen Jones* (Otto Preminger, 1954). She worked right up to her death in 1959, sometimes appearing only briefly in hackneyed maid and mammy parts, and noting: "I'd rather play a maid than be one." Sul-Te-Wan worked as a chorus girl in her sixties and was married for the final time at 70. Just imagine the tales she could tell, if anyone had been bold enough to ask.

Madame Sul-Te-Wan spent three weeks of January 1929 on *Queen Kelly*, right up to the final day of shooting. She may well have been there at the moment the plug was pulled and have her own version of the collapse. Naturally, one would love to know if she really thought she was playing a cook, though perhaps we can answer that question ourselves.

How did she feel about the Black priest performing the forced marriage? That might be a more complicated answer. Absent testimonies, such as that of Madame Sul-Te-Wan, are sadly another facet of *Queen Kelly*'s incompleteness.

1. Doris Denbo, "New Players Added to Cast of Gloria Swanson Picture", *The Los Angeles Evening Citizen News*, 8 January 1929, 11.
2. Quoted in Charlene Regester, *African American Actresses: The Struggle for Visibility, 1900–1960* (Indiana University Press, 2010), 21.
3. Grace Kingsley, "Four more with Gloria", *Los Angeles Times*, 9 January 1929, 10.
4. Denbo, 11.

16
The Axe

Once upon a time, when Gloria's financial situation was parlous, she fell into the arms of a White Knight. Not this time around. At the start of the 1930s, Gloria dusted herself off, reached out to old friends, and signed a million-dollar contract for four Special Feature Photoplays with United Artists. She was soon back to living the life of an international movie star, even if the films weren't always hits. She met her next husband, Michael Farmer, "a moody Irish playboy", when she was in Paris having fittings with Coco Chanel. She fell pregnant and hurriedly married him, first illegally in August 1931, then a few months later after her divorce from Henri came through. They skipped off back to Europe for a break from Hollywood. Gloria later claimed that in order to disguise the pregnancy in her Chanel costumes for *Tonight or Never* (Mervyn LeRoy, 1931) she invented the panty girdle. Their daughter Michelle was born in April 1932, in London, where Gloria was due to shoot *Perfect Understanding* (Cyril Gardner, 1933) with Laurence Olivier, but the marriage was already failing due to Farmer's aggressive jealousy and they divorced in 1934. During this time, Gloria contended with health scares, film-funding difficulties and press intrusion, as well as raising three children and making new movies. Despite all this, she finally finished, and distributed *Queen Kelly*. After a fashion.

Production manager Harry Poppe had written yet another version of the *Queen Kelly* script late in 1930, although it was never filmed. In 1931, however, Viola Lawrence cut a version that ended with Patricia jumping into the river. Gloria then hired Gregg Toland, who had worked as the second cameraman on *The Trespasser* (and would later find fame as cinematographer for films including *Citizen Kane*), to work with her on a very simple, sad and silent ending. "I did that finally in my own home," Gloria told Kevin Brownlow. "There were so many theatres throughout the world that still did not have talking equipment that I directed the scene myself… I shot that."

The new ending, shot on 24 November, replaces the existing African sequence and stays in Coburg Nassau. It opens with Queen Regina ordering Wolfram's release from prison—a scene that Boleslawski may already have shot—on the condition that he marries Patricia immediately and consummates the marriage before "the next sundown". If not, he must marry the Queen instead. Wolfram receives this news in his cell (a repurposed scene shot by Von) and goes to the convent, where the new footage begins. Wolfram is taken to see Patricia who is lying dead in the convent chapel, a set that had been in storage at Pathé since the shoot ended. Gloria presents as the most improbably glamorous corpse, while Byron appears a little changed. "He was so handsome," recalled Gloria, "and during the time I was doing the last part he had had an accident and he had broken his nose. He looked entirely different."[1] Wolfram, in his distress at losing Patricia, quotes the Heinrich Heine poem from their love scene, then draws his sword intent on killing himself, as the camera pulls back and the film ends. Some say Thalberg directed this, which would doubtless have enraged Von. He said it was Gloria, backing her claim. A score was composed by Adolph Tandler and recorded at the end of December. Why did Gloria claim this ending was shot in her own home, rather than at Pathé? Because as the later, bitter recriminations would reveal, she had cause to diminish Joe's involvement as much as possible. He had no wish to be associated with the film either. The title card for *Queen Kelly* features her name three times and Von's once, but not Joe's.

Gloria created this ending with the somewhat optimistic wish that United Artists would accept the completed *Queen Kelly* as one of the films in her contract. In this she was encouraged by Joe, who told her it was the best hope of keeping hold of her UA stock. Such dreams were dashed at the disastrous preview screening in Stamford, Connecticut on 26 January 1932. It was a blessing for Gloria that she was an ocean away. Lichtman reported that the audience were "restless" and "laughed at many spots that were intended to be serious".[2] *Queen Kelly* was now a quaint, silent relic in 1932, the year of such all-timers as *Scarface* (Howard Hawks), *Grand Hotel* (Edmund Goulding) and *Shanghai Express* (Josef von Sternberg). Quigley, co-author of the new Production Code, said it was "tragic to see Miss Swanson in that kind of a picture". *Motion Picture Herald* described the film as "a salvaged version of what probably constitutes one of the industry's most pretentious and most expensive failures… it is definitely 'dated'… Gloria Swanson's efforts may be construed as a libel upon her reputation."[3]

Lichtman's view was that UA should refuse the film, and Joe Schenck agreed, saying it was "terrible" and "entirely impossible to release… We could not even get the price of the prints out of the distribution of the picture."[4] *Queen Kelly*'s value had finally run down to almost nothing. It could only be palmed off abroad, where it could do no damage to star or studio. "*Queen Kelly*, Gloria Swanson's $800,000 tribulation, will shortly go on release for all foreign countries, in a revamped sound version,

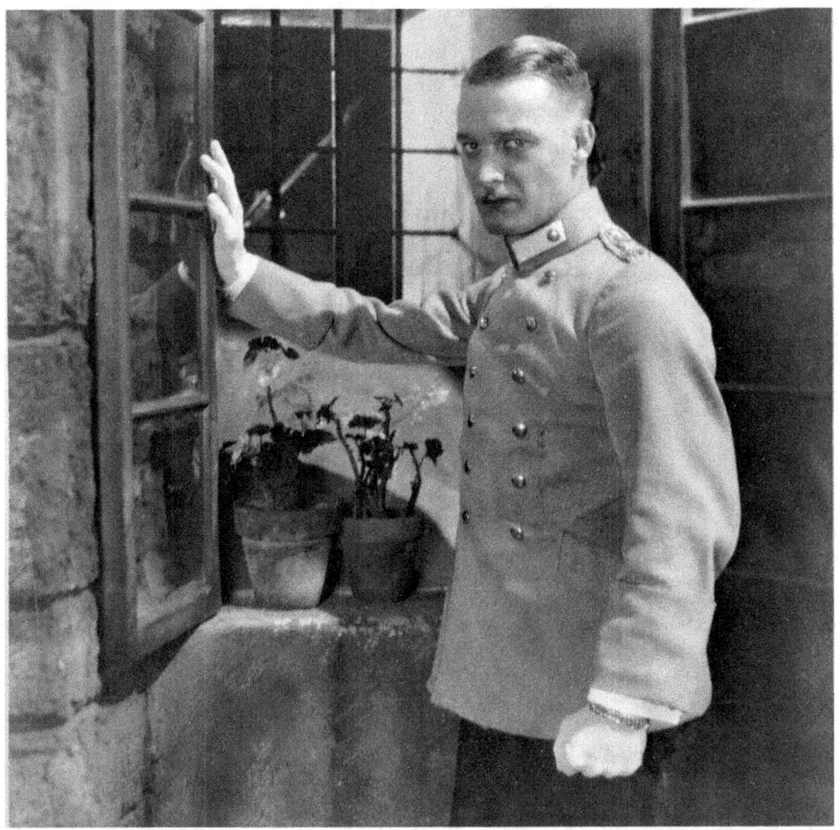

Wolfram in jail, a scene used by Gloria Swanson in her 1931 ending.
Harry Ransom Center/Milestone Film & Video.

with titles to suit the territories where sold," reported *Variety* in May. "United Artists, which will distribute, will not release the picture in the States."[5] In the end, *Queen Kelly*, with Gloria's truncated ending, was given a limited release in South America and Europe. The European release was well-received; a German critic called it "Ein Meisterwerk". Interest among cinephiles was high. The influential Film Society in London tried but failed to secure a screening.

Back home it looked like *Queen Kelly* had all but disappeared. It brought in very little money and Gloria was forced to sell her UA stock to Schenck after all. *Queen Kelly* seemed destined to be remembered as a glitch in Gloria's career, one of many debacles on Von's directorial CV and part of the bad luck that hindered Byron's attempt to become a movie star—if anyone remembered him at all. As the *Queen Kelly* saga had played out in public it could not entirely be entirely forgotten.

Gloria never made any attempt to brush it under the carpet, either. The press largely took her side on the story following Joe's disappearing act and Von's fall from grace, dutifully adding the film to the list of the many difficulties the star had faced so bravely in her career. *Photoplay* ran a profile headed "The Troubles of Gloria",[6] detailing the travails of a movie star, producer and mother. *The New Yorker* had already cooed in sympathy about "the wolf who howls periodically outside her golden door",[7] acknowledging that struggle and strife was part of her star persona as much as glamour and extravagance, or perhaps because of said glamour and extravagance. Gloria was living a lavish life by anyone's standards, travelling, buying clothes and jewellery, and keeping the children in boarding school in Gstaad. If she was reckless with money, she was also refreshingly frank on the subject, joking to a magazine in 1950, "When I die, my epitaph should read: 'She paid all the bills.'"[8]

Queen Kelly became the punchline to a joke that Gloria could tell at her own expense. In 1934, a Hollywood fan magazine gossiped that Gloria was redecorating her patio with chairs and tables scrounged from the *Queen Kelly* sets, with her quipping: "It is the only thing that I have ever been able to salvage from that picture."[9] Sometimes, the joke was more malicious. After the shoot of *Perfect Understanding* hit several bumps in the road, Gloria was less than polite about the inefficiencies of British film production in *Variety*. Fleet Street threw her own mistakes right back at her: "Every time she feels like placing all the blame on British incompetence," harrumphed *The Daily Telegraph*, "she should go down to the cellar and take another look at 'Queen Kelly'."[10]

The Telegraph was talking rhetorically. *Queen Kelly* was certainly not hidden in Gloria's cellar. Distribution prints existed in cities around the world. The world's first film archive was not established until 1935, at the Museum of Modern Art (MoMA) in New York, so *Queen Kelly* had not been stored by a benevolent third party—as yet. Joe had recouped everything he spent on the film from his profits on *The Trespasser*, while Gloria had spent the early 1930s paying back the loans Joe took out to pay for *Queen Kelly*'s costs while seeing very little return for her inflated investment. By 24 April 1935 Gloria had almost entirely paid off those loans; she owned *Queen Kelly*. That October, Joe and Gloria dissolved Gloria Productions on Joe's advice so she could sell Goulding the story rights to *The Trespasser* (he remade it at Warner Bros. with Bette Davis and Henry Fonda as *That Certain Woman* in 1937). Joe granted all the assets of the corporation to Gloria, which left her bemused and feeling slightly patronised, "as if a whole disastrous partnership had never been formed, as if bountiful were his middle name, as if I were a silly child who would forget to tie her shoes unless he left me specific instructions"[11].

One by-product of this dissolution was that the corporation sold the *Queen Kelly* footage to one Walter Futter, who one month later took delivery of "8 reels of negative action and track, and 8 reels of lavender print, action only" from the Consolidated Film Industries laboratory in Los Angeles. The following June he collected "the remainder of the negative action and track cutouts of this picture, consisting of 231 cans of film".[12] Futter got it for a song. Reports in the press varied from $2,000 to $10,000 to $25,000. He actually paid $250, but there was a condition: he was never to use a frame of the footage in which Gloria appeared (it isn't entirely clear whether she even knew about the sale). Futter was a filmmaker of travelogues and exploitation movies who together with his brother Fred had established a stock footage library sourced from amateurs and bankrupts, earning them the title of "the 'junk-men' of filmdom, because they've made a business of salvaging what the 'big brains' of the industry threw away"[13]. In the 1930s Futter was established on Poverty Row, having combined travelogue footage with live-action to make such "goona-goona" exploitation flicks as *Africa Speaks!* (1930) and *India Speaks* (1933). It seemed likely that Futter would be most interested in the reuse value of the Johnsons' Africa footage. After all this time, could Gloria have just sold her masterpiece for scrap?

Gloria's film career seemed to expire around the same time as this sorry deal was done. She had often predicted that a star's career finished around the age of 35, and this proved to be the case for her. After the financial catastrophe that was the operetta *Music in The Air* (Joe May, 1934), in which she co-starred once again with John Boles, Gloria didn't make another film for seven years. Box-office flops were one thing, but it didn't help her career that shortly after she signed with MGM, Louis B. Mayer caught her repeating a horrid antisemitic joke. On another occasion, when Harry Cohn of Columbia was cool on a play she wanted to star in, she hit the roof. "I flew into the greatest rage of my life. I told him exactly what I thought of him and all the other vulgar boors in the studios who wouldn't know a good story if it bit them."[14] She ripped the telephone cord out of the wall in her passion. The story was *Dark Victory*, which earned Bette Davis an Oscar nomination when she starred in it for Goulding at Warner Bros. in 1939.

Having burned her bridges with the movies, towards the end of the 1930s Gloria turned her attention to the business world. She had long been fascinated by technology and wanted to start an enterprise that would connect Jewish scientists in Germany with American labs—giving them a route to escape the Nazi regime and a chance to turn their inventions into profits. Henri would be a valuable contact in Europe. To set up the new business, Gloria had to use $200,000 of her own money. At this point, it seemed that the continued existence of *Queen Kelly*, ostensibly if not actually an asset, was a problem for her tax situation. There was a government lien on any profits that she made from its international sales, so in 1937 and 1938, after her lawyers had received assurances that there was no copy in existence in the US, Gloria ordered the destruction of prints of *Queen Kelly* overseas—in Holland, Havana and Rio de Janeiro, as well as the reels that UA identified as the original negative in Paris. To destroy a film print, or to mutilate it beyond any practical use, a large blade is used to chop the reel in two. As far as Swanson could ascertain, and as far as the American government was concerned, *Queen Kelly* had finally succumbed to the axe.

In 1939, in the first of many twists to this tale, and as further evidence that the Queen could not stay dead and buried for long, Futter announced a plan to resurrect the film. He would remove all Gloria's appearances and tell a story of "anti-democratic spy activities centered in a mythical Balkan kingdom"[15]. The news spread fastest in Britain, a juicy reminder of the new U.S. Ambassador's past as a film producer, chiefly because Herman G. Weinberg had reported on the announcement with horror in *Sight and Sound*, comparing it to the alleged reuse of footage from Sergei Eisenstein's unfinished *¡Que viva México!* in the Eddie Cantor vehicle *The Kid from Spain* (Leo McCarey, 1932). He lamented "throwing the glorious Gloria out completely!" and wondered whether Von would even receive a screen credit. "The films will go down in history as the first art on record that had such a cynical contempt for the creative work of the artist."[16]

Nothing ever came of this plan and no one seemed to remember much of it, except for a columnist called Harold Heffernan. In 1941, reporting on Orson Welles's difficulties getting *Citizen Kane* to the screen, he compared the debacle to the failure of *Queen Kelly*. Heffernan reminded readers of his syndicated column that:

A few years ago, Walter Futter, an independent producer, bought the 'Queen Kelly' negative for $25,000 figuring he could retrieve enough footage to make a feature based on a cowboy's adventures in Africa. He had to give it up. Miss Swanson was too prominently pictured all the way through it. You can buy 'Queen Kelly' from Futter today for $5,000. This unseen epic cost well over $1,000,000. It was, up to now, the most colossal blunder in movie history.[17]

No one took Futter up on the offer. Two decades later, he still had all the *Queen Kelly* material in his possession. At some point he gave it to filmmaker Dudley Murphy (who, improbably, had animated the title sequence of *What a Widow!*), who in turn donated the African footage to the Cinémathèque française in 1963. The rest was lost when Murphy's basement flooded.

Doubtless rising above any and all mention of Futter and his bargain-basement movie pitches, Gloria left Hollywood (but not before throwing an epic going-away party) and moved to New York. There she took up residence in a penthouse on Fifth Avenue and rented office space in the Rockefeller Center for her new business Multiprises. It never became a grand success, but it did introduce a valuable new technique for the manufacture of plastic buttons for clothes, and in the 1940s a couple of its scientists went to work for the U.S. government on the war effort.

Throughout the 1940s Gloria was busy, both as a businesswoman and a star. She returned to Hollywood to co-star with her friend Adolphe Menjou in RKO's *Father Takes a Wife* (Jack Lively, 1941), for the disappointing fee of $35,000. "A comedown as well as a comeback," Gloria told herself, but "exactly $35,000 more than any other studio had offered in seven years."[18] The reviews were kind, with critics dazzled by 42-year-old Gloria's youthful appearance ("she looks thirty tops, in the noonday sun"[19]), but that film also flopped, dashing any hopes of a revived Hollywood career for the time being. She made her Broadway debut in 1945, as Katherine in Harold J. Kennedy's comedy about adultery, *A Goose for the Gander*. The run was short, the reviews bad. "Miss Swanson is a victim of the circumstance that her role is silly, and last evening she seemed to be in a couple of moods about how to play it," wrote the *New York Times* critic[20]. Gloria hoped that her fifth marriage, in 1945, to investment broker William Davey, would enable her retirement, but he proved to be an alcoholic and they divorced acrimoniously a year later.

Gloria was still in touch with Joe, very occasionally, though they had grown further apart. He was deep into his political career, and while Gloria was increasingly advocating for the causes she believed in, she was squarely a Republican and Joe was a Democrat. They shared the same fears when their sons were called up during the war, at least. When Gloria's son was conscripted, she contacted Joe, who was able get him moved to a better-favoured unit. When Joe's first-born son, Joe Jr, a Navy pilot, was killed in action in 1944, Gloria sent him a letter of condolence. Despite the bitterness between them, their affair had been too serious to dismiss. They could be rude about each other to third parties. Joe claimed Gloria "wrecked my business, wrecked my health and damn near wrecked my life". While it's true that he suffered the ill effects of the smoking habit he picked up from her, the other claims are highly debatable. Privately, though, they stayed in touch and fairly friendly. Gloria even exchanged letters with Rose. Gloria's children viewed Joe as a father figure, of the distant but disciplinarian kind.

When a cheque for \$367.50 for foreign sales of *Queen Kelly* arrived in 1942, it was "a pleasant surprise from the past"[21], and welcome indeed. The truth was that *Queen Kelly* had indeed survived the chop. It is very possible that some of those prints ordered for mutilation had never been touched but preserved by archivists for whom destroying film history was anathema. Gloria shortly donated prints to archives, including one copy in 1945 to the MoMA Film Library. In 1948, MoMA started advertising revival screenings of *Queen Kelly* to the cinephiles of New York, first in April, then in November, as part of a double-bill with one of Gloria's old two-reel comedies, *The Danger Girl*.

Before the new decade arrived, the story of this unsinkable film would begin all over again. The following year, Gloria would be reunited with Von, and soon *Queen Kelly*, if only in a fragmentary form, would reach the nation's screens for the very first time.

1. GS interview with Kevin Brownlow, GSA.
2. Quoted, Koszarski, 257.
3. "To Deport Queen Kelly After Stamford Trial", *Motion Picture Herald*, 30 January 1932, 14.
4. Quoted, Welsch, 247.
5. "Swanson's Picture", *Variety*, 10 May 1932, 6.
6. Ruth Biery, "The Troubles of Gloria", *Photoplay*, June 1931 45 & 138-140.
7. Helena Huntington Smith, "Ugly Duckling", *The New Yorker*, 18 January 1930, 24.
8. "Gloria Swanson: What Makes Her Glamorous?", *Quick News Weekly*, 6 November 1950, 49.
9   Jack Grant, "Charles Ray Returns To Films — And Lives A Real Life Drama", *Movie Classic*, September 1934, 78.
10. "British Film Methods", *Daily Telegraph*, 1 April 1933, 8.
11. *SOS*, 446.
12. Letter from R.S. Rodgers to J.P. Curtin, 8 January 1957, GSA.
13. James Cunningham, "Asides and Interludes", *Motion Picture Herald*, 5 August 1933, 23.
14. *SoS*, 450.
15. "Hollywood scene", *Motion Picture Herald*, 27 May 1939, 47.
16. Herman G. Weinberg, "Celluloid Trumpet Blasts", *Sight and Sound*, Summer 1939, 59.
17. Harold Heffernan, "\$800,000 Blunder Looms for 'Citizen Kane' Film", *The Miami Daily News*, 15 March 1941, 9.
18. *SoS*, 466.
19. Malcom H. Oettinger, "She's Blitzing Father Time", *Screenland*, November 1941, 51.
20. Lewis Nichols, "Dead Duck", *New York Times*, 24 January 1945, 16.
21. Letter from Loyd Wright to GS, 12 January 1942, GSA.

17

The Scapegoat

"They gave me a knockout blow in Hollywood," Von told Henri Langlois and Lotte Eisner in Paris in the 1930s, "and I am still a little groggy."[1] *Queen Kelly* was almost, but not quite, the end of Von's directorial career.

"It is so sad about Erich von Stroheim," opined Cedric Belfrage in *Film Weekly* after he was dismissed from the set. "The kindhearted producers have done everything they could to help him turn over a new leaf. When, by all the rights of things, they could have spanked him and sent him home to mother in disgust, they have found it in their hearts time and again to forgive. 'Come back,' they have said. 'only be a better boy and we will let you spend still more of our money.' But Erich seems to be just naturally bad."[2] The May issue of *Picture Play* caricatured the director as someone who "may toss other people's millions away in a panoply of so-called production value" with "a reputation for extravagance and leisure in the making of his photo-plays. Scarcely a magazine goes to press without some subtle or blunt dig at him."[3]

As word spread around Hollywood that Von was out of favour, his peers speculated as to whether he had been conspired against or brought his troubles on himself. There was persistent gossip that Hays had Von in his sights as a producer who defied both the Code and the assembly-line methods of the Hollywood studios, and who had to be brought to heel. Others argued that Von did nothing to help his case. His peers frequently found his erratic behaviour infuriating. Hedda Hopper remembered Von causing hours of delays when playing a supporting role in the Greta Garbo vehicle *As You Desire Me* (George Fitzmaurice, 1932), then serving the cast and crew vintage champagne on the last day of the shoot. Anita Loos, who had admired Von ever since he arrived in Hollywood, was furious about the way he was treated: "Although it was understandable that he might be considered a financial risk, he was regarded as dangerously insane, repudiated, and allowed to go broke."[4] She called him "a tender-hearted lamb who staggered about in wolf's clothing".

In 1948, when Von delivered a eulogy at the funeral of D. W. Griffith, he entered into Hollywood lore one of its most popular axioms. "In Hollywood, you're only as good as your last picture. If you didn't have one in production within the last three months, you're forgotten, no matter what you have achieved 'ere this."[5] With the accumulated disasters in his career and the unmitigated failure of *Queen Kelly* to reach the screen, Von's worth had fallen to nothing.

He found himself briefly back at Universal in 1930, slated first to direct a talkie remake of *Merry-Go-Round* and then instead *Blind Husbands*, for which he prepared a massively detailed screenplay. Carl Laemmle fired him three days before the shoot was due to begin. In 1931, Fox hired Von to write and direct a contemporary film about two small-town kids falling in love in Manhattan, based on an unproduced play called *Walking Down Broadway*. Von's contract stipulated that he would shoot no more than 85,000 feet of film and produce a movie no longer than 95 minutes. Von's screenplay, handed over in August 1932, emphasised the characters' neuroses and was subtitled "An inconsequential story concerning small people along The Great White Way". He chose ZaSu Pitts to star and shot the film in 48 days for a budget of $300,000. But when the executives viewed what he had produced—a film about sexual obsession, deranged minds, suicide and violence—they were extremely disturbed. One studio employee claimed it was suitable only for showing at "a psycho-analysts' convention".[6] Fox fired Von and whitewashed the farrago by telling the press that he had shot too much footage as usual and that the performances were poor, thanks to his direction. Writer Edwin Burke and directors Albert L. Werker and Raoul Walsh were brought into rework the film, which was released in 1933 as the 61-minute *Hello, Sister!*—vastly different from Von's morbid intention, much more comic and sanitised, though with a lingering sense of his ambition and psychological complexity still intact. This strange hybrid film was a flop at the box office and considered lost for many years, but was rediscovered by film historian William K. Everson in the 1970s. After this fiasco, Von never called "Action!" again.

He did, however, secure his fame as one of the most famous and greatest character actors of his generation, in Hollywood and Europe, excelling in his screen persona as "the man you love to hate". Shortly after leaving *Queen Kelly* he played a deranged ventriloquist in his first talkie, *The Great Gabbo* (James Cruze, 1929); he even played a dictatorial Hollywood director, Arthur von Furst, in *The Lost Squadron* (George Achainbaud and Paul Sloane, 1932). He revived his old identity as a WWI German officer on both sides of the Atlantic, most notably with his triumphal performance as Captain von Rauffenstein, the commander of a POW camp in Jean Renoir's antiwar masterpiece *La Grande illusion*

(1937). Legends have been made from less. Partly thanks to the support of Renoir, in 1939 Von came close to directing again in France—a film about the decline of the house of Hapsburg, to be called *La Dame Blanche* but the outbreak of war brought the project to an abrupt halt before it could move into production. Von returned to Hollywood, where the demand for authoritarian German villains was shortly to soar once again.

All this time, however, Von felt that he had unfinished business in the swamp. He was determined to make the story that had fired his imagination, even if it had to be without the rest of *Queen Kelly*. He reworked the African scenario, with a new prologue, into a screenplay called *Poto-Poto*. Its heroine, Roulette Masha, is an itinerant gambler who stakes her body at the roulette wheel in the casino aboard an ocean liner travelling from Port Said to Zanzibar. She meets an American man and they spend the night together, but his wife kicks up a stink and has Masha evicted at an out-of-the-way stop called "Mombasa-Milindi". There she meets the grisly landowner Poto Jan, who makes a move on her but is outraged when she rebuffs him, and whips her viciously. They play roulette and he wins, so they are married "by a negro missionary" and Jan takes Masha back to his plantation in his Rolls-Royce. They are greeted by his housekeeper Bibi. He is bitten by a tsetse fly and falls sick, increasingly distrusting his doctor's treatment.

An American aviator, Captain Tim Hawks, is forced to abandon his plane and makes a parachute landing nearby. He befriends Masha and they fall in love. Bibi and Jan spy on the lovers while Jan plans a horrible revenge. He has Masha and Tim tied to a tree in the middle of the swamp; as the waters rise, crocodiles will get closer and closer. At home, Jan discovers Bibi posing in Masha's clothes and he whips her too. Jan's doctor alerts a local army captain, who mobilises a group of indigenous men and soldiers. Jan refuses to tell them where the lovers are but Bibi spills the beans and Jan shoots her in retribution. Back at the swamp, Masha and Tim are about to be crushed to death by a giant python and are falling unconscious when the search party arrives. To rouse the lovers, the doctor orders the bugler and drummers to make a tremendous racket while he pours hot sealing wax on their hearts. They awaken, knowing they are in love and finally safe from Jan, who has just died.

There was too much plot for a standard-length feature and the events are too outlandish even for early 1930s Hollywood. A script reader commented: "Atmosphere is handled with excellent effect and is the chief value here. The leading character has qualities and some 'business' that sell on the screen; but in the higher melodramatics he is too fiendish to be believed. The woman does not ring true at any point and does not win sympathy either as a siren or a regenerate. It is the 'villain's' story all through, and he has enough color and strength to be worthy, perhaps, of rehandling."[7]

The treatment was rejected, but the villain was seemingly "rehandled", without credit to Von in 1933's *White Woman*, directed by Stuart Walker for Paramount. In this seedy atmospheric melodrama, Carole Lombard plays Judith, an American widow who sings for the leering crowds at the "native café" in Malaysia. To avoid deportation, she agrees to marry the Cockney lecher Horace Prin (a drily camp Charles Laughton, with a lavish moustache), the self-styled "king of the river", who owns a rubber plantation deep in the jungle. He brings her back to his houseboat, where she discovers that he keeps his workers in line by threatening to feed them to the crocodiles. These workers include David, a dashing army deserter, played by Kent Taylor. David and Judith fall in love, and when Horace finds out he terrifies them with stories of the natives' violence to stop them from running away together. Only a new arrival called Ballister, a macho American fugitive played by Charles Bickford, has the nerve to stand up to Horace. When the Malays finally declare war on Horace, following years of his tyranny, David and Judith escape, assisted by Ballister, while Horace dies in a volley of spears.

The play that *White Woman* was officially based on, *Hangman's Whip*, dealt solely with the Horace and Ballister characters and the Malay revolt. The romance, so strongly reminiscent of both *The Swamp* and the 1926 play *Kongo*, is an interpolation. Years later, at a low ebb in his career, Von was working as a staff writer for MGM when he inserted another dash of *Poto-Poto* into a screenplay that eventually became *Congo Maisie* (H.C. Potter, 1940), the second in the popular series featuring Ann Sothern as a brassy Brooklyn burlesque dancer prone to far-fetched adventures.

Von's Hollywood career in the 1930s was beset by troubles. He found all his attempts to direct or write under his own name blocked. When MGM decided to remake *The Merry Widow*, Von thought he was in a strong position to negotiate for a chance to direct or for a greater slice of the profits of the silent film, but he had no leverage and was forced to take the $5,000 fee he had been offered and like it, while Ernst Lubitsch directed the movie. On the home front, things were worse. Von's wife Valerie was horribly burned in an accidental explosion at a beauty parlour, his son Josef fell seriously ill, and his second wife May was chasing him for child support payments. She would take him to court in 1934, prompting his Hollywood friends to hold a whip-round to bail him out. Von, who had been drinking heavily since Valerie's injuries, said the humiliation he felt following this well-intentioned gesture brought him to the brink of suicide. He threatened to kill himself on Christmas Eve.

Instead, Von moved to Paris (separating from Valerie) in 1936, which led to the reinvigoration of his acting career with *La Grande illusion*, in which he transformed his villainous aristocratic officer act into something more refined and sensitive, befitting one of his own romantic screenplays. With the money he earned, he tried to repay the Hollywood friends who had helped him out before he left. That's also when he met actress Denise Vernac, with whom he would spend the rest of his life. When Von returned to Hollywood in 1939, he was to enter a new phase, as a character actor and an occasional comedian. During the 1940s, he appeared in several low-budget films, with the occasional Hollywood hit such as *Five Graves to Cairo* (Billy Wilder, 1943), in which he had a supporting role as Field Marshal Erwin Rommel. "Mr. von Stroheim has all other movie Huns backed completely off the screen," enthused Bosley Crowther in *The New York Times*. "Just as he was in the last war, he is still the toughest German of them all."[8] In truth, Von's performance as the Nazi is the best thing about the film, a fully rounded portrayal of a stern authoritarian, one crack of his riding crop away from full brutality, but with a dash of the humanity that he had brought to Rauffenstein for Renoir.

Von had some success on stage too, playing Jonathan Brewster in the first touring production of horror comedy *Arsenic and Old Lace* in April 1941. When the play opened in Chicago, Gloria slipped backstage to see him after the show. "He looked grand, and we reminisced for hours,"[9] she recalled. *Queen Kelly* voice coach Laura Hope Crews was also in the cast, which perhaps facilitated what might otherwise have been an awkward reunion. Later in the year Von replaced Boris Karloff in the role on Broadway. All the time, every way he could, Von was trying to direct again, but he always ran into a brick wall. At the end of the war he returned to France, where he played leading roles in a series of often troubled productions. He made his way back to Hollywood only once more, in 1949. This was a special assignment with Wilder, Gloria—and the ghosts of silent cinema history.

Von never did direct *Poto-Poto*, but he did turn the story into a novel of the same name in 1933. It was eventually published in French in 1956, a year before his death. Loos enthusiastically bought a copy and found it "overwritten and unreadable" but admired its boldness: "Von was as shocking in his novels as in his pictures, and he was in the vanguard of all the modern writers of four-letter words."[10] When it was published, 71-year-old Von was in a hospital bed in Maurepas, a suburb of Paris, immobilised by the cancer that would eventually kill him. His novel was on the bookstands and *Queen Kelly* was about to play in the capital as part of a 10-day Stroheim retrospective. Glory attended him, but was just out of reach. "Offers are coming in from all over to do my memoirs,"

Von told *Variety*. "I've done about 200 pages and outlined the rest, just scratching the surface."[11] Von had in fact started work on his autobiography in 1950, envisaging four or five volumes; after a year of work, he had got only as far as his first days in New York. Right up to the end of his life he was writing, though, and dreaming up new films. "It's a funny thing," he told the reporter, "I'm more interested in what's happening today and what I may do tomorrow than in remembering yesterday."

Von died on 12 May 1957. On his deathbed he received what was probably his first genuine medal: France's Ordre national de la Légion d'honneur. Despite entreaties made on his behalf by Wilder, the Academy of Motion Picture Arts and Sciences declined to grant Von an honorary Oscar. Dismayed that the Cannes Film Festival failed to mark his passing with a moment of silence, Langlois and Eisner organised a retrospective of his films at the Venice Film Festival in 1958, including *Queen Kelly*—without Gloria's ending.

1.   Quoted in Richard Roud, *A Passion for Films: Henri Langlois and the Cinémathèque française* (Secker & Warburg, 1983), 73.
2.   Cedric Belfrage, *Film Weekly*, 25 February 1929, quoted, *Hollywood Scapegoat*, 77.
3.   Neville Reay, "The Stroller", *Picture Play*, May 1929, 55.
4.   *A Girl Like I*, 126.
5.   Quoted, Koszarski, 326.
6   Paul Rotha, *The Film Till Now: a survey of world cinema* (Twayne Publishers, 1960), 490.
7.   Arthur Lennig, *Stroheim* (University Press of Kentucky, 2000), 336.
8.   Bosley Crowther, "The screen in review", *New York Times*, 27 May 1943, 21.
9.   *SoS*, 482.
10. *A Girl Like I*, 127.
11. "Ailing Von Stroheim Still a Major Figure", *Variety*, 14 November 1956, 2.

18

The Hit

Billy Wilder was beside himself when he cast Von in the desert war movie *Five Graves to Cairo*, his second Hollywood job as a director. Wilder was born in what was then Austria-Hungary in 1906. As a teenager in Vienna, he had deeply admired his older compatriot's Hollywood movies. Although he saw his beloved Ernst Lubitsch seemingly thriving in America, he knew that Von's story was more tragic: a man of immense talent whose ambition had been stifled and his career thwarted by the Hollywood studio system. He confessed that his directing style was influenced by both men: the vivacious and the vicious, the fantasist and the realist. Wilder worked as a journalist in the 1920s and joked in a German magazine that in Hollywood Stroheim was known as Von, pronounced "one"—"because every company can shoot only one film with him, then it goes broke".[1]

For Wilder, Hollywood was a sanctuary because it had to be. He was part of the wave of Jewish emigrés who left the German film industry as the Nazi regime took hold in the 1930s, to find safety and opportunity in America. As Wilder pithily put it in 1945: "The optimists died in the gas chambers, the pessimists have pools in Beverly Hills."[2] The emigrés have been latterly acclaimed for the way that they brought that pessimism into their films, transforming the style and horror of German Expressionism into the shadows and nihilism of film noir. Wilder had a natural affinity with comedy but also mastered bitter films in the noir vein, such as the great *Double Indemnity* (1944) and *Ace in the Hole* (1951), and offered a stark vision of crumbling post-war Berlin, his home for many years before he emigrated, in the tremendous *A Foreign Affair* (1948). He saw the heartbreak that was the flipside of the happy ending and the darkness in the Hollywood sunshine. In getting to know the business, and getting to know Von, Wilder came to understand that Hollywood could be a terrifying, and brutal place.

When Wilder first met Von he told him he was ten years ahead of his time. Von disagreed: "Twenty." During the *Five Graves* shoot, Wilder enjoyed the fact that he had a genius on hand and that Von was bristling with ideas about his performance—that Rommel should be sunburned, but not under his cap, that he should carry two cameras, both with film inside, because "The audience will sense if the films aren't inside, they'll feel that they are merely props."[3] Wilder, although he knew that Von's German accent wobbled, that "he wasn't a 'von' at all and his accent belonged to one of the rougher suburbs of Vienna", also saw that he loved to play the part of a great man. "You could have gotten von Stroheim for nothing to play a king. He loathed playing enlisted men, but a general, that was absolutely right."[4]

Which is interesting, because the next role Wilder had in mind for Von was as a domestic servant. "Stroheim didn't mind playing a butler so long as the character had once been somebody important,"[5] remembered Wilder, and this butler had formerly been a great film director named Max von Mayerling. In 1948 Wilder had tried to make an adaptation of Evelyn Waugh's satire *The Loved One*, a novel about a British poet working at a Hollywood pet cemetery, but he couldn't get the rights, so he and his writing partner Charles Brackett worked in secret on an original screenplay. It was based on an idea of theirs that Paramount had rejected in the 1930s: "Silent picture star commits murder. When they arrest her she sees the newsreel cameras and thinks she is back in the movies."[6]

To protect their Hollywood satire from studio meddling, they told the Paramount executives that they were adapting a story called *A Can of Beans*, but instead they were creating *Sunset Boulevard*, the story of a silent film star living as a recluse in modern-day Hollywood, now an industry pariah, a ghost enveloped in the shadows. Former film critic D. M. Marshman Jr. made some key contributions to the screenplay. Pages went in batches to the Breen Office, out of a similar caution, and while cuts were imposed, the film's dark vision remained intact. Von was cast first, then Wilder went in search of his star, the imperious Norma Desmond. Mae West said no and the film switched from a comedy to something darker. Mary Pickford refused and, according to some sources, so did Norma Shearer and Greta Garbo. Pola Negri said yes but Wilder and Brackett were concerned about her Polish accent. Then George Cukor suggested Gloria. Wilder was more or less instantly convinced. The screenplay had been known as "the Gloria Swanson set up" ever since West had turned down the film.

"She had already been abandoned," Wilder told Cameron Crowe. "She was a death knell—she had lost a lot of money on the Paramount lot."[7] Wilder well knew all about that particular "death knell". He was one of the screenwriters on her 1934 flop *Music in the Air*—his first Hollywood gig and her last for many years. At her *Sunset Boulevard* screen test, the two touched on the subject "pleasantly but not at length", as she tactfully put it.[8] Gloria's impeccable performance at said screen test sealed the deal—and that was before Wilder remembered that two of his stars had been leading players in one of Hollywood's most epic disaster stories and that he would have something authentic for Norma Desmond to watch on her home projector after hours, while her director Max operated the machine.

The young yet already cynical screenwriter who stumbles into Norma's fly trap was mischievously named Joe, and he was played by William Holden, 19 years her junior. Montgomery Clift, two years younger still, had signed on to the role but changed his mind at the last minute—he didn't want to attract attention to his personal life and he was indeed seeing an older woman at the time. Gloria was 50, just like Norma, when she shot the film. If Gloria and Von had qualms about working together again, they surely swallowed them for the sake of the screenplay. Gloria claimed they had long since buried the hatchet but was vague about exactly when this happened, whether before or after she visited him backstage in Chicago.

Gloria hadn't exactly been languishing in obscurity when Paramount called in 1948; she had her own TV show, *The Gloria Swanson Hour*, on WPIX-TV in New York. But she relished a return to the big screen and the salary that accompanied it, even if it was a relatively modest $50,000. She decamped to Hollywood in early 1949 and set about preparing for the role of her life, collaborating intently with designer Edith Head on Norma's wardrobe. She arranged to run *Queen Kelly* for Wilder at MoMA so he could choose an extract, and he selected the close-up of Patricia praying and lighting a candle in the convent chapel. Wilder recalled spending only $1,000 for this clip, which eerily suits the disorienting tone of the film. That money didn't go to Gloria. "[S]ome nut claimed he had a claim," she recalled, "so because of that nuisance, Paramount paid him a couple of thousand dollars just so they could use that shot of me in the picture." The "nut" was probably Futter, although who knows? Gloria later claimed, unconvincingly, that it was a Boleslawski shot, but it is assuredly Von's work.

Out of context, the clip is both an image of youthful piety and of high Hollywood glamour: beautiful but somehow slightly vulgar, as the wax drips alarmingly close to Patricia's fluttering false eyelashes. Its appearance on screen precedes one of *Sunset Boulevard*'s most memorable shots, of Norma striking a pose in the projector beam, after delivering her indelible line about the silent era: "We didn't need dialogue, we had faces!" It's a thrilling moment, a tragic and simultaneously majestic conception of the film star wrapped up her own archaic image, trapped in celluloid aspic. In Paris, the young acolytes of Henri Langlois chose this image of a woman enveloped by her own archive to grace the front cover of the first issue of their new film journal: *Cahiers du cinéma*, crucible of the Nouvelle Vague.

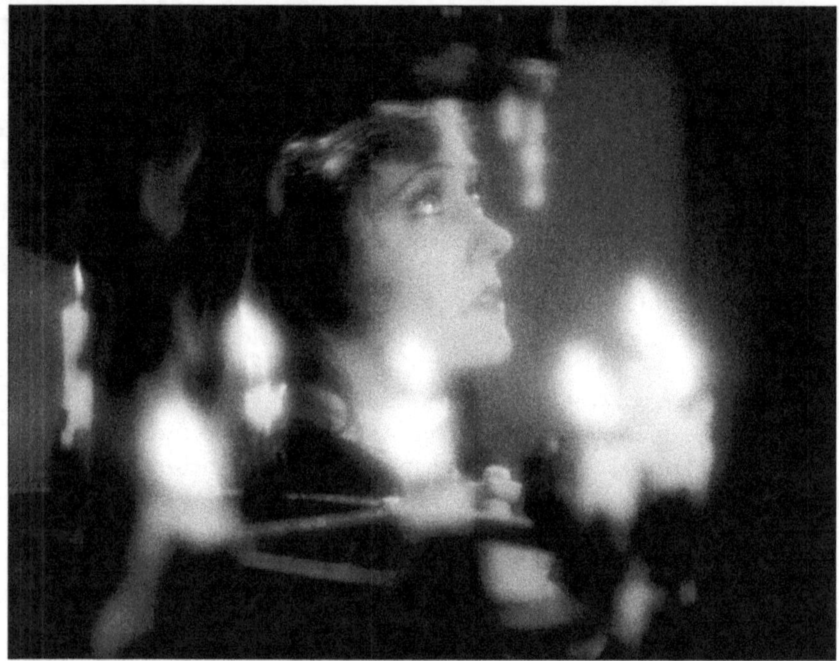

Patricia praying: the scene from *Queen Kelly* used in *Sunset Boulevard*.
Milestone Film & Video.

In *Sunset Boulevard*, Norma Desmond, a faded star of silent cinema, lives a reclusive life in a vast Hollywood mansion surrounded by her own memorabilia and with delusions of enduring grandeur enabled by her butler Max, who was once her director. Soon after screenwriter Joe wanders on to her property, she seduces him into a sexual relationship, making him a kept man. First, she demands his assistance with her new vanity project—not a comeback but what she proudly calls "a return to the millions of people who have never forgiven me for deserting the screen". She intends to write, produce and star in an adaptation of *Salome* at the studio where she made her name: "Without me there wouldn't be any Paramount Studios!"

A visit to DeMille at the Paramount lot brings tears to her eyes, while Max and Joe discover that the calls she had been receiving from the studio weren't about producing her screenplay but an attempt to rent her antiquated car for a period drama. More dispiriting new for Norma: Joe is really in love with pretty young script reader Betty (Nancy Olson). When he finally tries to leave her, Norma shoots him dead and his body falls into the swimming pool. The film is told in flashback, narrated by Joe's watery corpse. The final, magnificent scene sees Norma descending the stairs of her mansion. She is about to be arrested for Joe's murder but in her madness mistakes the waiting cops for a movie crew and the flashbulbs of the press photographers for the studio lights. Her arms outstretched towards the camera, she announces, "All right, Mr. DeMille, I'm ready for my close-up." It is beautiful and awful all at once, one of the greatest endings in any Hollywood film, up there with the desert deadlock that closes *Greed*.

If *Queen Kelly* had been a cursed production, *Sunset Boulevard* was a blessed one. "I shot *Sunset Boulevard* in about 60 days," recalled Wilder. "If only every picture could have gone so smoothly! I wanted Swanson, I got her. I wanted von Stroheim, I got him. I wanted DeMille, I got him. I wanted *Queen Kelly*, I got it. I wanted Paramount, I got it."[9] Von did double-duty, giving a terrifically unsettling performance, in his own clothes, as Norma's butler-director, who is revealed to be her ex-husband, and offering suitably unpleasant script suggestions to Wilder, some of which he embraced. It was Von's idea to make it plain that Max was writing all of Norma's fan mail, feeding her delusion. He also pushed for a shot of Max laundering Norma's underwear, which Wilder rejected. That could have been a reference to *Queen Kelly*. The film was, however, filled with silent Hollywood Easter Eggs: Norma sleeps in a boat-shaped bed from the set of *The Phantom of the Opera* (Rupert Julian, 1925).[10] Her bridge-party companions are Buster Keaton, Anna Q. Nilsson and H. B. Warner, who played Jesus in DeMille's *King of Kings*. Swanson got to spoof the Mack Sennett Bathing Beauties, reprise her excellent Chaplin imitation from *Manhandled*, and remind everyone she worked with Valentino.

Gloria put a lot of her own life history into the role, from the extravagant cars and DeMille's "Young Fellow" nickname to *Queen Kelly*, her complicated relationship with Paramount and even her own insecurities about the decline of her movie career. Gloria later wrote of her trepidation at taking on the part: "I grasped with fearful apprehension… that I would have to use all my past experience for props, and that this picture should be a very revealing one to make, something akin to analysis."[11] Perhaps because of this she must have known that she had delivered her best performance yet, one that would ensure her own lasting fame and credibility, even if it meant yoking her screen persona to the image of an insane, cruel woman. After she filmed the final scene Gloria burst into tears, wishing she could do it all over again. These had been 12 of the happiest weeks of her life.

When the film was previewed to Hollywood insiders at Paramount, reactions were mixed—and violent. Wilder recalled: "I remember Barbara Stanwyck kneeling down in front of Miss Swanson and kissing the hem of her garment in one of those ridiculous adulation things, and Louis B. Mayer shaking his fist saying, 'We should horsewhip this Wilder, we should

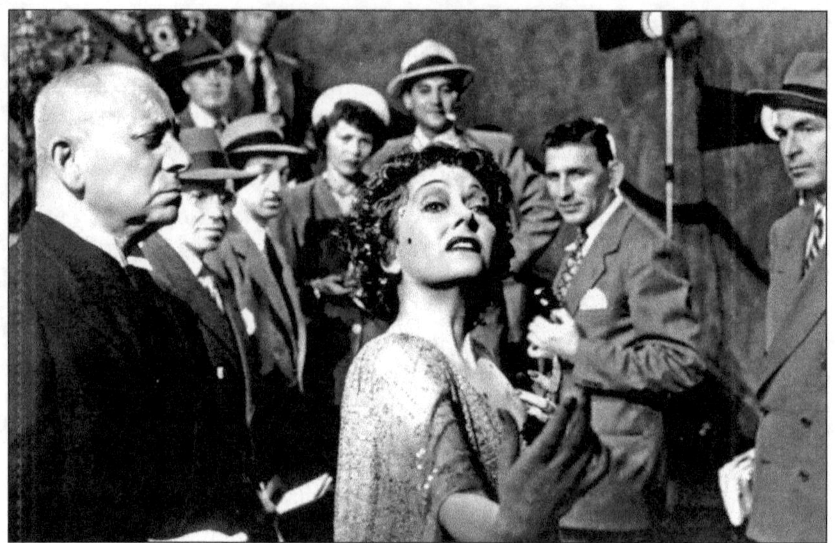

Gloria Swanson as Norma Desmond, watched by Erich von Stroheim as Max,
in the haunting final scene of *Sunset Boulevard*.

throw him out of this town, he has brought disgrace on the town that is
feeding him!'"[12] (Sometimes, when he recounted this story, Wilder added
that he told Mayer: "Why don't you go *fuck* yourself.") Mary Pickford
slipped out of a side door, so no one would see her sobbing, overcome
with emotion. Other stars cheered and bowed in homage to Gloria, which
prompted her cynical response: "All stars feel shaky about their careers…
They figured if a corpse could do it, they could too."[13] The most amusing
reaction to the film on record is one that is surely apocryphal but always
attributed to Mae Murray, Von's temperamental star from *The Merry
Widow*: "None of us floozies was that nuts!"

Sunset Boulevard was a box-office smash and a critical sensation
when it was released in the summer of 1950. "There is no use pretending
to discuss all the virtues, or even all the limitations, of this picture,"
wrote James Agee in *Sight and Sound*. "It is one of those rare movies
which are so full of exactness, cleverness, mastery, pleasure, and argu-
able and unarguable choice and judgment, that they can be talked about,
almost shot for shot and line for line for hours on end."[14] For decades on
end, he might have added. Gloria was a household name once again and
each review of her performance was more adulatory than the last. "It is
inconceivable that anyone else might have been considered for the role,"
raved *The New York Times*. "As the wealthy, egotistical relic desperately
yearning to hear again the plaudits of the crowd, Miss Swanson dominates the picture."[15]

Although Wilder held only brief rehearsals and gave the actors a few pages of the screenplay at a time, he seems to have coaxed from Gloria the most poised and meticulous performance she was capable of giving. Norma is monstrous, but she's also magnetic. It's impossible to tear your eyes away from her and the contortions of her face and claw-like hands. It's a performance seemingly without vanity, and yet Norma, decked out in silk and fur and diamonds, every curl in place and her eyes glistening as sharply as her jewels, is as beautiful as Gloria ever was in her heyday. Here is Steichen's leopardess, slightly dazed, slinking across the cinema screen.

Gloria, who was always completely in her right mind, insisted that she was nothing like Norma, and that's true in all in the most important ways. Yet she too had a terrible temper, and several people acknowledged a high-handed, sometimes malicious streak within her. Louise Brooks remembered a party when Gloria insisted on playing an obscure game that involved blindfolding the male guests and pushing their faces into a plate of honey. Brisk and resilient Gloria had none of Norma's tragic aura, though as John Russell Taylor pointed out in *Sight and Sound*, the mystery of *Queen Kelly* itself is what encourages the cross-identification between star and character: "Virtually the only one of her silent films that everybody knows something about (because it is virtually the only one made by a director who still rates) is *Queen Kelly*. And the image of *Queen Kelly*—for even today few of the people who know something about it have actually seen it—is of dark dramatic perversity in the best Stroheim manner."[16] Gloria's star persona was wrapped around an absence, a cinephile tragedy, and the suggestion of something too shocking to be shown. It's also true that in later projects when Gloria later played herself, as she so often did, she incorporated more of Norma's hauteur and the theatrical gestures—they suited her. As she put it, "You can impersonate Norma Desmond—the character that I play in a picture—or maybe my idea of Sadie Thompson, but you cannot impersonate Gloria Swanson."[17] Tell that to Marion Davies, who mimicked Gloria so brilliantly in *The Patsy* (King Vidor, 1928) or even Daggett in *Queen Kelly,* who flutters her eyelashes and pouts then pushes up her nose to impersonate Patricia for Jan.

Sunset Boulevard was nominated for 11 Academy Awards. It won three, for the screenplay, art direction and score. Wilder missed out on the direction prize and Gloria lost the Best Actress Oscar for the third time. Memorably, Bette Davis, whose success had dogged her decline, was nominated that year for playing another ageing actress in the Best Picture and Best Director winner *All About Eve* (Joseph L. Mankiewicz, 1950). Neither of them won—Judy Holliday did, for *Born Yesterday* (George Cukor, 1950). Gloria had to be content with the Golden Globe instead.

Costume designer Edith Head won two prizes, but not for *Sunset Boulevard*. Meanwhile, Von was insulted by his nomination—because it was in the Supporting Actor category.

Inevitably, the release of *Sunset Boulevard* prompted new interest in *Queen Kelly*. In London, the Film Society finally screened "the almost mythical *Queen Kelly*"[18] 18 years after its first attempt. In Antibes that summer, Henri Langlois' Festival of the Film Tomorrow screened the film to "a packed house", but not before Von insisted on the removal of Gloria's ending ("To make sure, he sheared it himself"[19]). The film was returned to the Cinémathèque française in its edited form. At MoMA in New York, the film played in its entirety yet again, with curator Iris Barry letting it be known it could get a regular slot if public interest was high enough, while her colleague Richard Griffith used clips from the film as part of a "Gloria Swanson Cavalcade", zipping through her career in 45 minutes.[20]

In 1951, Gloria capitalised on her newly restored fame by launching a clothing line called Forever Young, manufactured by the Puritan Dress Company, which was a going concern for decades. Her film choices weren't so savvy. She first starred in a feeble comedy, *3 For Bedroom C* (Milton H. Bren, 1952), as a film star stowing away on a sleeper train with her daughter. The chief attraction of the project was that they agreed to let her design her own costumes, but her soft, romantic character and the gently comic tone are a letdown after the gothic excesses of Norma Desmond and *Sunset Boulevard*. Following this flop, Gloria turned down a barrage of scripts about ageing movie stars, refusing to jump on the "hagsploitation" trend, epitomised by Bette Davis and Joan Crawford in *Whatever Happened to Baby Jane?* (Robert Aldrich, 1962). She took one more film role in the 1950s, in the Italian period comedy *Nero's Mistress* (Steno, 1956), opposite Vittorio De Sica and Brigitte Bardot. It wasn't a happy experience; she fell ill during the shoot and the film went unreleased in the US for another six years. "A great many of my scenes were omitted and those that were in were badly butchered as far as I am concerned,"[21] she fretted to a friend.

Her back catalogue was a better bet: Gloria was honoured twice at the George Eastman House, in 1955 and 1957. Fashion and television took up most of Gloria's time—as did the threat of a looming tax bill.

1.   Noah Isenberg (ed), *Billy Wilder on Assignment: Dispatches from Weimar Berlin and Interwar Vienna*, trans. Shelley Frisch (Princeton University Press, 2021), 148.
2.   Not for nothing do the heroes of two of his darkest Los Angeles films, *Double Indemnity* and *Sunset Boulevard*, die in a gas chamber and a swim-

ming pool respectively. Wilder's vision was too dark for the American audience: the gas chamber ending was cut out of the first film and scenes set in the morgue following Joe's demise in the pool were deleted from the second.

3. Charles Higham, "Meet Whiplash Wilder", *Sight and Sound*, Winter 1967, 22.

4. Quoted, Charlotte Chandler, *Nobody's Perfect: Billy Wilder, a personal biography* (Pocket, 2003), 112.

5. Quoted, Chandler, 148.

6. Quoted, Steven Cohan, *Sunset Boulevard* (BFI Bloomsbury, 2022), 21.

7. Cameron Crowe, *Conversations with Wilder* (Knopf, 1999), 47.

8. *SoS*, 479.

9. Quoted, Chandler, 160.

10. The director who completed *Merry-Go-Round*.

11. *SoS*, 481.

12. "Meet Whiplash Wilder", 23.

13. "Gloria Swanson: What Makes Her Glamorous?", *Quick News Weekly*, 6 November 1950, 50.

14. James Agee, "Films of the Month", *Sight and Sound*, November 1951, 284.

15. T.M.P., "Inner Workings of Filmdom", *New York Times*, 11 August 1950, 15.

16. John Russell Taylor, "Swanson", *Sight and Sound*, Autumn 1968, 202.

17. "I Am Not Going to Write my Memoirs!", 59.

18. "Tying a New Beau?", *Picturegoer*, 18 March 1950, 5.

19. "Antibes Tries to Share Film Festival Spotlite", *Variety*, 27 September 1950, 4.

20. "Swanson Cavalcade Being Assembled by N.Y. Film Museum", *Variety*, 27 December 1950, 3.

21. Letter from GS to Peggy, 26 October 1956, GSA.

19
The Remake

It was primarily the prospect of that heavy tax bill that motivated Gloria to pick up *Queen Kelly* again. When Gloria had reviewed the film with Wilder, she was pleased. "Erich and I even decided it had weathered the years very well, glowed like a classic, and might actually be rereleased, in a version better than the one that had been tacked together in the early thirties for release principally outside the United States."[1] In the wake of *Sunset Boulevard*'s box-office success, the time was ripe to attempt this "better version".

In 1955, Gloria went to call on Von at his home in Maurepas, a visit she recorded fancifully in one of her United Press dispatches (she was writing regular syndicated columns about her adventures in Europe). Gloria paints the prettiest picture, of reminiscing about the "silent but gay days in Hollywood" with Von and his guests. She offers fawning admiration of his past work as a director and excitement about the "humdinger" of a memoir he is writing, but she arrived with a purpose—to negotiate—and writes with another purpose: to promote the forthcoming revival of their film. With a straight face, she claims that Von answered the door thus: "Your servant, Max, has put out the golden carpet for 'Norma Desmond'—or are you 'Queen Kelly'?"[2] Although the shared memories may have been pleasant, Gloria was there to do business. Von had no contractual rights over *Queen Kelly*, having signed them all away long ago, but he felt entitled to a say in what happened to it next. Gloria was keen to appease him, whether out of moral obligation or expediency. Von imposed conditions on any release of *Queen Kelly*: it should only be shown in arthouse cinemas in Europe and Canada. For it to be released more widely, it must be completed, but properly.

In November 1956, *Queen Kelly* screened in Paris, both at Von's Cinémathèque retrospective and for two weeks at the beautiful La Pagode cinema. Gloria wrote a few gracious lines for the press, in French: "In its current form, I ask you to consider QUEEN KELLY as a document of a great era in cinema, a reflection of a past both very recent and very distant, still dear to our hearts." Dear, but not lucrative, sadly. She dismissed the rerelease to a friend as "fussing with the old pictures

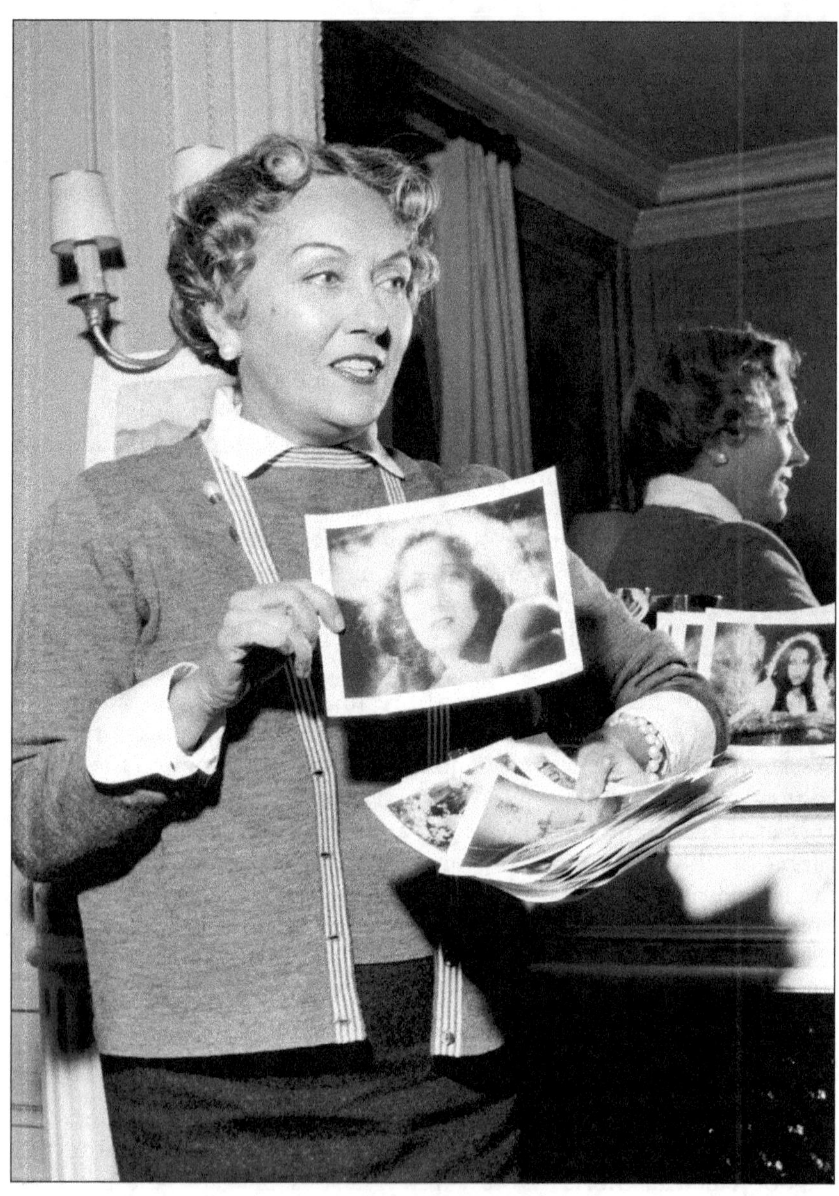

Gloria Swanson retells the *Queen Kelly* saga at a screening in Paris in 1956.
Everett Collection.

opening in a few little art theatres—nothing of any importance"[3], but the truth is that Gloria was severely disappointed with the poor financial return. She made a profit of just a few hundred dollars, 25% of which was guaranteed to Von. She had hoped for thousands. Demand for tickets was high and reports suggest that many of the Pagode screenings were full. "[T]he film held the audience firmly," wrote Hollywood publicist Herb Sterne to Gloria after attending two showings. "I became quite moist-eyed."[4] Gloria's lawyer, Lawrence Siegel, offered a handful of excuses for the poor returns, including a police blockade of local streets due to fears of protests connected to the Hungarian uprising and the increased price of fuel during the Suez Crisis. But reviews were good and cinemas in other European countries expressed an interest. Gloria wasn't bothered. She pulled the film from release in favour of a more interesting option.

In June 1956, Gloria and Von were talking seriously about the possibility of the better version of *Queen Kelly*, a full feature, with Von promising to send her "the basic outline of what I think the 2nd part should be".[5] They managed to locate Seena Owen, who laughed, "What could we do now?"[6] It was harder to find Byron, who was out of the business and suffering from multiple sclerosis, working and living in Long Beach. Hollywood reporter Sheilah Graham put out the call in her column and one of his friends, journalist Victor Carriere, happened to read it and supplied the details. He was excited, though perhaps keener to re-connect over tea with Gloria than to become a quinquagenarian matinee idol. Editor Viola Lawrence heroically unearthed the details of the Futter deal back in the 1930s; Siegel found the paperwork and Lawrence subsequently tracked down the footage itself. Siegel also did his best to dissuade Kirk Douglas from naming a new boxing film *King Kelly*—luckily he moved on to another project. With the progression of Von's illness, he was sadly unable to write much less direct the new scenes. Instead Gloria, with the help of Herman G. Weinberg, found an ideal candidate. Three decades after he had been tasked with cutting Von's *The Wedding March* down to size, Josef von Sternberg was called in to expand *Queen Kelly*.

Austrian-American director Sternberg, whose von was every bit as authentic as Stroheim's, was a Jew, born Jonas Sternberg in Vienna in 1894. His films were characterised by a rare elegance of composition and an emotional vividness that encompassed melancholy and vicious cruelty as well as romantic love and raw sexuality. His story, like his artistic sensibilities and his temperament, was similar to Von's own. He spent his teenage years in the States, became a US citizen in 1908, and started out in the Fort Lee, New Jersey film business in 1911. He served in the U.S. Army during WWI and made his way back to the American film industry.

He made his directorial debut with *The Salvation Hunters* in 1924, a poetic-realist film about drifters living in poverty. Paul Ivano photographed his next, *A Woman of the Sea*, produced by Charlie Chaplin but shelved and never released. He achieved great success at the end of the decade with the gangster film *Underworld* (1927) and a tragedy set in Hollywood, *The Last Command* (1928). He went to Berlin to make *The Blue Angel* (1930) and returned to America in triumph with his new star Marlene Dietrich, whom he directed in a string of intensely beautiful Hollywood pictures. However, Sternberg's career never fully recovered from the failure of his unreleased 1937 Roman epic *I, Claudius*, shot in London, the production of which was beset with power struggles and disasters. By the time he came to discuss *Queen Kelly*, he had already shot what would prove to be his final film, the Japanese war drama *Anatahan* (1953). In his consistently entertaining but unreliable memoir, *Fun in a Chinese Laundry*, published in 1965, Sternberg praised Von in the highest terms: "He influenced the visible and the invisible within the range of his camera; the air itself was charged with the electricity of his creative vitality. He was the first to propose that there should be no conventional limit to the length of a film, an edict now commonly and mostly unjustifiedly followed."[7]

Sternberg wasn't hoping to remake *Queen Kelly* or merely provide an ending but to do what Gloria called "something really constructive".[8] She praised his "super ideas as to what might be done with the picture (rather inexpensively), so that I could recoupe [sic] some real money" to producer Joseph Brandel, who had been in charge of the French release of the film. She reminded him: "Right now I am two thousand dollars out of pocket, plus $800,000."[9] Siegel, hoping to sell the idea to Joe, called it "a new, up-to-date, inexpensive sound version" for a cost of $100,000. Sternberg was able to view an existing cut of *Queen Kelly* in January 1957 and was determined that he could rework it into a new film narrated by Gloria, possibly with a song. He planned to shoot 1,500-2,000 feet of new scenes and see what he could repurpose from the Futter footage. He would also drop some close-ups "which many of those who have seen the film find meaningless and boring", delete all the intertitles and remove all "the dated, out-moded, gauche dialogue and scenes".

"In general terms the new film is planned as a vehicle for a unique piece of cinema showmanship—the presentation of Miss Swanson in two groups of sequences, photographed thirty years apart, in conjunction with von Stroheim's celebrated pageantry and cynicism, and shown in modern contexts devised by von Sternberg," wrote Siegel. The new director was relaxed about continuity. Having met Gloria and studied her appearance in the original film he concluded that "Miss Swanson, in 1957, looks essentially the same as in 1929." Gloria was to play a "vigorous, worldly woman", perhaps a New Orleans madam, "regaling her customer-listener(s) with the 'story of her life' related cynically, not tragically",[10] to explain how she came to be called Queen Kelly. One is reminded of Dietrich in Sternberg's *Shanghai Express*, drily quipping that "It took more than one man to change my name to Shanghai Lily."

Gloria and Siegel contacted Joe to discover whether the original costs could be written off as a tax loss. Joe, always one to cover his tracks, warned Gloria: "That was thirty years ago, and most of that stuff has been thrown out or destroyed and I think it might be very difficult to authenticate."[11] A month later he forwarded a very brusque statement from his accountant pointing out that all the losses had already been taken and that after 28 years, the statute of limitations meant that Gloria's hope was ill-founded. As far as the Sternberg plan went, Joe "wouldn't bet 10 cents in this new proposition", considering it improperly budgeted and, unless she found a distributor to back it, he was not going to get involved, deciding that it was a "waste of time and money".[12]

To say that this response inflamed Gloria's rage would be a serious understatement. She wrote back in the most furious terms, ready to hold Joe to account for the whole sorry saga of the film and her subsequent financial struggles: "There is no 'Statute of Limitations' on conscience— nor truth." She told Joe his claim that he stood the loss on *Queen Kelly*, "was, still is, and will be into eternity, <u>a falsehood</u> (as a lady would say)". She also implied that he had mislaid her tax papers on purpose and accused him of a very specific betrayal, of "your letting me down" during what must have been the process of shooting a new ending to *Queen Kelly* in 1931: "It was you who insisted [sic] on helping me finish the picture so that I <u>would not</u> lose my [United Artists] stock. And then what happened—why you proceeded to vanish into thin air—when every moment was so costly to me—leaving me with no alternative." It's a truly vehement tirade, which contains several references to God—"he is mine as well as yours, though I have not contributed money to his glorification"—to her humble existence living on her Puritan salary, and to a "diabolicle" dream she had about Joe ("not a pretty one, though you had a charming smile all the time").

Gloria further urged Joe not to respond with similar anger but to be "kind enough to be equally frank with yourself, so that such frankness on our part can ease our misunderstandings. Life is too short for any further—mistakes." In a postscript, she professed herself free of malice, "blessed with forgiveness" and hopes he is similarly "blessed with truth".[13] It really is an astonishing letter, revealing quite how much she was affected by the failure of the *Queen Kelly* project and Joe's behaviour during their affair. Formidably written, it is designed to make the reader squirm with guilt. And it was not dashed off in a passion but drafted, reworked, and typed up. Her specific accusations are backed up by a comprehensive five-page statement from Siegel's office debunking Joe's claims, which concludes: "If, on the basis of these facts and their independent records concerning 'Queen Kelly' and the knowledge of film financing, the Kennedy people reach an unfavourable conclusion, that is their privilege; but their fictions, inventions and inaccuracies are resented and deserve rebuke."[14] Joe's response to Gloria, if he ever made one, has not been saved for posterity. It was abundantly clear that this multimillionaire would not spare a cent to finish what he had started on *Queen Kelly.*

In spring of 1957, Gloria informed Byron that the film was "having birth pains again".[15] By September 1958 it was "still in the doldrums".[16] As late as February 1961, Hedda Hopper reported on this plan, prompting D. R. O. Hatswell, *Queen Kelly*'s costume advisor, to write to Gloria, enclosing his CV, saying that if the film were to be revived he hoped to be "in on it". Hopefully, he added: "Maybe I can serve to supply the von Stroheim touch!"[17]

Gloria and Sternberg never got as far as shooting their new *Queen Kelly* and eventually abandoned it altogether, likely due to the impossibility of raising the funds. It's a shame, because Sternberg would really have been the best man for the job—even more so had they hired him in 1929, thereby side-tracking him from *The Blue Angel* and Dietrich and changing the course of Hollywood history forever. The distributors and U.S. TV companies that Gloria invited to take a look at *Queen Kelly* also shook their heads at the prospect. But Gloria would never turn her back on the film for good, not until the day she died. This loud silence from Joe, as well as Von's death earlier in the year, meant that *Queen Kelly* was now Gloria's responsibility alone.

1.   *SoS*, 482.
2.   Gloria Swanson, "Von Stroheim Recalls the Silent, But Gay, Days", *The Cincinnati Post*, 4 November 1955, 29.
3.   Letter GS to Peggy 26 October 1956, GSA.
4.   Letter Herb Sterne to GS, 13 November 1956, GSA.
5.   Letter EVS to GS, undated, likely June 1956, GSA.
6.   Aline Mosby, "May Release 28-Year-Old *Queen Kelly*", *Syracuse Herald-Journal*, 1 August, 1956, 14.
7.   Josef von Sternberg, *Fun in a Chinese Laundry* (Collier Books, 1965), 34.
8.   Letter GS to Joseph Brandel, 13 December 1956, GSA.
9.   Letter GS to Joseph Brandel, 7 January 1957, GSA.
10. Letter Lawrence Siegel to JPK, JPK Papers.
11. Letter JPK to GS, 25 February 1957, JPK Papers.

12. Letter JPK to GS, 15 March 1957, JPK Papers.
13. Undated letter GS to JPK, GSA.
14. Memo Re: Queen Kelly, GSA .
15. Letter GS to Walter Byron, 10 April 1957, GSA.
16. Letter Walter Byron to GS, 11 September 1958, GSA.
17. Letter D. R. O. Hatswell to GS, 12 February 1961, GSA.

20

The Hard Sell

Maybe Joe would have had a change of heart about *Queen Kelly*, but we'll never know. He departs this story at the start of the 1960s, overwhelmed by illness and tragedies. It is difficult to know where to begin with the Kennedy woes. In 1941, without telling Rose, Joe had elected to give his 23-year-old daughter Rosemary a lobotomy to treat her mental illness and curb what was seen as her erratic behaviour. It was a horrible failure, leaving Rosemary almost completely incapacitated. She was institutionalised for the rest of her life. Joe never visited her, keeping her location secret from the family for years. She died in 2005.

As already mentioned, his eldest son Joe Jr was killed in the war in 1944. His daughter Kathleen, a widow since her husband had been killed by a sniper, also in 1944, died in a plane crash in France in 1948. Joe lived to see his son John inaugurated as President in January 1961, but in December of that year he had a stroke, which left him paralysed on his right side, mentally sharp but struggling with his speech. When Gloria heard the news she sent "Loving thoughts and prayers" in a telegram signed "Your Queen Kelly."[1] John was assassinated in November 1963, plunging the nation into mass mourning. The family mourned another Kennedy son five years later when Bobby, a senator tipped as another future president, was also assassinated. In 1969, Ted Kennedy, already sole survivor of a plane accident in 1964, crashed his car on a bridge in Chappaquiddick Island, Massachusetts, and abandoned the vehicle, in which his passenger, Mary Jo Kopechne, died. The ensuing scandal destroyed Ted's own presidential aspirations. Joe died in November 1969, having outlived four of his nine children.

Joe's dream of founding a political dynasty persists, despite everything. His grandson Robert F. Kennedy Jr, born in 1954, campaigned as an independent candidate for President in 2024 and when this book went to press was Donald Trump's Secretary of Health and Human Services—the most controversial living Kennedy, despite formidable competition. Among other things, any reader of American tabloids may come to the conclusion that marital infidelity has been passed down through generations of Kennedy men.

In the 1960s, Gloria's affair with Joe remained a real secret, more closely guarded than his son's widely gossiped-about philandering with women, including Marilyn Monroe. Those revelations would have to wait. Gloria was busy being Gloria, every inch the star. At the start of the decade, the Hollywood Walk of Fame had been inaugurated, with two stars for Gloria, honouring her work on film and television. She was painting and sculpting in her spare time, but also appeared frequently on stage and as a guest star on television, acting in episodic dramas or popping up on talk shows to promote her clothing line and advocate for healthy nutrition. Later she would do this alongside her new partner William Dufty, a writer, who published the best-seller *Sugar Blues* in 1975.

In all this time, Gloria never went public about Joe; *Queen Kelly* was the only skeleton in her closet that she was prepared to exploit. Which she did, cent by cent and franc by franc. She accepted a small fee to present and introduce *Queen Kelly* at film societies and college campuses; she updated the programme notes for MoMA's 16mm circulation prints. The film continued to be shown in French cinemas, now that the remake was off the table, and in 1959 she arranged for the film to be shown on European television, with a percentage of the revenue going to Denise Vernac, Von's partner.

In 1962 she cancelled this deal and negotiated a new one in 1965, without the contribution to Vernac, who protested a little. As Gloria pointed out to a colleague rather bluntly, the concessions she made to Von in 1956 were for the sake of his pride, and she was the sole owner of *Queen Kelly*. "I have complete ownership of the film to do whatever I wish with it, even to making postcards of it, and you can tell Mrs. Von Stroheim (?) anything you like."[2] She pointed out that there were obviously no considerations of TV rights in the *Queen Kelly* contracts, drawn up in 1928. Across the years, several people erroneously assumed that Von or Joe had some rights over *Queen Kelly*. Gloria, though, was the one who had paid off the loans and she was now the person in contact with archives across the world about prints and arranging screenings on TV and in cinemas. She made several attempts over the years to find out when the film had actually been copyrighted. The answer finally came in March 1979: it never had been. Von's screenplay had been copyrighted in 1928, but that had expired. *Queen Kelly* was legally a public domain orphan, but in reality was assiduously protected by its fierce mama Gloria.

Gloria's efforts to get *Queen Kelly* out to an audience were rewarded when she finally got a chance to show it on TV in the States, albeit on local public television, New York's Channel 13, in the *A Million and One Nights* strand. The first broadcast was on 28 March 1966, the day after

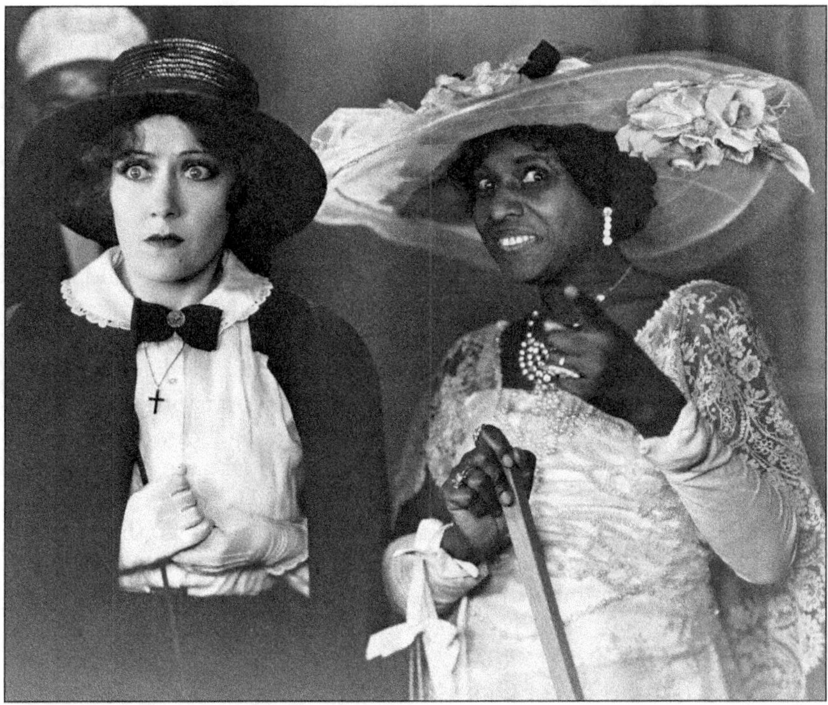

The African sequence of *Queen Kelly* was rediscovered in the 1960s and screened in London in 1965. Harry Ransom Center/Milestone Film & Video.

Gloria's 67th birthday. In the TV broadcast, she dropped a little secret, the whole truth of which she was trying to discover for herself. "In England, if you please," she said, "they have found some of the cut-out scenes in Africa, which were the censored scenes." This is the portion of the African sequence that was shot by Von and edited into the "misfit" cut in 1929. These scenes were removed not by any censor but most likely, at Gloria's request, by Viola Lawrence, to make space for her chapel ending. The National Film Theatre (now BFI Southbank) in London had screened *Queen Kelly* along with the African footage in 1965, which is apparently when Gloria heard about it too. The London screening was attended by several critics, including Kenneth Tynan, possibly the most notorious drama and film critic in Great Britain and no fan of censorship (later that year, he became the first person to say "fuck" on British TV). Tynan described the extra scene as "ponderous in its grotesquerie", adding little to the film, but was gratifyingly complimentary to Gloria ("I had forgotten how pertly and freshly Gloria Swanson plays the part") and to Von and his "coarse, opulent, inimitably sardonic imagination".[4]

After Lawrence Siegel investigated, it turned out that Henri Langlois had acquired this footage from Dudley Murphy, via Herman G. Weinberg,[5] for the Cinémathèque française to show once in 1963. But he never returned it. Now he had loaned it to the Brits too. This was part of the footage that had been sold to Futter in the 1930s, and now Gloria wanted it back. If the Cinémathèque was showing it in Paris, and the NFT was showing it in London, why shouldn't Gloria show it in New York? A year later she did, at the Beacon, and it changed the way that she talked about the film. Now it was not just her stillborn child but "a naughty little number", an artifact from the underground. This is when she started telling anyone who would listen that she was Hollywood's original rebel, and with good reason.

Gloria had started to turn her attention to formats other than film. She loudly insisted that she wouldn't write her memoirs (spoiler, she totally did), but there were a variety of other ways to cash in on her fame. In 1966 she drew up plans for a syndicated TV show called *Gloria Swanson's Movie Memoirs*, which would be supported by the publication of a picture book called *Sic Transit Gloria Swanson* and the release of an LP featuring numbers from the soundtracks of her films, including "Love, Your Magic Spell is Everywhere", and the love song Mickey Neilan wrote for her in the 1920s, "Wonderful One". These never materialised. In October 1966, Gloria's mother died after a short period of illness and following the loss, her doctor told her to take a period of rest. Despite her grief, she barely seemed to slow down at all: working, travelling, visiting her children and grandchildren, and stewarding *Queen Kelly* across the states.

Now that *Queen Kelly* had an added attraction in the form of the African scenes — a provocative new allure in the permissive 1960s — Gloria redoubled her efforts to get it shown more widely, contacting several TV stations as well as booking in-person screenings, and hoping to appear at festivals. For the most part, there was more interest in Gloria than *Queen Kelly*, though they came as a package deal. As Dufty wrote to one TV executive, reports of screenings introduced by Gloria "ran heavily to reviews of Miss Swanson's taxidermy and her survival seems always to have the effect of upstaging her celluloid work and image".[6] A few years later, Gloria told *Life* magazine that theatre audiences brought binoculars to her stage performances: "They want to see whether I'm retouched like a photograph or done up with wires."[7] When she was appearing in *Butterflies are Free* on Broadway in 1971, Swanson's *Playbill* biography read: "Name, nose, teeth, bosom, hair, kidneys — everything but the eyelashes — is real".

Gloria never abandoned the *Queen Kelly* mission. As late as 1975, a reporter could write, in all honesty, that Gloria "is still girlish enough to hop a plane anytime for practically anywhere to show the nostalgia crowd what it was all about when she was the silent movie idol of the '20s",[8] which meant screening *Queen Kelly*. She would spend the 1970s doing this while enjoying her celebrity as much as she had done half a century before, whether gracing primetime television with her anecdotes and sometimes a song, partying with Truman Capote in Studio 54 or lobbying for organic food and educating America on nutrition.

Although she preached old-fashioned romantic etiquette, called herself a "square" and told anyone who would listen that she had walked—no, run—out of the play *Lenny*, about the life of foul-mouthed comic Lenny Bruce, Gloria was probably more up to date and more broadminded than most septuagenarian great-grandmothers of her day. Her use of the term "underground film" when she talked about *Queen Kelly* suggests she had some kind of familiarity with the work of avant-garde directors such as those distributed by The Film-Makers' Cooperative in New York, founded in 1961. Indeed, she became friendly with the counter-cultural crowd in New York, and was regularly snapped with Andy Warhol at swanky parties in the 1970s. That's when she offered to direct one of his pictures. The mind delightfully boggles. One of her final screen appearances sees her hamming it up as a villain in Curtis Harrington's low-budget horror *Killer Bees*, which was an ABC Movie of the Week in February 1974. She plays Madame Van Bohlen, the sinister matriarch with a thick German accent who cultivates deadly bees at her vineyard.

There is just one intriguing what-if note from 1968, which is that Gloria copyrighted, but never published, a book called *Queen Kelly, Part 2: A Screenplay by Erich von Stroheim*. Why not share with the Swinging Sixties the story that made the Roaring Twenties blanch? The copyright was finally granted on 20 June, although the application was first made at the end of May.[9] It may be the case that the assassination of Bobby Kennedy on 6 June dissuaded Gloria from raking up family history by publishing the screenplay that Joe was meant to produce. Possibly she just couldn't find a publisher. Or perhaps she really was too tender to wade all the way into that swamp one more time.

1. Telegram from GS to JPK, GSA.
2. Letter from GS to Michéline Rozan, undated, GSA.
3. Syndicated interview with Philip K. Scheuer, "The indestructible Gloria Swanson", *The Morning Call*, 30 September 1967, 42.
4. Kenneth Tynan, "End of the Line", *The Observer*, 14 February 1965, 24.
5. In an interview in *Cahiers du cinéma* in October 1963 Weinberg asked Richard Griffith of MoMA if he knew where the African scenes were and

Griffith casually answered that Murphy had them and had promised them to MoMA a year and a half ago but Griffith was too busy to follow up. Herman G. Wienberg, "Entretien avec Richard Griffith", *Cahiers du cinéma*, October 1963, 13.

6. Letter from William Dufty to Harold Goldman, 13 July 1967, GSA.

7. Maggie Paley, "Gloria Swanson is back, full of organic beans", *Life*, 17 September 1971, 77.

8. Maryanne Conheim, "Great-Grandma Gloria Still Oozes the Glamour of Her Film-Queen Days", *Detroit Free Press*, 16 February, 1975, 53.

9. The delay was partly caused by the fact that the application had left Von's nationality blank on the form. It was resubmitted, erroneously stating that he was German.

21
The Lost

Everywhere Gloria went, from film societies to *The Dick Cavett Show*, she was asked about *Queen Kelly*, her great unrealised masterpiece. But not just that film. Fans who were reminded of her talent by *Sunset Boulevard* and repertory screenings of her silent classics clamoured for the impossible. Gloria was grilled for information on all her lost titles, films that she herself dearly longed to see again. Some of Gloria's proudest moments on screen — *Madame Sans-Gêne* and the final, crucial reel of *Sadie Thompson* — are still considered lost, unseen since the silent era. The reels may have been mislaid, destroyed, censored or wasted away due to nitrate decay, or gone up in flames like *The Honeymoon*, a victim of the stock's inherent flammability. Gloria herself was determined to find them. In 1968 she even travelled to the Soviet Union to search the archives in Moscow, but with no joy. Others now continue the hunt on her behalf.

One lost film that Gloria's fans longed to see was *Beyond the Rocks*, the Elinor Glyn-scripted romance she made with Rudolph Valentino. Her co-star's posthumous cult fame, including Norma Desmond's name-drops, kept the legend of this film burning until in 2003 the impossible happened. A print of *Beyond the Rocks* was discovered in a collection in Haarlem in the Netherlands. It was restored and screened in a near-complete form in 2005, and more material has since been found. It is now widely available, and although no form of film storage is 100 percent future-proof, the number of copies and formats circulating, as well as the modern blessing of state-of-the-art film archives, means it will almost certainly never be lost again. As for the rest of Gloria's work, lost silents are found now and again: just rarely enough to prompt a surge of joy and curiosity each time, and just often enough to keep the hope of finding discarded treasures alive.

Is there is more footage of *Queen Kelly* out there? Anything is possible. But Gloria herself and others, including FIAF (the international federation of film archives), hunted for every scrap they could get their hands on, and it is unlikely that there is more to found. Von loved to shoot multiple takes, but most of those that were printed would have been discarded if not used. Just like those tantalising scenes of Gloria and

Chaplin together in *His New Job*, these are certainly gone for good—lost to the cutting-room floor as the saying goes—like so much of Von's work.

Much of *Queen Kelly* is as irrevocably lost as the films that Gloria nearly made but never did. Her version of *Dark Victory*, for one, and a legendary unmade film of such grandiose and psychedelic aspirations it has become a cult item despite its non-existence. In the early 1970s, Alejandro Jodorowsky, the Chilean-French filmmaker of avant-garde, surreal spectacles, planned to adapt Frank Herbert's 1965 science fiction novel *Dune*, widely assumed to be unfilmable. Jodorowsky intended it to star his own 12-year-old son, as well as Salvador Dalí, Orson Welles, Udo Kier, Geraldine Chaplin—and Gloria. Scholars of Hollywood history, all too aware of the precedents, may have found Gloria's presence, alongside Welles, too much of a bad omen. The ghost of Von also haunted the project: Jodorowsky was working from a storyboard of 3,000 drawings, and envisaged a running time of 10 to 14 hours. Dalí demanded a helicopter and a fee of $100,000 an hour, which Jodorowsky honoured, intending to hire him for only 60 minutes of work, with the rest of his role played by a plastic robot. Dalí accepted on certain conditions, including that he could keep the robot in his personal museum and that his emperor character would sit on a throne that was a toilet shaped like two dolphins. Such bizarre stipulations were a matter of course for two like-minded artists, but studios were unlikely to be so accommodating.

Jodorowsky sent his script and artwork to several studios in the hope of finding backing for his vision. They all said no, but as a 2014 documentary about the film argues, the influence of these words and images, so widely disseminated, can be seen in such hit SF film franchises as *Star Wars*, *Alien* and *The Terminator*. Also, Jodorowsky and his storyboard artist Jean Giraud used many of the ideas in a series of graphic novels, *The Incal* (1980–2014). *Dune* was eventually filmed for the big screen, unhappily although quite brilliantly by David Lynch in 1984 and then to great acclaim in three parts by Denis Villeneuve. In these adaptations, Gloria's role, Reverend Mother Gaius Helen Mohiam, is taken by Siân Phillips and Charlotte Rampling respectively. It would have been quite something to see our Gloria, the convent girl of *Queen Kelly*, in the role of an alien Mother Superior, a truthsayer who is part of a superpowered sisterhood. The world of *Dune* is so vast as to inspire comparison with a panoply of analogues. Its degenerate empire, populated by aristocrats in dress uniforms with substance abuse problems, its exploited colony and its sacred sisterhood, has the whiff of an intergalactic *Queen Kelly*—at least Stroheim in space. Jodorowsky's *Dune*, like the later sequences of *Queen Kelly*, and the original cut of Von's *Greed*, may exist only in the imagination of film fans, but it takes up an impressive amount of space.

In the 2010s, the Canadian filmmaker Guy Maddin, whose fascination both for early and silent cinema and the more outlandish corners of film history and style has inspired much of his best work, set about reviving the dead. "Once I discovered that all my favourite directors from that first generation, who straddled the silent and talking picture era, had at least one lost film, I became really haunted by lost films," he told me. Lost-and-found films were already part of Maddin's oeuvre: he had already made films inspired by two "lost" Abel Gance films that turned out not to have been lost at all. Perhaps Maddin had the power to revive fallen film history? "I'm pretty secular, but when anyone holds a camera in their hands to make a movie, they get unbelievably narcissistic, and I just felt I had some spiritual connection with these movies," he says. "Once the internet became a big part of my life in the early 2000s, I started daydreaming about a lost film project where I could do this, not just to one or two films, but to many." Maddin chose not just to revive missing films, but unmade ones. "I started to think of unrealised projects as the unhappy spirits of things that would project themselves for people if they could, but can't and are left to wander the limbo land of cinema, just like a lost film."

Maddin's 2012 endeavour *Spiritismes* gathered a group of actors and crew in the basement of the Pompidou Centre in Paris, the first stop on a world tour, to recreate lost or unmade films, some distinguished and others thoroughly disreputable. Each morning would begin with a ciné-séance involving faux ectoplasm during which the assembled group would summon the spirit of that day's misbegotten movie before embarking on a re-enactment, still reeling under the influence of its supernatural energy. The actors would be "possessed" and act out the long-forgotten plot lines of these lost films. Each reconstruction cost half a million dollars to produce,[1] the kind of numbers that Von and Gloria could appreciate but might have Joe twitching in his grave.

I was honoured, Gloria might say fated, to be at the Pompidou on the day that Geraldine Chaplin and Udo Kier (her co-stars in the imaginary *Dune*) were performing a scene on a set dominated by a bed draped with a mosquito net. That bed immediately made me think of *Queen Kelly*. Not quite. Maddin was summoning the spirit of Von's *Poto-Poto*, his fetid tale from the swampland. Maddin's *Poto-Poto* was filmed that day in the museum, but also, at more personal risk, in icy waters. Maddin, along with his co-screenwriters Evan Johnson and Bob Kotyk, ventured out "in a rowboat on a little creek that snaked its way for half a kilometre toward Lake Winnipeg—if we tipped over, this boat would have destroyed the camera. I think it was early November, so it was very cold, but it was very beautiful." These riskily obtained images were used as rear-projection footage, to give the impression that the tiny set at the Pompidou was a room on a houseboat, steaming down the Mississippi river. Maddin's *Poto-Poto* hinges on the moment at the roulette table where Masha challenges Jan, and the wedding night scene, the last sequence attempted by the *Queen Kelly* crew. Maddin adds an extra mystical dimension, through the presence of an obscene deity named after the 1928 screenwriting manual *Plotto* by William Wallace Cook. There is a happy, if bizarre, ending. Masha grows in status and popularity as the new madam, while Jan is physically shrunk, a shrimp of a man, stranded without cash to stake at the roulette table.

Maddin was all too aware of the precedent set by *Queen Kelly*'s disastrous production history. "We should have cast someone to play Joe Kennedy to come in and like, turn the cameras off," he jokes. Maddin's production company is named after another of Von's incomplete films, *Walking Down Broadway*. Maddin filmed a version of that one too, in 1998; it was called *The Hoyden*. He isn't convinced it was a good omen for his filmmaking career. "It's just caused me one nightmare after another."[2] The *Spiritismes* project was thwarted by a run of bad luck and a lack of finance. After Paris, the project was due to move to MoMA, another key location in the *Queen Kelly* story, but they were replaced by an exhibition devoted to the Icelandic musician Björk. Soon, Maddin was on the brink of bankruptcy. His producer failed to raise the funds they needed for the ensuing shoots in Winnipeg and Sao Paolo, so the project came to a halt. For now, the Seances website where *Poto-Poto* was once hosted is no longer live. The blog written by one of the *Poto-Poto* actors, Maddin's ex-wife Kim Morgan, about taking part in the project, has also vanished from the internet. It is almost, but not quite, as if it never happened.

Poto-Poto exists in multiple, frustratingly ephemeral forms in the "limbo land of cinema": Von's own screenplay, as read and rejected by MGM, its appropriation in films including 1933's *White Woman*, Von's own French novelisation, published in 1956, and in Maddin's digital video footage of his reconstruction, subsequently folded into his 2015 feature *The Forbidden Room*. It also exists, lest we forget, as part of the expanding, semi-mythical *Queen Kelly* universe, a boundless cosmos of what-ifs and might-have-beens.

1. Andrew Pulver, "Guy Maddin: 'Keyhole will become crystal-clear upon your third viewing", *The Guardian*, 30 August 2012.
2. Author interview, 4 December 2025

22
The Memoir

Gloria's final appearance on the big screen was as herself, in mortal danger. She was dressed by Edith Head in black-and-ivory satin, clutching a red carnation. She was also, while dicing with death, doing something she had sworn she would never do—writing her memoirs. The producers of *Airport 1975* (Jack Smight, 1974), a sequel to the hit aviation disaster movie *Airport* (George Seaton, 1970), initially approached Gloria to pay an ageing, alcoholic actress aboard a seriously damaged Boeing 747. In this instalment, a jet flying from Washington DC to Los Angeles collides with a small plane, breaching the cockpit hull, and putting the pilots out of action. Disaster, or the threat of it, ensues. Gloria had no desire to be associated with either ageing or alcoholism, so by mutual agreement she agreed to play her best role—Gloria Swanson. As ever, ghosts of her former roles clung to her shadow on the screen. Nancy Olson, the ingenue from *Sunset Boulevard*, played the mother of a sick teenager (Linda Blair, of *Exorcist* fame) further back in the plane. For those devotees of *Queen Kelly*, there are even a couple of nuns on board, openly shocked by the thought of sharing the cabin with "one of those Hollywood persons". "An actress?" "Or worse."

As she enters the airport, Gloria is followed by reporters, eager for quotes, which she graciously delivers: "My life is a surprise. One surprise after another." During the flight she is accompanied by an assistant, relaying last-minute queries from her publishers about the draft of her memoirs. Who were her two Hollywood friends who didn't cave under studio pressure? Gloria picks up the tape recorder to name Carole Lombard and Grace Moore—an initially baffling response until one remembers that both stars died in plane crashes. "I was a rebel, too," she adds.

As disaster looms, Gloria tips her diamonds out of her bomb-proofed jewel-case and into the confused assistant's lap, stashing the memoir tapes in the box instead. One more recording for posterity: "Here you are darlings, it's all yours. I never wanted to have the damned thing published while I was alive, anyway!" It's deliciously camp, but the message is as clear as the brilliance of those Cartier jewels. Even if Gloria's body goes up in the flames, her most important legacy will survive her: the unvarnished truth about Hollywood. Only Gloria could make a late-career appearance in an ensemble film slated by Pauline Kael as "processed schlock… a box of rotten candy for movie junkies and TV dipsos"[1] into a valediction on her stardom and a commercial for her next project. Kael's argument was that the star cameos in such films were just exercises in humiliation: "They're not cast for their abilities; they're exploited for the public appeal they used to have and the aura that lingers around their names, and they get a stale, used-up look."[2] Gloria defies that assessment. She glows with health on screen and her theatrical pose, the hands thrown up, eyes raised to the heavens, sets her apart from the rest of cast. She was well practised at this part and knew how to exploit it for her own ends. She was advertising her forthcoming bestseller—no matter that it wasn't written yet.

This was just the second phase in Gloria's hype campaign for her autobiography. The first phase was strenuous denial, always guaranteed to stoke anticipation. "No, no, no. I am not going to write my memoirs," Gloria told a journalist in 1969. "Because I want to become famous as the one and only who hasn't. Everyone writes their memoirs. I don't want an epitaph on my grave."[3] And yet, Gloria had been recording herself on audio tapes since the 1950s, with just such a project in mind, and she had been keen for her sixth husband William Dufty, a former journalist whom she met in the mid-60s and married in 1976, to help her make it into a reality. They had already collaborated on 1975's *Sugar Blues*, a nutrition book about the dangers of the sweet stuff, which Dufty wrote and Swanson promoted heavily. After the release of *Airport 1975*, Gloria began dangling the prospect of her forthcoming tell-all book in front of the world. At a 1977 cocktail party in Los Angeles to celebrate the publication of *Ginger, Loretta and Irene Who?*, a book of Hollywood history circa 1933 by George Eels, Gloria told reporters that she and Dufty were hard at work on her autobiography. She promised dynamite. When it was published, she said: "There are going to be a lot of bodies twirling in the ground."[4] She knew already that her revelations would expose the 1974 publication of Rose Kennedy's memoir, *Times to Remember*, as a whitewash. She was also by this point attempting to sue Kenneth Anger for his own inflammatory tales in *Hollywood Babylon*. It was time to set the record straight, and Gloria knew she had a salacious story up her sleeve that even Anger hadn't had the nerve to tell.

Gloria and Dufty were indeed working on the book, along with English screenwriter and producer Brian Degas—who would later become Gloria's lover. Degas told Gloria, "Your life should read like a novel."[5] Degas sat with her for hours going through her old files and talking to her about her lovers, her films, every step of her non-stop life.

Then Dufty, relegated to a separate corner of the apartment, wrote it all down. Degas pitched the book to Jacob Epstein at Random House, who offered a $450,000 advance ($2.2 million today). In 1979 they brought in Wayne Lawson, a freelance editor and a friend of Degas, who had lots of ideas about how the story could be structured for maximum impact, and how to rewrite Dufty's text—to make it not just novelistic but a block-buster. The title was to be *Swanson on Swanson*.

Lawson likened the process to *Sunset Boulevard*. Degas was William Holden, the desirable younger man writing Gloria's manuscript, while Dufty was Von, the discarded husband lurking in the shadows. There was one chapter that Dufty refused to let Lawson see before it was sent to Epstein. "It was a lengthy diatribe about Joseph Kennedy," recalled Lawson. "In addition to being a crook in business," Dufty said, "Kennedy was a thorough degenerate who led a dissolute life." It seems Epstein did not consider it publishable. His response to this text was only to ask if it was some kind of joke. It is important to note that Rose was still alive—she died in 1995. "I have no idea what happened to those pages," wrote Lawson. "No part of them got into *Swanson on Swanson*, and very soon Dufty was out of the picture."[6] Another episode that escaped the manu-script: the end of Gloria's marriage to Dufty and the onset of her affair with Degas. When Lawson had a complete draft, Gloria read it through meticulously, adding hundreds of queries and notes, and then the job was done. Lawson was paid double the agreed fee and he didn't see Gloria again until the book launch.

Swanson and Swanson was published in 1980 and became an instant bestseller, selling 450,000 copies. It is probably the greatest film star autobiography ever written, thanks to both its style and substance. It has panache and flow, and while of course it flatters its subject-author, it is also breathtakingly candid: about Gloria's lovers, husbands and abor-tions. Although we may be able to see the omissions in her tale of *Queen Kelly*, it was the fullest account of that ill-fated shoot that anyone had ever shared. Janet Maslin in *The New York Times* raved about the book. "Movie stars' memoirs don't get any better than *Swanson on Swanson*, a peppery account of a clever and headstrong individual… Whatever else she may have been, Miss Swanson was never confused."[7]

The story of her affair with Joe, confirmed in print for the first time, made headlines and in 1981 got her on the ABC news show *20/20* for an interview with Barbara Walters, which she kicked off by serenading her interviewer with "Wonderful One". Things got decidedly more sticky after that when Walters asked her about Joe. First, Gloria refused to confirm that she had been in love with Joe, and in fact she's very believ-able when she says she just doesn't know. However, when Walters asked her whether she felt guilty for having an affair with a married man, Gloria became outraged. "Guilty? I went through absolute hell." Her misgivings, she suggested, were no match for his persistence, and his obsession. It's rare to see Gloria as flustered as she is under Walters' questioning, telling her that she wrote the book, at least in part, to quash any rumour that Brother was Joe's illegitimate son. When Walters asks why she never answered Ted Kennedy's requests to write a tribute to his father, Gloria becomes tight-lipped. "Because what was I going to write?" It could well be true that the unpublished chapter of *Swanson on Swanson* was strong stuff. As it was, the Kennedy family condemned the book in no uncertain terms. Eunice Kennedy Shriver, Joe's daughter, wrote to *The Washington Post*, denouncing Gloria's book for "parading warmed-over 50-year-old gossip that accuses the dead and insults the living".

Most of Gloria's interviews were much softer, which was welcome news because in 1980 and 1981, this sleek octogenarian was suddenly everywhere again. She went on an extensive international book tour, accompanied by Degas. She also appeared on TV in Kevin Brownlow's oral history of the silent era, *Hollywood*—scenes she had taped in 1977. Brownlow devoted half an episode to her, and naturally covered *Queen Kelly*. She appeared on stage at the National Film Theatre in London, telling former *Times* critic John Russell Taylor about her life as a Hollywood rebel; Ingrid Bergman, praised in Gloria's book for her personal defiance during her own affair with Roberto Rossellini, turned up to see her. In September she was photographed by Richard Avedon for *Vogue*, a blaze of energy in white curls, with her Hollywood smile crinkled into a joyful expression. It was rare to see Gloria so free and uninhibited in front of the camera. She posed more pensively for a Blackglama furs ad campaign, in a mink coat and leather elbow gloves. The tagline: "What becomes a legend most?"

Away from the cameras, Gloria was interested in the facts, not the legend. She appointed New York-based archivist Raymond Daum to take care of her personal papers, and when in 1982 she sold her files to the Harry Ransom Center at the University of Texas in Austin, he moved with them. It is mostly thanks to this extensive collection, as well as *Swanson on Swanson*, that we know as much as we do about *Queen Kelly*—and the hypocrisies of silent Hollywood. If she couldn't find all those lost reels of her favourite films, if she was never able to play Queen Kelly on screen, she was at least able to reclaim the truth, as she saw it, for future generations.

Gloria died in New York Hospital on 4 April 1983, aged 84, two weeks after suffering a mild heart attack. She had returned to the city from the Portuguese Riviera, where she was resting—for once. After she died, many of her belongings, including her jewels and film memorabilia, were sold by private auction. Her legacy is dispersed across the world, wherever her films are shown and her treasures shared. While I was working on this book, her art deco rock-crystal-and-diamond bangles were on display in London's Victoria and Albert Museum, as part of an exhibition dedicated to the Cartier jewellers. She had bought them in 1932 and wore them in a few films, including *Perfect Understanding* and *Sunset Boulevard*—making them almost as much of a signature as her beauty spot and her red carnation. In *Sunset Boulevard*, you can see them sparkle in the beam of the arc light, when Norma visits DeMille at Paramount Studios, dressed in her finest finery. Gloria also wore them to the Academy Awards for the same film. But in 2025, a far more expensive object, equally as dazzling, was also out in the world. *Queen Kelly* itself was back on the screen.

1. Pauline Kael, "The Current Cinema", *The New Yorker*, 28 October 1974, 72.
2. Ibid, 71.
3. "I Am Not Going to Write my Memoirs!", 109.
4. "Ginger, Loretta and Irene Who?", *Hollywood Studio*, April 1977, 39.
5. Wayne Lawson, "Swanson Song", *Vanity Fair*, Hollywood 2023, 113.
6. Lawson, 116.
7. Janet Maslin, "A Star Remembers", *New York Times*, 9 November 1980, 12.

23
The Revival

Queen Kelly was a film made by hard, painstaking labour by a team working long into the early hours. It was remade the same way. In late 1983, just months after Gloria died, Dennis Doros was working the Erich von Stroheim shift, grafting late into the night to bring *Queen Kelly* back from the dead.

Doros, 26, worked for Kino International, a distributor founded in New York City in 1976 by Bill Pence and purchased a year later by Donald Krim, formerly of United Artists—the studio that was to distribute *Queen Kelly* back in 1929. Krim's cousin, Arthur B. Krim, along with his partner Robert Benjamin, had bought United Artists in 1951; they left in 1978 to found Orion Pictures. Donald had worked first in the 16mm rental division then helped found United Artists Classics, the first arthouse division of a major studio. Still in operation as Kino Lorber after a merger with Lorber Digital in 2009, Krim's company has to date been responsible for bringing thousands of silent, classic and independent films to international audiences.

Krim had *Queen Kelly* in his sights from early on, and applied, unsuccessfully, to Gloria herself for distribution rights. After she died, he tried again via Benjamin, by then the lawyer for her estate, and this time he scored. Originally the plan was to release the 1931 edit separately, as sourced from a nitrate print in her collection at the Harry Ransom Center, and the African scenes, discovered in 1963, which were on 35mm. Doros, a recently employed 16mm salesperson at Kino, suggested a more ambitious plan. Would it be possible to combine them both and create something that came close to Von's original vision? "I guess I must have volunteered," Doros tells me.[1] "Then Don asked if I could do it and I lied. I had learned to splice film when I was a 16mm projectionist in college, but that's not exactly the same thing." Doros had given himself the challenge of turning the extant parts of *Queen Kelly* into a whole movie. At the same time he would be doing a similar fix for the missing reel of *Sadie Thompson* and continuing to report for his day job.

"I was a non-theatrical salesman, and in only a year, in 1984, the division had gone from \$35,000 to \$100,000," says Doros. "Don was very happy with me making him money because the company never had any. He was a great man, probably not a great businessman, but if you stick to your guns and you stick to your priorities, who's going to make money? I don't think he ever acquired a film just to make money. He was my inspiration in many ways.

"Don said, 'If you do your work during the day, you can do this at night. And I can't pay you.'" So after working 9-to-5 at the Kino offices in Manhattan, Doros took the bus home to New Jersey and drove his mother's car to Janice Allen's Cinema Arts lab in Park Ridge, about an hour away, to work on Gloria's movies from eight or nine in the evening to two in the morning. "Janice taught me how to hot-splice film. She taught me how to work with negatives. We didn't have a Steenbeck, so I cut reel-to-reel. I had no previous negative-cutting experience; I just imagined what it should look like and tried to do my best."

It was a phenomenal effort. "I would get back home at three, wake up at 6.30, and repeat this day after day—for a year and a half," recalls Doros, explaining why some of his memories of the project are "blurry". But he was determined enough to put in the double shift. "At 26, everybody has something to prove. I wanted to do something that was worthwhile, and this was my chance."

Doros's plan was to use all the footage and some of the stills to piece together the film in a similar fashion to American Film Institute archivist Robert Gitt's 1971 reconstruction of Frank Capra's *Lost Horizon* (1937), or Ronald Haver's 1983 reconstruction of George Cukor's *A Star is Born* (1954), a process he later described as "like putting a jigsaw puzzle together with a blindfold on".[2] Where production stills were used, they were animated by a longtime documentary cinematographer/stills animation expert, Bob Lee, to shift the audience's attention to particular details and characters that help to move the story forward. Surprise, surprise—an original nitrate copy of the soundtrack to the 1931 version had survived, with Adolph Tandler's score and sound effects specified by Von. With the help of retired curator James Card, Doros "bribed his way into the George Eastman House film archive late at night to locate and label the 'missing' soundtrack so it could be 'found' by the staff later that week".

Viola Lawrence's edit of the first section of the film, up to Patricia's suicide attempt in the river, was more or less complete. Doros needed to remove Gloria's interposed ending and build a bridge between that section and her arrival at her aunt's African brothel. Then he had to find a way to give the film an ending—Von's ending. With so many original papers retained by Gloria, new intertitles could be made using Von's own dialogue. The difficulty was choosing which of the many different screenplays to follow. For expediency's sake, Doros tried to go with the last, shorter version. Sean Coughlin, the film preservationist who later became the founder of Cinetech, prepared the intertitles, ready to be cut into the film, for its premiere at the Berlin Film Festival in February 1985. "The weekend before the premiere, the intertitles hadn't been shot, and that Saturday, Sean was going to get married, but he had to come into work to do them," recalls Doros. "To this day, he says I ruined his wedding. I'm not sorry about it. Janice and I worked, I think, 48 straight hours that weekend to get it to Berlin."

But for once, *Queen Kelly* would meet a deadline. The Berlin screening, at the Akademie der Künst, was a triumph, and *Queen Kelly* seemed to be a hit wherever it played. After more than a five-decade wait, the film finally went on release in the United States, kicking off with the Los Angeles premiere its makers could only dream of, in March at the Bing Theatre—the start of a month-long retrospective dedicated to Von. In the *Los Angeles Times*, critic Kevin Thomas opined: "So painstaking, so beautifully paced is Doros' 96-minute restoration, incorporating stills and explanatory titles, that the film is actually a surprisingly satisfying and even meaningful experience."[3] Writing in *The New York Times* when the film opened in Manhattan, Stephen Harvey called it "a poignant reminder of just what the screen was abandoning in the headlong rush toward sound".[4] There were screenings across the world, including not just the 1985 Berlinale but the Venice Film Festival and the Giornate del Cinema Muto in Pordenone, Italy, where the world's silent film buffs congregate.

"It grossed over half a million dollars around the world. It played in something like forty countries. Studio executives were sneaking into the premiere in Los Angeles and getting thrown out," says Doros. "That took me by surprise. I thought I was a fraud. I had no training. I had no expertise. I was a non-theatrical salesperson, and all of a sudden I'm an archivist that everybody wants to meet. And yet, at the same time, the archives hated my guts because I wasn't one of them. I was commercial. I was selling Stroheim's genius by cutting together what I thought was best, even though they were doing this themselves with other films. I was forthright about it."

As Von could tell you, nothing ventured, nothing gained. *Queen Kelly* was the start of a long and impressive career in film restoration as well as distribution for Doros. In 1990, with his wife Amy Heller, he founded Milestone Film and Video, which has looked after the descendants of *Queen Kelly* for 35 years, restoring and distributing outsider films, independent films made by women and people of colour: by Lois Weber, Nell Shipman, Charles Burnett, Kathleen Collins, Jane Campion, Shirley Clarke, Ayoka Chenzira and more. It's a small but mighty business, run, in Doros's words, by "two short but adorable Jewish people out of their home in New Jersey".[5] Doros and Heller are also the co-presidents of Missing Movies,[6] an initiative to save more *Queen Kelly*s, bringing films that are unavailable back into circulation and helping to reunite filmmakers with their lost works. This began when they brought Nancy Savoca's *Household Saints* (1993) back into cinemas after it had been unavailable for years. Milestone has been a force for good, and a progressive voice, in the world of archive cinema. As this book went to press, Heller and Doros were making plans for their retirement, but their catalogue has already been entrusted to new Milestone president, archivist and scholar Maya Cade.

Before Doros could retire, he had one final date to keep with *Queen Kelly*. Kino's distribution rights to the Gloria films expired in 2015, and as Doros puts it, "They were my first cinematic children… I got a little nostalgic." So Milestone acquired the rights, but the negatives from Doros's first reconstruction weren't so easy to find. That's when the George Eastman House revealed that its archive contained three nitrate prints as well as outtakes for *Queen Kelly*, and within those reels there were two scenes that had never been placed in any other version of the film.

"They had kept this from me for forty years," says Doros. "That's when I realised I could start from scratch. I could digitise everything from the original nitrate. That became even more daunting, because if I'm going to start all over again, I have to consider my choices in 1985, and I knew I hadn't made all the right choices then because I hadn't seen enough silent films."

Not just more footage but more information came to light. "Ted Kennedy had refused me access to his father's papers in 1984 and probably rightfully," says Doros. "It was only four years since Gloria had told the world that Daddy and Gloria had an affair, and it was probably still upsetting to the family." Now Doros had access to the relevant papers from the Kennedy archives, making *Queen Kelly* "the most documented film in restoration history". He could take inspiration from these discoveries, including the fact that one economy suggested in January 1929 was to recycle a shot of cathedral bells ringing from *The Wedding March* for the nuptial finale. Doros and Heller have retained the rights to their "cinematic children" in perpetuity, so this second reconstruction, what they call a "reimagining"—because Von's intentions cannot be exactly replicated—is their own project. "What I did is exactly what Don Krim did, forty years ago: going to our own bank accounts and spending all our money to restore this film again." And like Gloria before them…

The result—a 4K restitution of *Queen Kelly*, from the beautiful nitrate sources that do justice to Von's gorgeous vision of Mitteleuropean

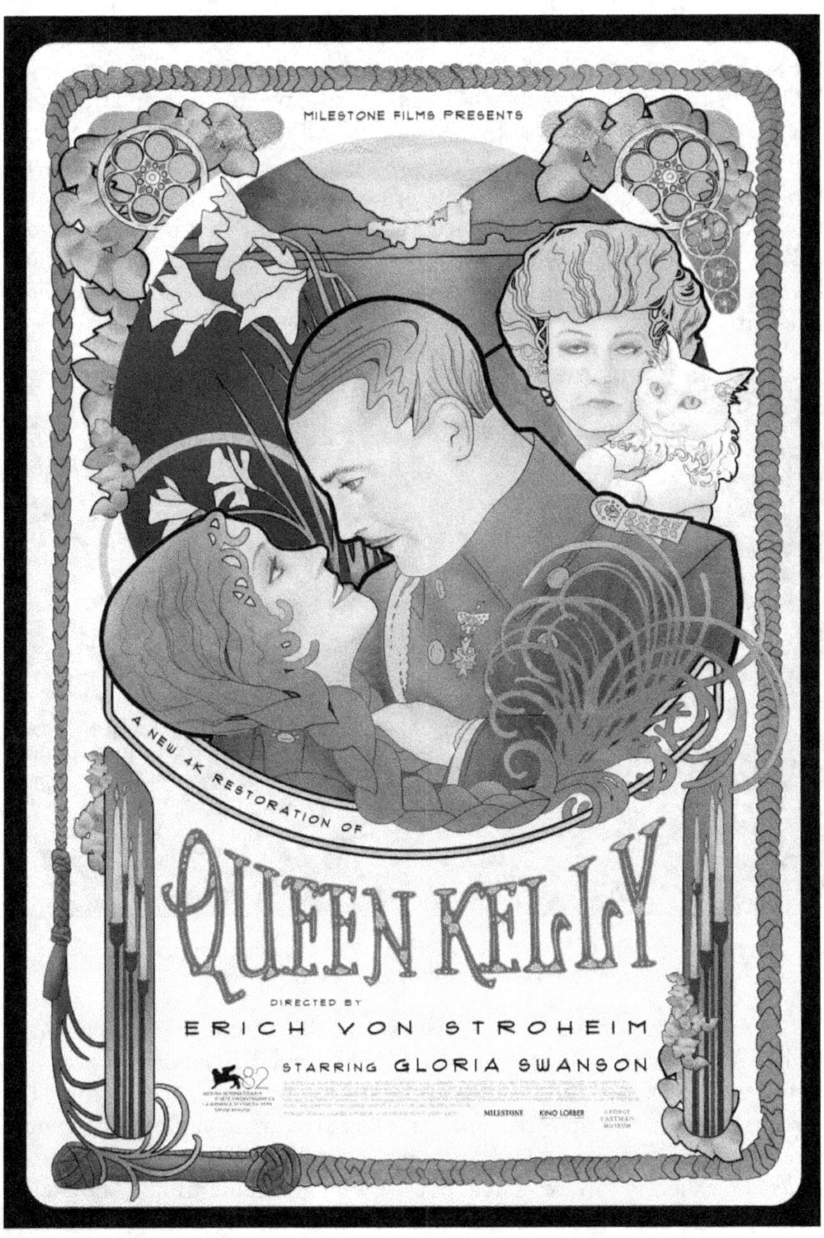

The poster for the 2025 'reimagining' of *Queen Kelly*, designed by Lauren Caddick.
Lauren Caddick/Milestone Film & Video 2025.

decadence and to Gloria's sensual performance—looks tremendous. And it sounds wonderful too, with a newly composed orchestral score by Eli Denson. It's the closest we can get to sitting with Gloria, Von and Joe in the screening room in 1928, awestruck at the rushes, excited by the possibilities of this story. What wouldn't they all have given to see their film premiere, as this version did, at the 2025 Venice Film Festival, to a full house that included Francis Ford Coppola and Alexander Payne, with the Syntax Ensemble playing Denson's score? Coppola, director of such troubled and long-gestating projects as *Apocalypse Now* and *Megalopolis* (2023), is surely the one man living who can most identify with Von and his struggles in his quest for cinematic greatness. No wonder he wanted to see it.

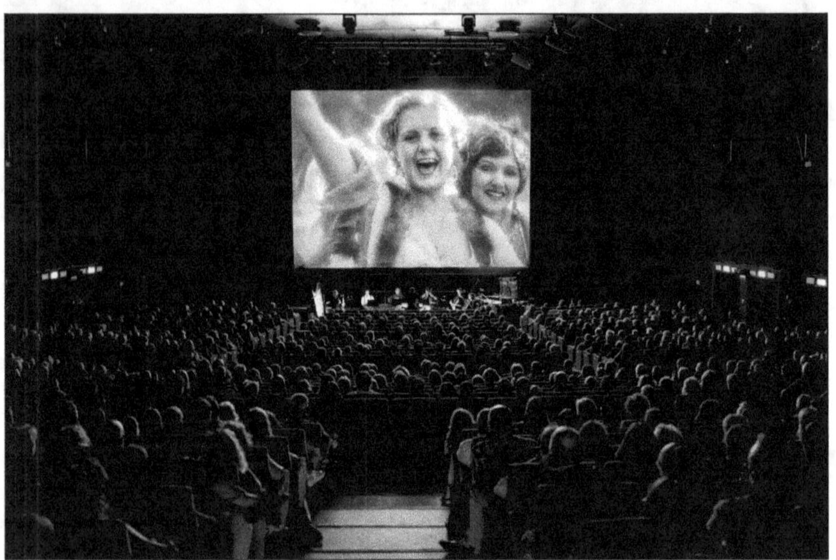

The 'reimagining' of *Queen Kelly* screens at the Venice Film Festival, 2025.
Valerio Greco/Milestone Film & Video.

The director of the festival, Alberto Barbera, told the audience that he had a personal connection to the film's "cursed director". "I was just a student," he said, "and I wrote my first monograph on a director. That director was Erich von Stroheim. An obsessive, manic auteur with enormous ambitions, beyond Hollywood's capabilities." Introducing *Queen Kelly*, he called it "an excessive, overflowing, extreme film". The Swiss-Italian newspaper *La Regione* reviewed the screening, saying: "The film lives today not as an object or a memory but as a cinematic emotion, necessary in its vibrant essence, cruel in its extraordinary narrative, a true lesson in cinema."[7] Previewing the film's subsequent appearance at the

New York Film Festival a month later, *New Yorker* critic Richard Brody wrote: "The surviving version, augmented with additional footage, proves the film to be a spectacular, fanatically ornamental, yet harrowing masterwork of erotic ecstasies and horrors."[8]

Queen Kelly still retains its fatal allure: troubling yet erotic, a lesson in cinema. Doros, who has spent so many hours of his life watching the film frame by frame, is still moved by it. "I still see Paul Ivano's brilliance. I see more clearly now the transgressiveness of Stroheim," he says. "The way I feel about this film is that it's part of me now. It wasn't meant to be. I gave it up 35 years ago. But you know, Kevin Brownlow has *Napoléon* [Abel Gance, 1927], Bob Gitt had *Becky Sharp* [Reuben Mamoulian, 1935].[9] Archivists who live a long time usually come back to their films."

Despite her best efforts, Gloria never quite got to finish her film or to screen any kind of reconstruction at glittering international film festivals. But Doros has—and now we can see *Queen Kelly* in almost all of her glory and discover her story. "This is our farewell tour," say Doros and Heller. "It's a happy ending for us too."

1. Author interview, 31 October 2025.
2. "Ronald Haver, 54; Was Film Restorer Of 'A Star Is Born'", *New York Times*, 21 May 1993, 8.
3. Kevin Thomas, "Queen Kelly to launch tribute to 'a madman'", *Los Angeles Times*, 24 February 1985.
4. Stephen Harvey, "Queen Kelly opens—more than 50 years late", *New York Times*, 22 September 1985, 17.
5. Amy Heller and Dennis Doros, "Thank you to the Art House Convergence and Spotlight Cinema Network!", 3 February 2029, milestonefilms.com
6. missingmovies.org.
7. Ugo Brusaporco, "*Queen Kelly* e Sorrentino come nuvole aprono Venezia", *La Regione,* 27 August 2025.
8. Richard Brody, "What to see in the 2025 New York Film Festival's first week", *The New Yorker*, 25 September 2025.
9. Both of whom helped Doros with the 1985 restoration and he thanked in his speech at Venice.

24
The Curse

Gloria, Von and Joe all had one unusual trait in common. They believed they could see the future. Since she was a young woman, Gloria had been aware of "some kind of muscles in my mind that I had never used before",[1] which gave her forewarnings of events, including the death of Rudolph Valentino. She had another such premonition at the outset of shooting *Queen Kelly*. Gloria was fascinated by the subject of parapsychology and studied it almost as keenly as she did nutrition. Ever since a gypsy woman read his palm and told him his future lay in Universal City, Von had put his faith in fortune-tellers. "I'd be simple-minded," he told *Photoplay*, "not to believe in things that have been proved to me so clearly. Go on and laugh if you want to. You'd have laughed a few years ago at somebody who'd have predicted all the wonders of radio, too, wouldn't you?"[2] Von even learned to read palms himself, under the tutelage of a Professor Winton, who displayed moulds of the hands of his famous clients in the window of his premises in Santa Monica. Joe didn't read tarot cards or tea leaves; he read ticker tape. Renowned as a strategist, always plotting one or two steps ahead in business deals, he read the markets as easily as other people read paperback novels. His ability to predict which way a stock would turn was the basis of his fortune. When the world lamented the Wall Street Crash of 1929, Joe had used his uncanny business savvy not just to protect himself but to profit from the stock market's fall.

The question remains: why did such clairvoyants march forward into a scheme that almost everyone else predicted was doomed to fail? That the papers would consistently label "ill-fated"? That Gloria and Joe would both describe as cursed? It wasn't rational for Gloria and Joe to believe they could complete the film Von planned to make—either to fund it or get it past the censors. Why would Von go to work for a man who believed only in commerce, with no experience of producing a prestige film? For all three, *Queen Kelly* was something of a last-chance saloon, the choice you make when all the others are off the table. Gloria had already proved to her satisfaction that she did her best work by disobeying either Hollywood's business practices (*Madame Sans-Gene*) or its censors (*Sadie Thompson*).

Von was running out of producers and studios who would give him any kind of opportunity. And Joe could see this would be his last chance to complete his foray into Hollywood by making a picture of lasting significance before the coming of sound made the industry unpredictably volatile. The curse of *Queen Kelly* was, you could say, merely the industry biting back against three people who had dared to challenge its rules.

Indeed, all three soon came to consider the project "ill-fated". But this trio of risk-takers *nearly* got away with it. Gloria's acting career slowly sank but she came back with *Sunset Boulevard* and was a star to her dying day. Von's directorial days were done but he would still make great films, not least *La Grande illusion*. Joe walked away intact having profited from his movie career overall. He lost the lover but kept the wife, and moneywise recouped more than his stake—with interest. Derr worked as a successful Hollywood producer until 1943. Others weren't so lucky. Walter Byron, who gave up a promising career in Britain to make it in Hollywood, never did become a star. Maybe he never would have, but spending the best part of two years tied up in *Queen Kelly*—and the subsequent blemish on his CV—meant he never had a chance. The film did little to nothing for anyone else's career either. Of all the people who tried to save the film, Richard Boleslawski went on to a successful career as a Hollywood director, which likely would have happened anyway, but Josef von Sternberg never did make another film. This was not the last chance he needed.

Despite her optimistic outlook, Gloria remained damaged by *Queen Kelly*. As hard as she worked to save and share it, she surrounded herself with a cloud of failure, and to the industry she was the figurehead of one of Hollywood's most epic disasters. However much she might try to reclaim it as a statement of artistic ambition, a provocation to Hollywood's sexual hypocrisies and simply as a beautiful movie, *Queen Kelly* was the reason she most resembled Norma Desmond. The only way to truly lift the curse of the film during her lifetime would have been to see it released, acclaimed and turning a tidy profit. We can hope that Gloria has enjoyed a posthumous respite from the jinx, thanks to the efforts of Dennis Doros and colleagues.

I asked Guy Maddin whether he felt the curse of *Queen Kelly* had affected him when he made his version of Von's *Poto-Poto*. The answer he gave me was surprising, and distressing. "It feels like everything I've been doing since I got hooked up with these doomed, sad spirits, everything about my career has been cursed," he said. "So if I lifted the curse off that film, it fell onto me, like cleaning snow off a roof with a rake—it just all lands on you. So maybe the spirit of *Queen Kelly* is much happier now." I hope this isn't true, and in all seriousness, Maddin rejects the idea of a curse—partly, you sense, because it lets him off the hook for the folly of taking on a project as unwieldy as *Spiritismes*. "I'm not going to say it was cursed. I think it's all my fault. It was just a mad project. I was going to make well over a hundred movies and there was no way to fund them. It's a little more romantic to say the whole thing was cursed, but I'd say a more accurate assessment is that it was stupid—but it was romantic, ultra romantic."[3]

Could the curse of *Queen Kelly* be mobile, travelling to associated projects? Ask any fan of musical theatre and you may find an enthusiastic yes. There is, according to theatre pundits, such a thing as "the curse of *Sunset Boulevard*", attached to both the stage show and its stars. It all begins, of course, with Gloria. In 1953, she tried to get a stage musical adaptation of *Sunset Boulevard* off the ground. A 12-week film shoot with Billy Wilder wasn't enough; she wanted to play Norma every night. She worked with a pair of young songwriters, Dickson Hughes and Richard Stapley, who had recently completed a musical revue about *Time* magazine. Blood, sweat and tears went into the project, but it eventually foundered. For one thing, after a long time spent wavering, Paramount finally decided not to grant the rights, fearing it would diminish their revenues from reissuing the movie. The writers felt the studio had been stringing Gloria along all the time, just as the fictional Paramount indulged Norma in the movie. Then there was the problem of sex. Allegedly, Gloria fell for Hughes, but he did not return her feelings. Far from it: he was discreetly in a relationship with Stapley. Gloria threw a Norma-sized fit when she discovered the truth. Footage exists and is floating around online of Gloria singing one of the songs, "Wonderful People", on *The Steve Allen Show* in 1957. In the 1990s, Hughes and Stapley repurposed their score in a nightclub show—about this backstage intrigue.

The movers and shakers of musical theatre stepped up to the challenge. In the 1960s, Hal Prince wanted a go and asked Stephen Sondheim to write it, with Angela Lansbury in mind as the star, which is a delicious idea. Then, at a cocktail party, Sondheim met Wilder, who spooked him out of it. "You can't write a musical about it, it has to be an opera," said Wilder. "After all, it's a story about a dethroned queen."[4] After Sondheim backed out, Prince turned to John Kander and Fred Ebb. It never happened, but it was too good an idea to die.

Finally, in 1993, the English composer and impresario Andrew Lloyd-Webber brought *Sunset Boulevard* to the stage with libretto and lyrics by Don Black and Christopher Hampton, but not without massive unpleasantness—bitter fights, legal complications, spiralling costs, and dethroned queens. First, the great stage star Patti LuPone, who opened the show as Norma in the West End, was promised she would get the lead role when the show opened on Broadway. Then Lloyd-Webber gave it to Glenn Close, who had starred in Los Angeles. Then he switched again and gave the role to Faye Dunaway. Then he changed his mind, saying Dunaway's singing voice wasn't up to scratch and reverted to Close. Both LuPone and Dunaway sued Lloyd-Webber; both times he settled out of court, for eye-watering sums. LuPone bought a swimming pool and named it after him. But the saga didn't end there. Despite being a critical success, *Sunset Boulevard* failed to break even, partly due to the extravagant blockbuster sets ordered by Lloyd-Webber. And it was Close's turn to fall out with the boss, when she accused him of manipulating the box-office data.

The show is now performed "semi-staged" or on minimalist sets, and remains popular, which raises the prospect of another beleaguered project. Starting in 2005, Close worked to get the musical produced as a film, which finally went into pre-production in 2019 but hit the bumpers during the Covid-19 pandemic. Nicole Scherzinger is the new Norma, garlanded for her performance in Jamie Lloyd's revival of *Sunset Boulevard* in the West End and on Broadway in 2023–4. She is hoping to reprise the role on film. "There has been some talk," she told *the Hollywood Reporter*. "That is my dream, so I'm manifesting that right now."[5] All that is left is to make an opera about the making of *Queen Kelly*. That, after all, really is a story about a dethroned queen. Maybe that could lift the curse.

It is one thing for theatrical people to talk about curses, with their break-a-leg and Scottish Play superstitions, but surely the movie business doesn't work that way. *Au contraire*. Hollywood has long banked on superstition. The business loves to titillate audiences by, say, depicting voodoo rites in lurid 1930s melodramas or teenagers pursued by the spectre of death itself in the 21st-century *Final Destination* horror franchise. But Hollywood has long romanticised its own business practices with the mystique of movie magic and associated hoodoo. An actress with a string of one or two flops is "box-office poison"; one who wins an Oscar is expected to bestow good fortune on her next film. And yet the Best Actress "curse" predicts a failure to follow. Furthermore the "Oscar love curse" is said to jinx the romantic life of anyone who wins an acting award. If it sounds inconsistent, well, of course it is.

When anthropologist Hortense Powdermaker visited Hollywood in the 1940s, she was struck by how irrational the business could be, with producers working on "instinct" and the groupthink of the industry censors creating a whole new set of powerful taboos. "Hollywood bustles with frenzied activity, and makes use of the most modern technology," she wrote. "Yet at the same time it gives the impression of being only half awake in its slow emergence from a dim prehistoric past of illusions, fears, and magical thinking."[6] In the same way that the Melanesians of Oceania were secretive about "black magic", Powdermaker found that Hollywood producers were furtive about "net profits". Von nailed it at Griffith's funeral when he said, "In Hollywood, you're only as good as your last picture." Screenwriter William Goldman was even more concise: "Nobody knows anything." A curse is merely a story we tell ourselves about a failure, an excuse we make instead of learning from what we have done wrong.

Queen Kelly, spoken of in hushed tones even by Steven Bach and the other producers of *Heaven's Gate*, is a special kind of cautionary tale in an industry that doesn't like to learn lessons from failure. *Queen Kelly* is that unhappy bad luck story of a beleaguered production, escalating in cost, that doesn't have a happy ending, unlike say *Titanic* (James Cameron, 1997), which after a long and difficult shoot broke box-office records, won Oscars and launched careers; or even *Cleopatra*, which made its money back in the long run. This is the real curse of *Queen Kelly*, which has become a kind of *Macbeth* of the movies—not to be spoken of. No one can quite agree on why the "Scottish play" became associated with bad luck, but the most sensational story is the one that says a coven of witches hexed the play because they were enraged that Shakespeare had transcribed one of their spells in the text. The credulous enjoy listing the number of mishaps that have befallen productions of *Macbeth* over the years, from an actor killed by a wound obtained in an onstage sword fight in 1947 to theatre fires, a riot, a suicide, and even terrible reviews. Filmmakers are not immune. Dario Argento claimed his horror film *Opera* (1987), set in a theatre staging Giuseppe Verdi's *Macbeth*, was beset by the play's curse. No wonder Bach and his colleagues felt that likewise, the *Queen Kelly* curse could be activated by speaking its name aloud.

If we consider Macbeth in classic style as a tragic hero, brought low by his fatal flaw of ambition, we are reminded of another path by which a curse attaches itself to *Queen Kelly*—via Joe. This, if it were true, would be the most serious malediction of them all. Just a few months before Joe died, his son Ted walked away from that car crash in Chappaquiddick, leaving his passenger to die. Speaking publicly in the aftermath of the event, Ted put a voice to a fear that many had shared, wondering aloud whether "some awful curse did actually hang over all the Kennedys".[7] The idea of a Kennedy curse was not new. The family had suffered a devastating series of losses, starting with Joe Jr's death in the war and most famously the assassinations of John and Bobby. These incidents were just as well known to the public as the family's material blessings.

Over the years, with more stories added to the legend, the idea of a Kennedy curse has grown, and unscientific as it may be, lodged in the public's imagination. For many people, the curse begins with Joe, the patriarch and founder of the Kennedy clan. His must be the original sin that brought about the punishment. And there is no shortage of tales to tell against Kennedy, true or not, beginning with those bootlegger rumours and ending with whatever Gloria wrote in her memoir that was not deemed fit to print. In her recent book, *Ask Not*, Maureen Callahan sets out the alleged crimes—and many of them are deadly serious—of three generations of Kennedy men. She identifies the Kennedy curse not as a groundless superstition but as a term to encompass a serious pattern of misogynistic, violent and reckless behaviour. For Callahan, it indeed begins with Joe, although she identifies his original sins as incidents that took place long after *Queen Kelly*, including his open support for Hitler at the outset of World War II, and his decision to lobotomise Rosemary. In terms that might resonate with Gloria, Callahan describes "a pathology passed down from the father, a kind of negative life force, this treatment of women as accessories, broodmares, chattel. It was in the Kennedy DNA, and there didn't seem to be a cure."[8] If the Kennedy curse were real, then maybe it started to make itself known earlier. After all, Joe told Gloria that he experienced his first failure at the age of 40, and that failure was *Queen Kelly*—with its sacrilegious scenes and its adulterous origin.

The idea of a Kennedy curse is an unusual case of superstition and sensationalism colliding with a series of terrible facts. The idea persists whenever a new sorrow visits the family. Most recently, in December 2025, JFK's grand-daughter Tatiana Schlossberg died aged just 35 of a rare cancer that was diagnosed within hours of her giving birth to her second child, giving her a year to live. Before her death, she wrote: "Now I have added a new tragedy to [my mother's] life, to our family's life, and there's nothing I can do to stop it."[9]

Gloria was more officially the target of a curse, an unsuccessful one, cast her way later in life. People had long said that her association with Norma Desmond was a kind of hex, veiling her true persona as a beloved star and a first-rate comedienne, with the shroud of a madwoman, a murderess. One of her enemies tried to flesh out that horror. Kenneth Anger may not have been party to mainstream Hollywood's magical thinking, but he was a true devotee of the occult, practising "cinematic magic" in his movies. When Gloria took him to court in 1977 for the liberties taken in *Hollywood Babylon*, he hit back with every trick in his paranormal arsenal. He sent Gloria poison-pen letters attacking her work and her personal life, saying that she had finally become Norma. Mocking her campaigns against sugar consumption, he signed these notes "Uncle Sugar" or "Uncle $C_{12}H_{22}O_{11}$". He made a voodoo doll out of a picture of her and Valentino, he wrote spells, sometimes in

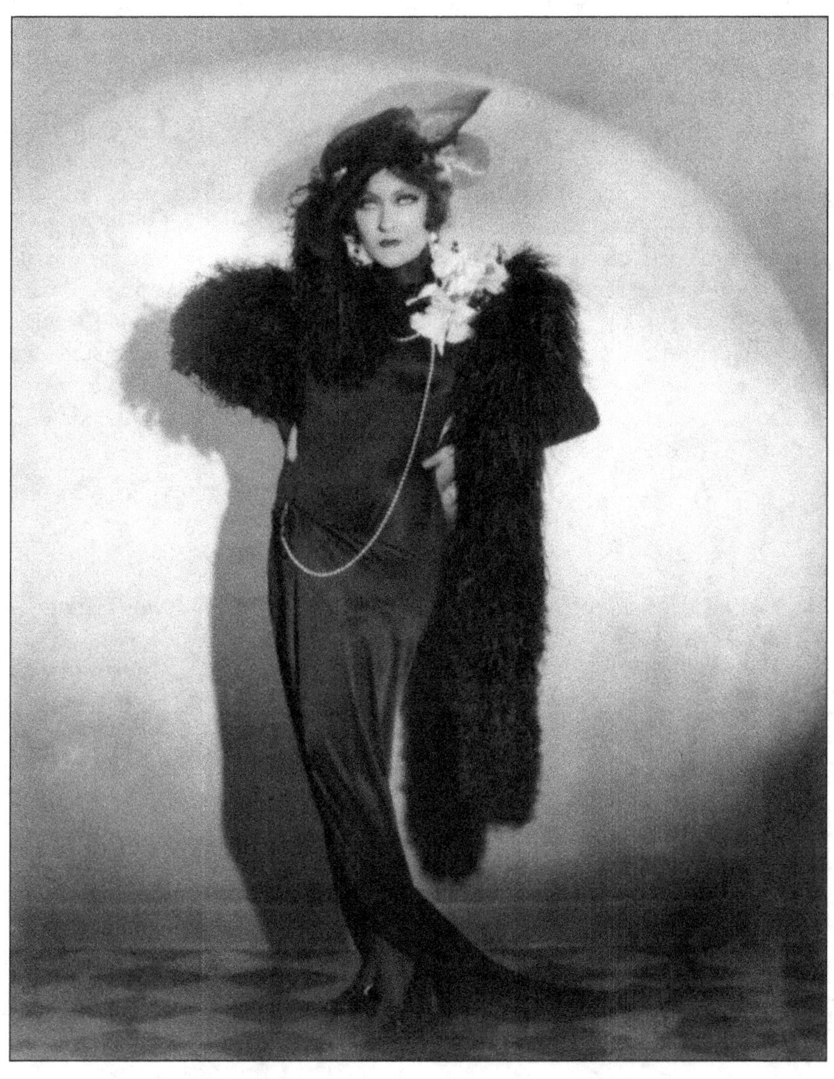

Gloria Swanson never gave up on *Queen Kelly*,
her 'child that somehow didn't want to be born'.
Milestone Film & Video.

Latin, and he filled a miniature coffin with sugar, painted "Hic jacet [here lies] Gloria Swanson" on the top, and mailed it to her apartment. Gloria doesn't mention this hate campaign in her memoir, but she did preserve all these damned artefacts in her archive. She wouldn't memorialise such vindictive behaviour in print but she didn't mind future generations knowing that she had once again triumphed over a setback that would throw a weaker woman off course.

After all, believing in a curse is just another way of giving up your own power, which is something Gloria would never do. She certainly never gave up as far as *Queen Kelly* was concerned. She saved the reels, she told its story, and she kept its name alive. Just as she did with Anger's grim invocations, she left a few clues in her archive to fill in the gaps. This Hollywood rebel knew a thing or two about defiance. And she didn't believe in curses any more than she adhered to the new-fangled taboos concocted by the Hays Office. To banish the hex, if ever it existed, we should take up Von's invitation to laugh. In fact, we should follow our queen, who never was dethroned after all, throw our chins in the air, and cackle: "Curses—me foot!"

1.   *SoS*, 118.
2.   Harry Lang, "Exposing the Occult Hocus-Pocus in Hollywood", *Photoplay*, December 1928, 99.
3.   Author interview.
4.   Quoted in Cohan, 92.
5.   Lexi Carson, "Nicole Scherzinger on How Her 'Pop Star Mentality' Prepared Her for *Sunset Blvd.*, 'Manifesting' a Film Adaptation and First Tony Nom", *The Hollywood Reporter*, 8 May 2025.
6.   Hortense Powdermaker, *Hollywood, the Dream Factory: An Anthropologist Looks at the Movie-Makers*, (Little, Brown, 1950), 281.
7.   "Kennedy's Television Statement to the People of Massachusetts", *New York Times*, 26 July 1969, 10.
8.   Maureen Callahan, *Ask Not: The Kennedys and the Women They Destroyed* (Mudlark, 2025), 131.
9.   Tatiana Schlossberg, "A Further Shore", *The New Yorker*, 8 December 2025, 15.

Acknowledgments

First and foremost, I want to thank Dennis Doros and Amy Heller of Milestone, for saving *Queen Kelly*, for trusting me to tell its story, and supporting this project every step of the way. Also, Paul Cronin, who makes fast decisions and gave me this wonderful opportunity. Cari Beauchamp, while she was alive, was a font of wisdom and encouragement. Through her work on Joseph P. Kennedy and Hollywood, she has also been at my side throughout this process, which has been as poignant as it was precious. Richard Koszarski, the maven of Stroheim studies, and Mike Mashon were both incredibly generous with their time and their valuable scholarship. I am grateful also to Guy Maddin for sharing his war stories of reviving *Poto-Poto*, and for savouring the strangeness in this melodramatic history.

I am deeply indebted to the resources of the Harry Ransom Center, George Eastman Museum, The John F. Kennedy Presidential Library and Museum, Georgetown University Library, New York Public Library and the Margaret Herrick Library (Academy of Motion Picture Arts and Sciences), as well as the boundless riches of Media Lantern and Newspapers. com. In particular, I would like to thank Steve Wilson of the Harry Ransom Center and Nancy Kauffman of George Eastman Museum for providing images. Thanks also to my homes away from home, the BFI Library and the British Library—and closer at hand, to Worthing Library.

This book was blessed by having good friends. For support, expert knowledge and advice I am grateful to so many people that I have to alphabetise this list: Julie K. Allen, Karie Bible, Rob Byrne, Bryony Dixon, Thomas Flew, Adrian Garvey, Kate Howell, Sheldon Hall, Lies Lanckman, Michael Leader, Henry K. Miller, Andrew Moor, Laura Mulvey, Heather Osborn, Tim Robey, Daniel Rosenthal, Amy Sargeant, Gavin Smith, Dan Streible and Jay Weissberg. An extra loud thank-you, which should be in all caps, to the friendship and feminist uplift of Kate Saccone and Maggie Hennefeld, who provided feedback on a key chapter. To Anna Bailey for good sense and oat cappuccinos.

Endless thanks to Tony, Diana and Stephen Hutchinson, the three greatest cheerleaders a writer could have. To Elsie and Lana for feline fellowship. Above all to Nicky Bason for believing in me and in this book, for his "punchy" advice and boundless enthusiasm.

Index

¡Que viva México!, 160
"Love, Your Magic Spell is Everywhere", 132, 190
"Wonderful One" (song), 28, 190, 199
7th Heaven (Borzage), n.48

Abercrombie, Milo, 74
Abie's Irish Rose, 83
Academy Awards, 46, n.47, 128, 134, 148, 159, 168, 175, 201, 214, 215
Ace in the Hole (Wilder), 169
Aldrich, Robert, 176
Allen, Janice, 204
Anatahan (von Sternberg), 182
Anger, Kenneth, 28, 198, 216-8
Anger, Zia, xv
Apocalypse Now (Coppola), 141, 208
Arbuckle, Roscoe, 25, 100
Argento, Dario, 215
Arsenic and Old Lace (Capra), 167
Ask Not (Callahan), 216
Associated Negro Press, 143-4
Avedon, Richard, 37, 200
Awakening, The (Fleming), 74

Bach, Steven, 141, 216
Bachrach, Ernest, 86
Bardot, Brigitte, 176
Barbera, Alberto, 208
Barrymore, Lionel, 44-45, 89
Beau Geste (Heyes), 76
Beacon Theater, The, ix, x, xi, xiii, xiv, xv, 190
Becky Sharp (Mamoulian), 209

Beggars of Life (Wellman), 93, 94
Beery, Wallace, 3, 21-2, n.30, 41, 64
Beeston, Alix, xv
Beeston, Fred, 33
Belfrage, Cedric, 107, 163,
Bell, Monta, 54
Belloc, Hilaire, 33
Benjamin, Robert, 203
Bennett, Constance, 133, 137, 139
Bergman, Ingrid, 200
Berlin Film Festival, 205
Berlin, Irving, 136, 138
Bern, Paul, 116-7
Bertini, Francesca, 12, 90
Beverly Hillbillies, The, xii
Bibo, Irving, 136
Bieler, Dr, 44
Big Parade, The (Vidor), 55
Billington, Francellia, 15
Birinski, Leo, 131
Birth of a Nation, The (Griffith), 3-4, 42, 152
Blair, Linda, 197
Blue Angel, The (von Sternberg), 182, 184
Boleslawski, Richard, 135, 154, 171, 212
Borelli, Lyda, 90
Bowker, Virginia, 3, 133
Brackett, Charles, 170, n.30
Brandel, Joseph, 182
Breen, Joseph, 147, 170, 175, 204
Bren, Milton H., 176
Brent, Evelyn, 34
Brief Encounter (Lean), 89
Brody, Richard, 209
Brooks, Louise, 175

Brownlow, Kevin, 141, 142, 155, 200, 209
Bruce, Lenny, 191
Buckland, Wilfred, 24
Burbridge, Ben, 60
Burnett, Charles, 205
Burroughs, Marie, 9
Busch, Mae, 17
Bushman, Francis X., 1-2
Byron, Walter, xii, 74-75, 80, 98, 105, 110, 113, 114, 131, 134, 156, 157, 181, 184, 212

Cade, Maya, 206
Cahiers du cinéma, 171, n.192
Callahan, Maureen, 216
Campion, Jane, 205
Cannes Film Festival, 168
Cantor, Eddie, 160
Capote, Truman, 191
Card, James, 204
Carmen Jones (Preminger), 153
Carriere, Victor, 181
Cartier, 197, 201
Centre Pompidou, 195-6
Chanel, Coco, 155
Chaplin, Charlie, xi, 21, 40-1, 100, 173, 182, 194
Chaplin, Geraldine, 194, 195
Charles III, King, 85
Cheat, The (DeMille), 22
Chenzira, Ayoka, 206
Cinémathèque fançaise, 39, 57, 160, 176, 179, 190
Citizen Kane (Welles), 96, 155, 160
Clarke, Shirley, 206
Cleopatra (Mankiewicz), xiv, 141, 215
Clift, Montgomery, 171
Close-Up, 14, 95, 142-3
Close, Glenn, 214
Collins, Kathleen, 205
Cochrane, Robert H. 31
Cody, Lew, 138
Cohen, Milton, 60, 62-3
Cohens and the Kellys, The (Pollard), 83

Cohn, Harry, 159
Colbert, Claudette, n.30, 153
Cole, Rufus, 11, 12
Columbia Trust, 4, 5, 8, 9
Compson, Betty, 9
Congo Maisie (Potter), 166
Cooper, Miriam, 44
Coppola, Francis Ford, 141, 208
Coughlin, Sean, 205
Crawford, Joan, 46, 176
Crewe, Regina, 79
Crews, Laura Hope, 94, 132, 134, 136, 167
Crossman, Grace, 61
Crowe, Cameron, 170
Crowther, Bosley, 167
Cukor, George, 78,
Currier, Guy, 9, 31

D'Arcy, Roy, 54
Daggett, Rae, 98, 120, 127, 151, 175
Daily Telegraph, The, 85, 158
Dalí, Salvador, 194
Dana, Viola, 34, 83
Daniels, Bebe, 24, 153
Daniels, William H., 51
Dark Victory, 159
Darling, Candy, xi
Daum, Raymond, 200
Daves, Delmer, 136
Davey, William, 161
Davies, Marion, 10, 115, 175
Davis, Bette, 158, 159, 175, 176
Day the Clown Cried, The (Lewis), xiv
De Forest, Lee, 94
De Grasse, Sam, 15
de La Falaise, Henri, 38, 39, 40, 42, 43, 46, 61, 62, 63-64, 78, 84, 91, 94, 99, 100, 101-2, 118, 120, 121, 122, 126, 131-2, 133, 135-6, 137-8, 139, 155, 159
De Sica, Vittorio, 176
Degas, Brian, 198-200

DeMille, Cecil B., 22-24, 27, 28, 29, 34, 36, 68, 90, 95, 96, 111, 129, 147, 149, 153, 172-3, 201
Denson, Eli, 208
Derr, E.B., 32, 61, 62-3, 93. 94, 104, 115-17, 120, 122, 126-7
Dietrich, Marlene, 182, 183, 184
Dismond, Geraldyn, 142-3
Doros, Dennis, 203-9
Double Indemnity (Wilder), 169, n.176
Douglas, Kirk, 181
Dove, Billie, 97
Drain, Émile, 38
Dufty, William, 188, 190, 198-9
Dunaway, Faye, 214
Dune (novel and film adaptations), 194-5
Dwan, Allan, 21, 35-6, 38, 42, 94, 136, 138

Edington, Harry, 127
Edward VIII, King, 84, 85, 115
Eels, George
Eisenstein, Sergei, 160
Eisner, Lotte, 163, 168
Emerson, John, 4, 13
Epstein, Jacob, 199
Epstein, Jeffrey, 85
Essanay Studios, 1-3, 22, 152,
Ex-Wife (Parrott), 134
Exhibitors Herald, 33, 95
Eyre, Laurence, 134, 136

Fairbanks, Douglas, 6, 13, 25, 40, 42
Farmer, Michael, 139, 155
Farmer, Michelle, 155
FIAF, 192
Film Booking Offices of America (FBO), 12, 31-4, 35, 43, 60, 52, 79, 80, 83, 95, 96, 115, 117-8
film maudit, xiv
First National Pictures, 95-6, 97
Fitzgerald, F. Scott, xv
Fitzgerald, John F. (Honey Fitz), 4, 5, 6, 10, 12, 146

Fitzgerald Kennedy, Rose, 4, 5-6, 9, 32, 33, 59, 64-5, 78, 91, 100, 101, 117, 126, 133, 138, 139, 145-7, 161, 187, 198
Times to Remember, 198
Fitzmaurice, George, 13, 163
Fleming, Victor, 74, 138
Flesh and the Devil (Brown), 44, 74
Fonda, Henry, *158*
Ford, John, 76
Foreign Affair, A (Wilder), 169
Fox, 42, 43, 164
Fox, William, 34
Francis, Madam, 102, 109
Frazier, Robert,143, 144
Fuller, Dale, 17, 18
Fun in a Chinese Laundry (von Sternberg), 182
Futter, Walter, 149, 160-1, 171, 181, 182, 190

Garbo, Greta, 44, 97, 163, 170
Gasnier, Louis J., 11-2
Gaynor, Janet, 46, 142
George Eastman House, 147, 176, 204, 206
George, Maude, 17, 57
George, Prince, Duke of Kent, 100
Germonprez, Louis, 97
Germonprez, Valerie, 14, 15, 49, 166-7
Gibson, Florence, 98
Gilbert, John, 44, 54, 55, 84, 110, 117
Gish, Dorothy, 4
Gish, Lillian, 14, 44, 90, 97, 153,
Gitt, Robert, 204, 209
Giuffre, Virginia, 85
Glazer, Benjamin, 78, 94, 116-7, 122, 128, 129, 132
Glyn, Elinor, 27, 55, 105, 193
Godless Girl, The (DeMille), 95
Gold Rush, The (Chaplin), 41, 43, 67
Goldman, William, 215
Goldwyn studios, 50, 51, 74
Goldwyn, Samuel, 22

Gone With the Wind (Fleming), 138
Gorilla Hunt, The (Burbridge),
    60-1, 88
Goulding, Edmund xi, 116-17, 122,
    129, 132, 134, 138, 156, 158, 159
Gowland, Gibson, 15, 50, 52
Graham, Sheilah, 181
Grand Hotel (Goulding), 156
Gravina, Cesare, 50
Gray, Bill, 10, 12
Great Gatsby, The, xv
Griffith, D. W., 3-4, 13, 14, 17, 40,
    41, 98, 152, 153, 164, 215
Griffith, Richard, 176, n.192

Hall, Mordaunt, 46, 51, 55, 56, 86,
    139,
Hallelujah (Vidor), 144-5, 153
Halsey, Forrest, 37, 38
Harrington, Curtis, xi, 191
Harrison's Reports, 52, 89
Harry Ransom Center, 200, 203
Harvard University, 5, 12, 34-5, 42,
    44, 60, 61, 101
Hatswell, Donald Robert Overall,
    76, 184
Haver, Ronald, 204
Hayakawa, Sessue, 22, 83
Haynes, Daniel L., 144
Hays Formula 26, 43, 52, 72, 106,
Hays Office, xi, 26, 40,42, 43, 45,
    46, 69, 72, 76, 78, 88, 107, 112,
    117, 119, 125, 127, 141, 142,
    146, 147, 148, 218,
Hays, Will, xi-ii, 26-7, 29, 32,33, 34,
    35, 43, 44, 46, 59, 113, 143-4,
    145, 147, 149, 163
Hayworth, Rita, 46
Head, Edith, 171, 176, 197
Hearts in Dixie (Sloane), 143
Heath, Lance, 86
Heaven's Gate (Cimino), xiv, 141, 215
Heffernan, Harold, 160
Heller, Amy, 205-7, 209
Her Man (Garnett), 139
Hersholt, Jean, 50, 52

Hertz, Joseph D., 31
Hitchcock, Alfred, xiii, xiv
Hoberman, J., xiv
Holden, William, 171, 199
Hollywood (TV series), n.15, 200
Hollywood Babylon (Anger), 28,
    198, 216
Holmes, Gerda, 2
Hopper, Hedda, 146, 163, 184
Howard, Sidney, 138
Howey, Walter, 31
Hubert, René, 38, 41, 133
Hunt, Madge, 98
Huston, John, xiv

I, Claudius (von Sternberg), xiv, 182
Imitation of Life (Stahl), 153
Intolerance (Griffith), 13, 98, 153,
Ivano, Paul, 102-4, 106, 107, 109,
    111, 125, 182, 209

Jazz Singer, The (Crosland), 62, 130
Jodorowsky, Alejandro, 194-195
Johnson, Evan, 195
Johnson, Martin and Osa, 89, 115,
    134, 159
Jones, May, 13, 166
Joplin, Janis, xiii
Julian, Rupert, 50, 173

Kane, Robert, 46
Karloff, Boris, 167
Keaton, Buster, 173
Kennedy curse, 215-6
Kennedy Jr, Robert F., 187-8
Kennedy Shriver, Eunice, 200
Kennedy, Bobby, 189, 191, 215
Kennedy, John Fitzgerald (JFK), 9,
    63, 146, 147, 216
Kennedy, Joseph Jr, 6, 161, 187, 215
Kennedy, Joseph P.,
    Affair with Gloria Swanson, xv,
        60-1, 62-4, 78, 81, 91, 138-9,
        146, 161, 183-4, 188, 199-
        200, 206

ambassadorial career, 32, n.47,
    145, 147, 160
antisemitism, 10, 32, 33, 60,
    95-96
as producer, xii, 33-4, 35, 59, 60-
    1, 65, 67, 73-4, 76, 78-9, 81,
    96, 104, 134, 135-9, 142,
    143, 146-7, 148-9,
Banking career, 5, 8-9
Catholicism, 5, 33, 65, 67, 91,
    145-7
early life and education, 4-5
Exit from Hollywood, 147, 149
FBO career, 12, 31-4, 35, 60, 62,
    79, 83, 95, 96, 115, 117, 118
First National Pictures career,
    95-6
Fore River Shipyards, 9
Fred Stone Productions, 10-11
Harvard lecture series and *The
Story of the Films*, 34-35, 42, 44,
    60,
Hayden, Stone, 9-10, 11
Illness and death, xii, 187
K-A-O investments, 95, 96
Marriage to Rose Fitzgerald, 4,
    5-6, 9, 59, 64-5, 78, 91, 100,
    101, 126, 133, 138, 139, 145-
    7, 187,
Pathé career, n.47, 62, 95, 96,
    117, 118, 126, 132, 135, 139,
    147, 156,
Relationship with Will Hays, 27,
    32, 33, 34, 35, 147,
Robertson-Cole career, 11-2
Securities and Exchange
    Commission, 145
Stock manipulation, 9-10, 31, 81,
    133, 145, 211,
Wall Street bomb attack, 1920,
    7-8
Wall Street Crash of 1929, 148, 211
Kennedy, Kathleen, 187
Kennedy, Patrick Joseph (P. J.), 4, 5,
    10, 131, 132
Kennedy, Rosemary, 187, 216

Kennedy, Ted, 117, 187, 200, 206, 215
Kerry, Norman, 44, 49-50, 74
Keystone, 17, 22
Kid from Spain, The (McCarey), 60
Kier, Udo, 194, 195
Kimball Young, Clara, 24, n.29, 41
King Kong (Cooper/Schoedsack),
    96, 153
King of Kings, The (DeMille), 34,
    95, 96, 173
Kino International, 203-4, 205
Kismet (Gasnier, 11-2, 33
Kongo (Cowen), 88-9, 90, 166
Kopechne, Mary Jo, 187
Kosher Kitty Kelly (Home), 83
Koszarski, Richard, 3
Kotyk, Bob, 195
Krim, Donald, 203-4

Laemmle, Carl, 11, 12, 15, 16, 18,
    19, 20, 23, 68, 164
Langlois, Henri, 39, 57, 163, 168,
    171, 176, 190
Lansbury, Angela, 213
Lasky, Jesse, 22, 23, 25, 26, 28, 29
    34, 128,
Last Command, The (Sternberg), 182
Laughton, Charles, 166
Lawrence, Viola, 97, 155, 181, 189, 204
Lawson, Wayne, 199
LeBaron, Wiliam, 35, 78, 97, 104,
    107, 111, 119, 122, 128, 129
Lee, Bob, 204
Lehár, Franz, 54, 136-8
Leisen, Mitchell, 24
Leonard, Robert Z., 134
Leone, Sergio, xiv
Lichtman, Al, 94, 117, 131, 156
Life, 190
Linder, Max, 12
Lloyd, Frank, 34, 153
Loew, Marcus, 32, 34, 44
Lombard, Carole, 166, 197
Loos, Anita, 4, 13, 107, 163, 167
Lord, Father Daniel A., n.29, 147
Loved One, The (Waugh), 170

Lowe, Edmund, 74-5
Lubitsch, Ernst, n.30, 57, 107, 166, 169
LuPone, Patti, 213-4
Lynch, David, xiv, 194

Macbeth, 215
Maddin, Guy, 195-6, 212-3
Magnificent Ambersons, The
    (Welles), xiv
Maid of Salem (Lloyd), 153
Margulies, William, 104
Marion, Frances, xiv-v, 33, 118
Marshall, Tully, 54, 97, 124, 125
Marshman Jr., D. M., 170
Martinelli, Giovanni, 94
Maslin, Janet, 199
Mathis, June, xiv, 51
Matieson, Otto, 131
Maugham, Somerset, 42-3
Mayer, Louis B., 51, 54, 81, 159, 173-4
McCarey, Leo, 160
McKinney, Nina Mae, 145
McLaglen, Victor, 42, 75
McPherson, Aimee Semple, 79
Megalopolis, 208
Merry Widow, The (operetta), 54, 136
MGM, xiv, 23, 32, 34, 41, 44, 51, 54,
    74, 88, 95, 136, 137, 159, 166, 196,
Miles, Harold, 96, 97
Milestone Film and Video, 205-9
Million and One Nights of Film, A
    (Ramsaye), n.xvi, 189
Mix, Tom, 33
MoMA, n.47, 158, 162, 171, 176,
    188, n.192, 196
Monroe, Marilyn, 188
Moore, Colleen, 97
Moore, Eddie, 10, 12, 31, 33, 61,
    115, 122, 126
Moore, Grace, 197
Moore, Owen, 138
Morgan, Ann, 105,
Mountbatten-Windsor, Andrew, 85
Movietone, 57, 79, 93, 122

MPPDA (Motion Picture Producers
    and Distributors of America),
    26, 27
Muir, Florabel, 147
Murnau, F. W., xii
Murphy, Dudley, 160, 190
Murray, Mae, 54-5, 68, 84, 109, 174

Napoléon (Gance), 209
National Film Theatre
    (BFI Southbank), 89, 200
National Legion of Decency, 147
Nazimova, Alla, 90-91
Negri, Pola, 170
Neilan, Marshall "Mickey", 27-8, 190
New York Times, The, 19, 42, 46,
    56, 79, 95, 133, 161, 167, 174,
    199, 205,
New Yorker, The, 158, 209
Nielsen, Asta, 90
Nilsson, Anna Q., 173
Number 13 (Hitchcock), xiv

O'Connell, Cardinal, 6, 101, 145-6,
O'Leary, Ted, 61, 136
Olson, Nancy, 172, 197
Osso, Adolphe, 38
Owen, Seena, 98, 107-109, 134, 181

Pagode, La, 179, 181
Paramount (Famous Players-
    Lasky), 22, 23, 25, 29, 33, 35,
    39, 40, 41, 44, 46, 55, 56, 57, 60,
    79, 95, 134, 136, 166, 170, 171,
    172, 173, 201, 213
Parker, Albert, x, 41
Parrott, Ursula, 134
Parsons, Louella, 52, 79
Pathé, n.47, 62, 63, 95, 96, 115, 117,
    118, 119, 135, 139, 147, 156
Patsy, The (Vidor), 176
Payne, Alexander, 208
Peeping Tom (Powell), xiv
Peper, William, xiii
Perret, Léonce, 37, 38
Peter Pan, 40

Phantom of the Opera, The, 173
Phillips, Siân, 194
Photoplay, 19, 32, 33, 37, 39, 42, 51,
    65, 158, 211
Pickford, Charlotte, 60
Pickford, Jack, 25
Pickford, Mary, 25, 40, 60, 72, 90,
    100, 170, 174
Pitts, ZaSu, 50, 52, 55, 164,
Pollock, Gordon, 102
Polo, Malvina, 17
Poppe, Harry, 155
Powdermaker, Hortense, 214
Powers, Pat, 12, 31, 55, 56, 57, 61,
    65, 67, 74, 76, 115
Production Code/Lord-Quigley
    Code, 26, 33, 147, 149, 156, 214
Puritan Dress Company, 176, 183

Queen Kelly,
    appearance in *Sunset Boulevard*,
        171, 173,
    as a film maudit or cursed film,
        xiv, xvi, 132, 135 140, 141,
        212-3, 215, 218,
    as a musical operetta, 136
    as a Ruritanian film, 88
    first cessation of filming, 124-9,
        141, 148-9
    as a sound film, 93-5, 121
    as an underground film, ix, xi,
        xv, 142, 190, 191,
    as an unfinished film, ix, xi-ii,
        xiii-iv
    broadcast on European TV, 188
    broadcast on US TV, xii, 189, 190
    casting, 74-6, 97-8
    characterisation of Queen Kelly,
        83-4, 86-8, 90, 91
    commentary by Black journalists,
        142-3, 143-4,
    concerns over content, 72-3, 78,
        10-7, 112-3, 119, 122, 124-5,
        126-17, 141-2, 143-5, 146, 147
    contribution of Paul Stein, 131-2
    contribution of
        Richard Boleslawski, 135
    copyright status, 188
    depiction of monarchy, 83-5,
        107, 109
    depiction of Tanzania
    destruction of prints, xiii, 159-60
    disagreements on set, 102-4
    discovery of African footage,
    dismissal of Erich von Stroheim,
        127-8, 130, 134-5,
    escalating costs, 93, 96, 115, 117,
        131, 134, 138,
    final cessation of filming, 138,
        141, 148-9
    shoot, 101, 102-9, 110, 111, 114-
        6, 119-126, 131-2
    Gloria Swanson's replacement
        ending, 155-6, 183
    influences on African setting,
        88-90
    limited release in early 1932,
        156-7
    opinion of Allan Dwan on, 136
    opinion of Edmund Goulding
        on, 129, 134
    planned adaptation by Josef von
        Sternberg, 181, 182-3, 184
    pre-production, 73-6, 80, 81, 93,
        96-7
    preservation status, 160, 162,
        193-4, 203, 204, 206,
    Priest played by a Black actor,
        143-4, 145
    production design, 96-7
    promotion by Gloria Swanson,
        ix-xiii, xiv-xv, xvi, 188-9, 193
    Publicity, 79, 86,
    reasons for abandonment,
    reconstructions and re-releases,
        189-90
    repertory screenings, 162, 176,
        179-81, 188, 189-90, 191,
        193
    report by Eugene Walter, 126-7

sale of footage to Walter Futter, 159, 160,
screenplay revisions, 73, 76-8, 97, 115-7, 120, 122
Swamp, The (screenplay), 68-74, 76-8
title change, 83
Quigley, Martin J., 33, 147, 156
Quirk, James R., 33, 39-40

Rampling, Charlotte, 194
Ramsaye, Terry, 32, 65
Ranger the Wonder Dog, 59, 107
RCA Photophone, 62, 93, 94-5
Red Badge of Courage, The (Huston) xiv
Redemption of David Corson, The (Thomson), 74
Rée, Max, 97
Reefer Madness (Gasnier), 12
Regeneration (Walsh), 42
Reid, Wallace, 4, 25, 40
Reinhardt, Harry, 75
Reinhardt, Heinrich, 75
Reinhardt, Max, 97
Réjane, 37
Renoir, Jean, 164-5, 167
RKO, 96, 97, 104, 115, 117, 139, 161
Robertson-Cole Distributing Company, 11-12, 55, 83
Roosevelt, Franklin D., 145
Rothafel, Samuel "Roxy", x
Rossellini, Roberto, 200
Rowland, Richard A., 40
Roxy, The, x-xi, xii, 34, 42
Russell Taylor, John, 175, 200
Ruth, Babe, 11

Salvation Hunters, The (Sternberg), 182
Sarecky, Louis, 104, 119, 129
Sarnoff, David, 63, 96
Savoca, Nancy, 206
Scarface (Hawks), 156
Schenck, Joseph, 41-3, 60, 61-2, 94, 154, 157

Schenck, Nick, 41
Scherzinger, Nicole, 214
Schlossberg, Tatiana, 216
Scollard, Pat, 62, 134
Sea Hawk, The (Lloyd), 34
Sennett, Mack, 22, 63, 173
Seymour, James, 35, n.47
Shanghai Express (Sternberg), 156, 183
Shearer, Norma, 134, 170
Siegel, Lawrence, 181, 182-3, 190
Sight and Sound, 39, 160, 174, 175
Sills, Milton, 34
Sherwood, Robert E., 52, 78
Shipman, Nell, 205
Skinner, Otis, 11, 12
Smith, Al, 145
Smith, Agnes, 52
Solomon, Stefan, xv
Somborn, Herbert, 24-25, 27, 28-29, n.30, 35, 38, 41
Sondheim, Stephen, 213
Sothern, Ann, 166
Spiritismes (Maddin), 195-6, 213
Squaw Man, The (DeMille), 22
Stanwyck, Barbara, *173*
Steichen, Edward, 37, 46, 80, 175
Stein, Paul, 131-2
Steno, 176
Stern, Julius, 19
Sterne, Herb, 181
Sternheim, Carl, 105
Stone, Fred, 10-1
Stone, Galen, 9
Stotesbury, Mr and Mrs, 63, 64
Street Angel (Borzage , n.48, 142
Stroheim, Erich von,
allegations of espionage, 13-14
attitude to sound films, 94, 130
beginnings of film career, 3-4, 13-14
belief in clairvoyance, 211
career decline, 166-7
Catholicism, 55, 65, 67, 143
early life and first years in America, 3

harsh treatment of actors, 18, 50,
    54, 109
illness and death, 163-4, 167-8
long working hours, 102, 163
name change, 3, 84
perceived anti-Americanism,
    19-20
perfectionism, 14, 15, 16-18, 56,
    73, 96-7 102, 105, 110, 115-
    6, 117-118, 122
Poto-Poto (novel), 167, 195, 196,
    212
Poto-Poto (screenplay), 165-6
screenwriting, 14, 89-90, 94, 164,
    165
sensitivity and depression, 14, 166
villain persona, 13-14, 164-5, 167
FILMS AS ACTOR:
    As You Desire Me, 163
    Birth of a Nation, The
      (see separate entry)
    Five Graves to Cairo,
      169-70
    Grande Illusion, La, 167, 212
    Great Gabbo, The, 164
    Heart of Humanity, The,
      13, 14
    Sunset Boulevard
      (see separate entry)
    Lost Squadron, The, 164
    Old Heidelberg, 4, 57, 98
    Sylvia of the Secret Service,
      13-4
FILMS AS DIRECTOR:
    Blind Husbands, 11, 15-16,
      21, 23, 68, 164 (*Pinnacle,*
      The, 14-15, 21, 23)
    Devil's Pass-Key, The, 16, 17
    Foolish Wives, 16-20, 33, 49,
      57, 148
    Greed, xiv, 50-2, 54, 56, 57,
      69, 98, 148, 173, 195
    Honeymoon, The, 56, 57, 193
    Merry Widow, The, 54-5,
      74, 79, 81, 84, 98, 110, 115,
      148, 166, 174

Merry-Go-Round, 49-50,
    51, 55, 74, 164
Queen Kelly (*see separate*
    entry)
Walking Down Broadway/
    Hello, Sister!, 164, 196
Wedding March, The, 55-7,
    61, 65, 67, 72, 75, 76, 80,
    84, 105, 109, 117, 181, 206
Sugar Blues (Dufty), 188,
    198
Sul-Te-Wan, Madame, 98, 120, 127,
    143, 151-4
Sullivan, Charlie, 32, 43, 61, 93, 94
Sunset Boulevard (Wilder), ix, 21,
    22, n.30, 91, 170-176, n.176,
    179, 193, 197, 199, 201, 212,
    213,
Sunset Boulevard (Lloyd-Webber),
    213-4
Sunset Boulevard (Hughes &
    Stapley), 213
Sunset Boulevard (Prince,
    Sondheim, Kander & Ebb), 213
Swanson Somborn, Gloria, 24, 27, 28
Swanson, Gloria,
    abortions, 22, 38, 64
    affair with Joseph P. Kennedy,
      xv, 60-1, 62-4, 78, 81, 91,
      138-9, 146, 161, 183-4, 188,
      199-200, 206
    as a film producer, xv, 37-8, 40,
      41-44, 46, 104, 141-2, 155-6,
      158
    beginnings of career, xi, 2-3, 21-2
    death, 200
    diet and nutritional advocacy, x,
      44, 188, 191, 198, 211
    early life, 1
    enduring youthfulness of, x, 161,
      190-1
    fashion style, x 1, 2, 21, 28, 41,
      176, 197, 200, 201
    father's death, 37
    Forever Young, 176, 183

invention of the panty girdle,
    155
journalism, 179
mother's death, 190
Multiprises, 161
premonitions, 101, 211
stardom, ix, 21, 37, 40, 41, 44-5,
    46, 60, 62, 63, 67, 68, 83, 84,
    126, 137, 133, 155, 158, 161,
    171, 174, 175, 176, 188, 197-
    8, 199, 212, 216,
Swanson on Swanson, 198-200
TV and talk show appearances,
    xii, xiii, xiv, 171, 176, 189,
    190, 191, 193, 199-200,
FILMS:
3 For Bedroom C, 176
Affairs of Anatol, The, 23, 24-5,
26
Airport 1975, 197-8
Beyond the Rocks, 27, 193
Bluebeard's Eighth Wife, 29,
n.30
Danger Girl, The, 22, 162
Don't Change Your Husband,
22
Father Takes a Wife, 161
Great Moment, The, 136
Humming Bird, The, 36
Killer Bees, 191
Love of Sunya, The x, 34, 41-2,
44, 62, 94
Madame Sans-Gene, 37-8, 39,
67, 84, 193, 211
Manhandled, 21, 35, 173
Music in the Air, 159, 170
Nero's Mistress, 176
Perfect Understanding, 155,158,
201
Sadie Thompson, 43-6, 59, 60,
62, 64, 67, 68, 69, 72, 80, 83, 84,
88, 107, 115, 124, 125, 128, 134,
142, 175, 193, 203, 212
Society Scandal, A, 35-6
Stage Struck, 36

*Sunset Boulevard (see separate
entry)*
Teddy at the Throttle, 22
Tonight or Never, 155
Trespasser, The, x, xi, 132-4, 137
139, 155, 158
What a Widow!, 138, 139, 160
Zaza, 35
PLAYS:
Butterflies are Free, 190-1
Goose for the Gander, A, 161
Reprise, xii
Swanson, Joseph ("Brother"), 28,
    59, 78, 138, 161, 200
Talmadge, Constance, 97
Talmadge, Norma, 41
Tan, Sandi, xv
Tandler, Adolph, 156, 204
Taylor, Kent, 166
Taylor, William Desmond, 25
Ten Commandments, The, 34, 96
Thalberg, Irving, 18, 49-50, 51, 54,
    134, 136, 137, 156
That Certain Woman, 158
Thief of Bagdad, The, 42
Thomas, Olive, 25
Thomson, Fred, 33, 62, 118
Time, 213
Times, The, 85, 200
Titanic, 215
Toland, Gregg, 156
Travers, Richard, 2
Tynan, Kenneth, 189-90

Underground cinema, xi, xv, 142,
    191
Underworld, 182
United Artists, 40-1, 43, 60, 61-2,
    67, 80, 83, 94, 117, 127, 129,
    131, 132, 134,135-6, 141, 142,
    155, 156-7, 160, 183, 203
United Press, 179
Universal, 11, 12, 13, 15, 16, 17-19,
    34, 49, 55, 57, 83, 93, 109, 143,
    164, 211

Valentino, Rudolph, 27, 40, 41, 173, 193, 211, 216
Vanity Fair, 37, 46, 80
Variety, 19, 138, 143, 144, 157, 158, 168
Venice Film Festival, 168, 205, 208
Vernac, Denise, 167, 188
Victoria and Albert Museum, 201
Vidor, King, 55, 143, 175
Vitaphone, 34, 94
Vogue, 37, 200
von Brincken, Wilhelm, 74, 76, 98
von Sternberg, Josef, xiv, 56, 156, 181-3, 184, 212,
von Stroheim, Erich Jr, 13, 166
von Stroheim, Josef, 49, 166
von Stroheim, Margaret, 3
Walker, Elisha, 95
Walker, Stuart, 166
Wall Street bomb attack, 1920, 7-8
Wall Street Crash, 7, 134, 148, 211
Walsh, Raoul, 42-5, 46, 67, 75, 164
Walter, Eugene, 126-7
Walters, Barbara, 199-200
Ward, Sport, 78
Warhol, Andy, xi, 191
Warner Bros, n.47, 62, 93, 96, 158, 159
Warner, H. B., 173
Warner, Henry, 34
Washington Post, The, 200
Waugh, Evelyn, 170
Weber, Lois, 205
Weinberg, Herman G., 86, 160, 181, 190
Welles, Orson, xiv, 49, 52, 96, 194
West of Zanzibar, 89, 143
West, Mae, 86, 170
What Price Glory, 42, 75
Whatever Happened to Baby Jane (Aldrich), 176
White Woman, 166, 196
Wilder, Billy, ix, 21, 91, 167, 168, 169-71, 173-4, 175, 179, 213
Woman of Paris, A, 41
Woman of the Sea, A, xiv, 102

Wood, Sam, 24, 27, 28, 29, 136
World Journal Tribune, xiii
Wray, Fay, 55, 56-7, 109

Yellow Cab Company, 31

Zéro de Conduite, xiv
Zukor, Adolph, 23, 28, 32, 34, 60
Zuro, Josiah, 122, 135

Sticking Place Books (stickingplacebooks.com) is a New York-based publisher specializing in cinema, offering interview books, memoirs, critical and historical studies, screenplays, and essay collections. Our titles include:

Lessons with Kiarostami, edited by Paul Cronin

In the Shadow of Trees: The Collected Poetry of Abbas Kiarostami

Still Film Crazy (After All These Years) by Patrick McGilligan

It's Only a Movie by Bruce Joel Rubin

Three Visionary Screenplays by Bruce Joel Rubin

Playing Among the Stars: Conversations with Damien Chazelle by Nathan Réra

The Magic Eye: The Cinema of Stanley Kubrick by Neil Hornick

A Shared Cinema: Conversations with Michael Ciment by N. T. Bihn

The Naughty Bits: What the Censors Wouldn't Let You See in Hollywood's Most Famous Movies by Nat Segaloff

Mexico: The Aztec Account of the Conquest by Werner Herzog

Werner Herzog/Rogue Filmmaker by David LaRocca

De Palma on De Palma: Conversations with Samuel Blumenfeld and Laurent Vachaud

Publication as Autobiography: Occasional and Forsaken Texts— and Endangered Cinema Species by Scott MacDonald

Filmmakers Thinking by Adrian Martin

Secret Cinema: The Rise and Fall of the Blue Movie by John Baxter

Casualties of War: An Investigation by Nathan Réra

Hollywood on the Tiber by Hank Kaufman and Gene Lerner

What Made Cinema? Essays on Visual Culture and Early Film by Ian Christie

Travels in the Cities of Cinema: Conversations with Jonathan Rosenbaum by Ehsan Khoshbakht

Camera Movements that Confound Us by Jonathan Rosenbaum

Upon Open Sky by Guillermo Arriaga

Ambrose Chapel by Brian De Palma

Russian Poland by David Mamet

The Archival Impermanence Project by Ross Lipman

These Fragments I Have Shored Against My Ruin by Caveh Zahedi

Cinema Now and Then: Conversations with James Naremore by Craig S. Simpson

Circle of Lions by Anthony Ray

Peace of Mind: A Paul Williams Anthology, edited by Paul Cronin

Flashbacks: A Passion for Film by Peter Cowie

Haneke on Haneke: Conversations with Michel Cieutat and Philippe Rouyer

Darkness Visible: The Cinema of Jonathan Glazer by John Bleasdale

Let Me Dream Again: Essays on the Moving Image by Luke McKernan

O Brother, What Might Have Been: Three Lost Screenplays by Preston Sturges

Mister Everywhere: Conversations with Pierre Rissient by Samuel Blumenfeld

Every Movie is a Miracle: A Colloquy Between Leonard Maltin and Nat Segaloff

High Contrast Hollywood by Julian Upton

Charles Chaplin's The Freak: The Story of an Unfinished Film by David Robinson

Jump Cuts, Tracking Shots, and Scherzos by David Sterritt

A Cinephile Under the Influence: Conversations with David Sterritt
    by Mikita Brottman

My Life is the Cinema by Esfir Shub

I Killed Bette Davis by Larry Cohen

HeadHunter by Larry Cohen

I Loved Movies, But... by Joseph McBride, Conversations with Danny Peary

A Reluctant Film Critic by Gerald Peary

The Zen of the Director by Peter Markham

Adventures in Auteurism: A Crusade for the Criminally Neglected
    by Daniel Kremer

Persistence of Vision: A Collection of Film Criticism
    Edited by Joseph McBride

Writings and Relics 1990–95 by Michael Almereyda

My Strange Love: Selected Film Reviews and Essays, 2001–2021
    by Stuart Klawans

The Autobiography of Jane Brakhage by Jane Wodening
    with P. Adams Sitney and David E. James

The Curse of Queen Kelly by Pamela Hutchinson

Lost Screenplays of the 1970s by Jim McBride

My Lunches with Henry Jaglom by Daniel Kremer